MUSLIMS
IN STORY

MUSLIMS IN STORY

Expanding multicultural understanding through children's and young adult literature

GAURI MANGLIK
and **SADAF SIDDIQUE**

ALA
Editions

CHICAGO 2018

Gauri Manglik is the CEO and founder of KitaabWorld.com, a literary organization that spreads awareness about South Asian children's literature. As a first-generation immigrant mother raising her two boys in California, she felt strongly about advocating for increased diversity in children's literature in schools and libraries. Prior to founding KitaabWorld, Manglik practiced law for more than twelve years and advised a number of start-ups as they disrupted conventional ways of doing things. Inspired by their innovative thinking, Manglik followed her own passion to disrupt the world of children's literature and bring marginalized voices to the table. She has written numerous articles and research papers in various journals including *Tax Notes International* and *Teaching Tolerance.*

Sadaf Siddique is cofounder and chief creative officer at KitaabWorld. Her background in journalism and her work in print, documentaries, and online media in India and the United States has focused on innovative ideas for social change. She was part of the research and editorial team on social impact-investing at Omidyar Network. She led editorial strategy at Link TV's *Dear American Voter*, an interactive project on global perspectives on the 2008 U.S. election. Siddique also has experience in managing content acquisitions as editorial manager for *Imagining Ourselves*, an award-winning, multilingual and multimedia online exhibit, and she was part of the team at Devi Pictures that produced female-oriented films such as *Unlimited Girls*. Her writings have appeared in *Hyphen Magazine*, *San Francisco Bay Guardian*, *Dawn*, *The Hindu*, *Indian Express*, and the *Times of India*.

ISBN: 978-0-8389-1741-1 (paper)

Library of Congress Cataloging in Publication Control Number: 2018023567

Book design by Kim Thornton in the Adelle, More Pro, and Source Sans typefaces.
Cover image © ori-artiste / Adobe Stock.

♾ This paper meets the requirements of ANSI/NISO Z39.48–1992 (Permanence of Paper).

Printed in the United States of America

22 21 20 19 18   5 4 3 2 1

Stories are a communal currency of humanity.

—Tahir Shah, *In Arabian Nights: A Caravan of Moroccan Dreams*

CONTENTS

FOREWORD

Let's Counter Islamophobia through Stories

I OFTEN GIVE TALKS IN SCHOOLS AROUND THE COUNTRY, DRAWING ON MY own books to talk about the experiences and points of view of Muslim and immigrant teenagers, especially in a post-9/11 world. Recently, when visiting a rural community in upstate New York, I asked students to give a few responses to the terms *teenage*, *watched*, and *Muslim/Islam*. For *teenage*, they wrote the usual—*bored, drama, pressured*. For *Muslim/Islam*, most wrote: *Discriminated against. Terrorism. Middle East.*

Such narrow terms! Yes, Muslim Americans clearly face discrimination and bear the stigma of terrorism. But surely we can find a way to widen young readers' associations to attain a greater breadth of experience and history. Surely we can find a way to take their sense of what it means to be a teenager and make them realize that a Muslim teenager experiences this too. Surely they can learn that Islam stretches deeper and further than the war-torn images of the Middle East.

In the mid-1990s, while researching a nonfiction book on immigrant teenagers, I quickly realized that Muslim teenagers, and especially girls, were completely invisible in young adult literature. This was after Gulf War (1990–91), and girls would tell me of the taunts they'd get just walking home from school, or the difficulty they had finding an in-between cultural space. Their experience was both similar and different from the other teenagers I interviewed. Since then, we can see that the field of books on Islam and the Muslim and Muslim American experiences has been steadily growing.

That's why *Muslims in Story* is so crucial, so vital to our libraries, and so important for the soul of our country. It widens the path of knowledge, imagination, and curiosity. It is a resource that will help to illuminate the past, our history of Islam and Muslims in America, and our present, with all its complexities and pressures. It will help to deepen what our readers know about the Muslim American experience, and to understand the larger scope of Muslims in the world. And it will give young Muslim readers a chance to see themselves and their own culture and history reflected in the pages of books. Most of all, it will counter the dreadful, dehumanizing images of Muslims that haunt our media.

What is a book? Books are bridges, an opportunity to use our fundamental human traits of curiosity and empathy. Books are places where we stretch ourselves, but where we also find some common contours of human experience. Since 9/11 this has become ever more urgent for our young readers. Muslims, once invisible, have suddenly became hyper-visible, flattened under the glare of demonizing headlines. Rumor becomes fact, and groups of people become scapegoats. Our country, and our children, need this stretching in order to find their common experiences and stretch into the unknown, and explore that which we do not know. Too often, as I saw with the students I speak to, their images of Muslims are drawn from sensational news headlines, misinformation, a sense of otherness, and perhaps fear.

Librarians and educators stand at the entrance to the book-bridge, getting young readers to cross over and stretch to see what might be right in front of them, and what lies beyond the borders of their lives. Librarians are also the ones to put a book into the hands of a young person who may never have seen herself depicted in the pages of a book. They quietly whisper to them: You are here. I see you.

This book is extraordinarily researched. In the course of reading it, I found that there was much I knew, but there was also much that I did not know. For instance, I didn't know that Thomas Jefferson owned a Quran and even hosted an *iftar* (the evening meal eaten by Muslims during Ramadan) at the White House in 1805.

This book's curated list of titles, with its excellent suggestions for activities, will allow our readers to pause and look around them with different eyes. Some will see themselves in the titles we recommend. Others will see what was not even visible before. We are given such a variety of books, from a simple tale about sharing scant resources in a refugee camp, to the gorgeous gold-leaf illustrations in picture books on Rumi and Muhammad. There are gentle lessons about fitting in; there are others about the span of holidays within Islam and across cultures; and there are many serious and funny coming-of-age novels about whether to wear a hijab (headscarf), identity, bullying, and even Urdu poetry. Or I think too of nonfiction books that would appeal to my own son, who is more of a factoid reader: *1001 Inventions and Awesome Facts from Muslim Civilization*, or the story of the *Grand Mosque of Paris: How Muslims Helped Jews during the Holocaust*. For older teenagers, there are sophisticated, edgy graphic novels taking on the here-and-now of politics, such as *The Arab of the Future* and *Persepolis*. A favorite part of this guide for me comes at the very end, with the appendix "Frequently Asked Questions on Islam" by Sumbul Ali-Karamali. What I like about this part of the book is its tone: so commonsensical, so down-to-earth and accessible in its treatment of all the misconceptions that surround Islam and Muslims.

As I finished this volume, I was reminded of two images from where I grew up, in Queens, New York. In a corner of the cemetery where my parents are buried is the Tatar section—turn-of-the century tombstones bearing Cyrillic and Arabic inscriptions, crescent moons, and stars. This is an area reserved for the American Mohammedan Society, Muslim immigrants from Russia and Poland who came to the United States and built the first mosque in North America—a lost, forgotten history. Just a few miles away, in an area that has become known as Little Bangladesh, stands a relatively new mosque; during Ramadan hundreds of Muslims pour on to a nearby high school lawn to pray. These two images are the invisible past and the teeming, transforming present, all in one borough of New York City. And this is the America we are living in right now. This is what we can begin to see and learn about.

Next time those answers about Muslims and Islam come back from the students, I think of the many books we can put in their hands. I think of how much farther and wider their imaginations, their curiosity, and their hearts can go.

Marina Budhos

ACKNOWLEDGMENTS

The journey of a thousand miles begins with one step.
—Lao Tzu

AS WE EMBARKED ON THIS JOURNEY, WE'VE BEEN SUPPORTED BY A NUM-ber of people who have not only helped guide us with practical advice, but have buoyed our spirits with a shared vision. For their encouragement and belief in us, we are truly humbled and honored.

We would like to thank Mary Mackay, ALA's Associate Executive Director for Publishing for setting us on this path from an online campaign to a book. To our editor, Jamie Santoro, we are grateful for all your encouragement and guidance, and your thoughtful review of our work. To the team at ALA Editions, thank you for green-lighting this project and working with us to get this book to print in a speedy manner.

We are also grateful for the invaluable feedback and assistance from librarians Jennifer Wilkins and Lucinda Abbott at the Menlo Park Library. We have a renewed appreciation for the efficient, robust, and well-stocked public library systems we used, and we would especially like to thank our local San Mateo County Libraries for providing us with many of the books we chose to review in this book. Also, a heartfelt shukriya to Naheed Senzai for taking the time to help us shape our ideas and for giving us more to think about.

To all the authors we interviewed for this book: Rukhsana Khan, Hena Khan, Jeanette Winter, Reem Faruqi, Emma Apple, Shahrukh Hussain, Naheed Senzai, Sally Mallam, Randa-Abel Fatteh, Fatima Sharafeddine, Michael Hamilton Morgan, SA Chakraborty and Sumbul Ali-Karamali, our sincere gratitude for believing in this project.

We are also very grateful to all the librarians, educators, bloggers, parents, and others who shared and supported our *Counter Islamophobia through Stories* campaign, and kept the hope that there are more allies and friends who cherish and respect people of all stripes against the fury of those who spread fear and hatred.

Lastly, we would like to thank our families for taking our late nights, rushed meals, and shortened bedtimes in their stride. And to our wonderful little boys—you are the inspiration for all that we do. We hope that one day, all young readers will find their own special way to light the way forward.

INTRODUCTION

ON THE EVENING OF NOVEMBER 8, 2016, WE STARED IN DISBELIEF WHILE watching the results of the U.S. presidential election. We had already felt troubled by the Republican campaign and its candidate, who used his platform to incite fear of anyone who appeared different. We had spent the last few months doing just the opposite. We had started a company to focus on South Asian children's books, and we had built an online resource of diverse books. We then introduced these multicultural stories to parents, librarians, and educators in the community in order to help build bridges of cultural understanding.

As reports poured in of increased hate crimes in the months that followed, we saw young children dreading going to school, fearful for their parents, and troubled by comments from their peers and others at school. We could not sit back and do nothing. Our work had led us to find ways to help children make connections with one another, so we researched ways that we could help Muslim children feel safe and understood. In January 2017, we launched our campaign named "Counter Islamophobia through Stories" in order to flip the narrative and feature positive stories of Muslims.

We sought to address misinformation on Islam and Muslims by seeking out books featuring Muslim children, we curated book lists to facilitate their discovery, and we interviewed authors whose books we featured. In addition to the online campaign, we reached out to various communities of parents, teachers, and librarians in order to expand our reach. We led diverse storytimes, teacher

workshops, and presentations in the course of our campaign. Rather serendip-
itously, we submitted a proposal to present our work at the American Library
Association's 2017 Annual Conference. Shortly thereafter, we began work on
writing this book for ALA Editions in order to expand our campaign's sphere of
influence to educators and librarians all over the world.

This book is divided into two parts. Part I creates a broader context around
the issue of Islamophobia. We provide a brief history of Muslims in America,
and we connect it to the present with a detailed chapter on understanding Islamophobia and its impact on children. This background outlines the problems, the
pressing need for creating long-term change, and the reasoning behind our
possible solution.

In Part II of this book, we present a solution. We feature curated book lists
around four different themes, with ideas for educators and librarians to share
these books with children for year-round engagement. Author interviews
interspersed throughout this part offer their personal insights and motivations to tell their own stories.

Through the titles reviewed in this book, our hope is that we can all work
together to build bridges of cultural understanding book by book, and story by
story.

PART I

Why Counter Islamophobia through Stories?

Chapter 1

An Overview of Muslims in America

THE UNITED STATES IS OFTEN HAILED AS THE LAND OF FREE-dom and opportunity. The sights, sounds, and feel of America—imposing city skylines, the birthplace of jazz, a hotbed of commerce, medical and technological innovation, and a multicultural meeting ground of immigrants—all make up an idea of a country and its people that are leading the world in all aspects of progress and modernity.

People from all over the world have chosen to migrate to America and make it their home. Some such as the Irish, Jews, or more recently the Syrians, were fleeing persecution in their home countries. Others came to pursue educational or professional opportunities. This microcosm of diversity and multiculturalism is reflected in many American cities. For example, Queens, one of the most diverse boroughs of New York, is home to more than 138 languages.[1]

Many different communities, often built around languages, countries of origin, and religious preferences, have become part of the American fabric. One such community that has recently garnered a lot of attention is Muslims. Muslims in America are a diverse group of people from all over the world. African Americans, South Asians, and Arabs comprise more than three-quarters of all the Muslims in the United States.[2] This diversity is reflected in the different ethnic groups, ideologies, sects, and traditions of Islam, and also in the social, racial, and economic makeup of Muslim Americans. While some Muslims integrate Islam into their daily lives, others are nonpracticing and see being Muslim as just part of their culture. Irrespective of their adherence to their faith, all Muslims in America—from refugees forced to flee their home countries, to people who came here looking for better jobs and lives—feel a sense of belonging here. This drives them to actively participate in the social, cultural, intellectual, and civic spheres of American life.

Muslims in America have impacted all aspects of American life, from commerce and business to the sciences, civil society, and the arts and popular culture. Sports heroes such as Muhammad Ali, Kareem Abdul Jabbar, and Ibtihaj Muhammad have trailblazed new paths for American athletes. The architect Fazlur Rahman Khan changed the landscape of American cities by designing structural systems for towering skyscrapers. Dr. Ayub Ommaya invented neurological methods to treat brain tumors, while Ernest Hamwi rolled up his waffle-like *zalabia* into the first edible ice-cream cone. The hip-hop artist Rakim and classic rap albums have influenced other Muslim artists such as Mos Def, Ice Cube, and Busta Rhymes. Dave Chappelle, Aziz Ansari, and Hasan Minaj have entertained audiences through various forms of media and stand-up comedy. Most recently, Mahershala Ali was the first Muslim American to win an Academy Award in 2017. From serving in the military to serving their constituents in the U.S. Senate, Muslim Americans' contributions are interwoven into the fabric of the nation.

Muslims make up one percent of the U.S. population and comprise an estimated 3.45 million people of all ages in America today.[3] Of these, some arrived as immigrants or refugees, and others are converts, but most of them are American-born Muslims descended from the many Muslims who have been a part of the American story for decades and even centuries, and even back to the formation of the republic.

Muslims as Part of the American Story

Historical mentions of Muslims in America predate Columbus and some are known to have been aboard his 1492 expedition as well. In the 1530s, the African explorer Estevanico, also known as "The Moor," referencing his North African Muslim origins, "is said to have explored Arizona and New Mexico in search of gold and treasure."[4] Muslim sounding names are also recorded in Spanish colonial documents.

The transatlantic slave trade that began in the seventeenth century led to the forced migrations of many Muslims from Africa to America. Some of these Muslim slaves were well-educated and literate in Arabic, which helped them rise to leadership positions within plantations. Enslaved Muslims often made attempts to return to their homelands, and their writings help us trace their history.

Job Ben Solomon Jallo, sold as a slave to a Maryland planter, continued to practice his faith and made multiple attempts to escape. He managed to reach England as a free man in 1733, and returned to Africa in 1773. Abd Al-Rahman Ibrahima, a well-educated prince, was sold into slavery in Mississippi. Though he married and started a family, he wrote letters in the hopes of securing his freedom. His letter eventually reached the king of Morocco, who secured his release in 1828. Ibrahima embarked on a wide tour of the United States to raise money for his family's freedom. He returned to Africa in 1829 but died of illness soon after. Omar ibn Said worked as a house slave in South Carolina. Despite having converted to Christianity, he remained loyal to his Islamic heritage, as recounted in his autobiography.

While most of these accounts are of individuals retaining their Muslim religious identity, there is also evidence of Islam being practiced in communal settings. In the communities around the Georgia and South Carolina coasts, "African American Muslim slaves and free men and women of color practiced Islam in the nineteenth century and perhaps into the early twentieth century as well."[5]

On Sapelo Island off the coast of Georgia, a Muslim slave called Bilali served as an overseer and even prepared the slaves to fight off the British in the War of 1812. Records from the Revolutionary War indicate that Muslim soldiers fought on the American side. This legacy continued with 292 Muslim soldiers fighting in the Civil War.[6]

As America began to take shape as a nation, the Founding Fathers too were cognizant of Islam and sought to include it within the ambit of religious freedom. John Adams praised the Prophet Muhammed in his writings; Benjamin Franklin was open to the preaching of Islam[7] in the United States; and Thomas Jefferson owned a copy of the Quran and hosted the first *iftar* (breaking of the Ramadan fast) at the White House for the Tunisian ambassador in 1805.

By practicing Islam, enslaved Muslim black men and women were reclaiming their lost religious and spiritual heritage. Though some practiced their faith in secret, many had to abandon their religion and undergo forced conversions.[8] As these slaves died off, Islam eventually petered out among second-generation African Americans. The loss of identity and culture as a result of the slave trade continues to impact the African American consciousness. Even after the abolition of slavery and the Great Migration of blacks from the South to the North in the twentieth century, they continued to face prejudice and discrimination. African Americans felt a pressing need to regain their dignity, and they found a way to rediscover their African roots in Islam.

Within the African American community, two homegrown movements were inspired by Islam in the twentieth century. The Moorish Science Temple established in 1925 preached a doctrine of shedding slave identities, and adopting new names and appearances with a focus on black unity and social and economic independence. The Nation of Islam founded in 1930 gave each of its followers an X in lieu of their last name to "represent an identity that has been stolen from them during slavery."[9] Muhammad Ali and Malcolm X were the most prominent members of the Nation of Islam. Though inspired by Islam, the core principles of both these movements were contrary to the teachings of orthodox Islam. In the 1960s, Malcolm X adopted mainstream Islam, and eventually the Nation of Islam merged with the Sunni tradition of Islam. Since then, there has been a resurgence of Islam in African American communities. Conversion is a way for many African Americans to connect to their Muslim past and honor their ancestors. Today, African Americans form 60 percent of native-born U.S. Muslims.

Many scholars have argued that it is problematic to view Muslims as "foreign" or as "threats to the United States." On the contrary, they argue that African American Muslims are well integrated into American society. Through their style, music, and activism in hip-hop, sports, and the recent Black Lives Matter movement, they have played a key role in shaping the American history of resistance and popular culture.[10]

Growth of Muslim Communities in the United States

Over the years, Muslim immigrants have come to the United States for better educational and economic prospects, while others have come as refugees escaping war and conflict. Some of these refugees eventually returned to their home countries, but many others have settled permanently in the United States. These first-generation immigrants had families and formed large communities of Muslims, all of whom call America their home.

The first wave of immigrants came between 1890 and 1920 mostly from Syria, Lebanon, and Palestine, territories that were under the rule of the Ottoman Turks. They settled in working-class neighborhoods of Detroit, Chicago, and the Midwest and earned a living as peddlers and factory workers. The United States then passed the National Origins Act in 1924, which limited immigrants to Christians from northern and western European countries. However, global events such as World War II, the achievement of Indian and Pakistani independence from Great Britain in 1947, the Arab-Israeli War in 1948, and the attainment of independence by many former British and French colonies in Africa and the Middle East in the 1950s and early 1960s, resulted in continued immigration of many displaced people, including another wave of Muslim immigrants to the United States. Muslims came from India, Pakistan, Palestine, and Yugoslavia.

In 1965 President Lyndon Johnson signed the Hart-Celler Act (also known as the Immigration and Nationality Act), which "banned discriminatory quotas based on national origins."[11] This led to many more Muslim immigrants from Asia, Africa, and the Middle East entering the country. Although the act stated that all immigrants would be given equal opportunity, only people with a certain level of education could apply. Many of these newer immigrants were well-educated professionals who settled in the suburbs.

Numerous overseas conflicts that began in the 1960s and have continued to the present day have led Muslims to flee their homelands and come to the United States. Among these conflicts have been the Six-Day War between Israel and its Arab neighbors in 1967, the Islamic Revolution in Iran in 1979, the Soviet invasion of Afghanistan in 1979, civil wars in Lebanon, Somalia, and Sudan, the 1991 Gulf War, the disintegration of Yugoslavia, and the ethnic cleansing in Bosnia-Herzegovina. Additionally, the U.S. invasions and occupations of

Afghanistan and Iraq that began in 2002 and 2003, and, more recently, civil wars in Libya and Syria, have created unprecedented numbers of Muslim refugees. Many of these refugees came to the United States in search of safety and security. The U.S. Office of Immigration Statistics states that between 2000 and 2013 approximately one million Muslim immigrants came to the United States.[12]

Muslims in America today are one of the most diverse and vibrant communities of Muslims anywhere in the world. From the Muslims descended from those who fought in the American Civil War, to the influential all-Muslim jazz band, to sports heroes, hip-hop pioneers, architects, and even the creator of the humble ice-cream cone, American Muslims—known and unknown—fully participate in the American dream.

When viewed through this prism of historical continuity and contributions to American society, the singular idea of Muslims as outsiders is refracted into the colorful spectrum of the diversity of people and experiences that make up being an American Muslim.

Notes

1. While there is no precise count, some experts believe that New York City is home to as many as 800 languages—far more than the 176 spoken by students in the city's public schools, or the 138 that residents of Queens, New York's most diverse borough, listed on their 2000 census forms. Sam Roberts, *New York Times,* 2010, www.nytimes .com/2010/04/29/nyregion/2910st.html.

2. Toni Johnson, "Muslims in the United States," 2011, Council on Foreign Relations, https://www.cfr.org/backgrounder/muslims-united-states.

3. "U.S. Muslims Concerned about Their Place in Society, but Continue to Believe in the American Dream," findings from PEW Research Center's 2017 Survey of U.S. Muslims, 2017, www.pewforum.org/2017/07/26/demographic-portrait-of-muslim-americans/.

4. Edward E. Curtis IV, *Muslims in America: A Short History* (Oxford: Oxford University Press, 2009), 4–5.

5. Curtis, *Muslims in America,* 15.

6. Edited by Edward E. Curtis IV, Encyclopedia of Muslim-American History (New York: Facts on File, an imprint of Infobase Publishing, 2010), 561. See url: https://books.google .ca/books?id=owZCMZpYamMC&pg=PA561&dq=Yusuf+ben+Ali+and+Bampett+Muhamed &hl=en&sa=X&ei=Db25U_DTLLD60gWezYDwAg#v=onepage&q=Yusuf%20ben%20Ali% 20and%20Bampett%20Muhamed&f=false.

7. Benjamin Franklin, *Autobiography*, 1771, ushistory.org, www.ushistory.org/franklin/autobiography/page49.htm.

8. Sylviane A. Diouf, *Servants of Allah: African Muslims Enslaved in the Americas* (New York: New York University Press, 2013), 54.

9. Anbara Zaidi, *Muslims in America* (Understanding Islam) (Philadelphia: Mason Crest, 2016), 60.

10. Su'ad Khabeer, *Muslim Cool: Race, Religion and Hip-Hop in the United States* (New York: New York University Press, 2016).

11. Curtis, *Muslims in America*, 72.

12. Zaidi, *Muslims in America* (Understanding Islam), 48.

Chapter 2

Islamophobia
and Its Impact

ESPITE THE LONG HISTORY OF MUSLIMS IN AMERICA AS set forth in the preceding chapter, there continues to be a perception of Muslim Americans as separate or "foreign" from other Americans. Muslims have been often discriminated against or treated differently as a result of this perception. Such discrimination is often referred to as "anti-Muslim prejudice" or as "Islamophobia" in a broader sense.

While the literal meaning of the term *Islamophobia* is "fear of Islam," our use of the word *Islamophobia* encompasses a wide range or actions that are rooted in anti-Muslim prejudice. In fact, Islamophobia has frequently been defined as "an exaggerated fear, hatred, and hostility toward Islam and Muslims that is perpetuated by negative stereotypes resulting in bias, discrimination, and the marginalization and exclusion of Muslims from America's social, political, and civic life."[1] This definition acknowledges the broader impact that Islamophobia has on the daily lives of Muslims in our society.

The term *Islamophobia* apparently first came into use in 1970s, but it only gained formal acceptance in the late 1990s due to a report by the Runnymede Trust's Commission on British Muslims and Islamophobia that was entitled *Islamophobia: A Challenge for Us All* (1997). The report states: "We did not coin the term Islamophobia. It was already in use among sections of the Muslim community as a term describing the prejudice and discrimination which they experience in their everyday lives. For some of us on the Commission, it was a new term, a rather ugly term . . . it is evident from the responses which we have received that Islamophobia describes a real and growing phenomenon—an ugly word for an ugly reality. Hardly a day now goes by without references to Islamophobia in the media."[2]

Twenty years later, this ugly reality continues and has gained even more ground both in Great Britain and in the United States, in terms of both its reach and impact. There was an acute escalation of Islamophobia in the United States after the devastating terrorist attacks of September 11, 2001. To this day, Islamophobic sentiments often see a spike immediately after terrorist attacks in the United States or abroad. The actions of extremist Muslim groups such as al-Qaeda and ISIS continue to vilify Islam and all of its followers.

Deeply prevalent personal prejudices are often inflamed by politicians in order to stoke fear and hostility towards Muslims. Most recently, the 2016 U.S. presidential election and events since then have resulted in a resurgence of Islamophobic incidents and sentiment in the United States. The campaign for the election saw a strong anti-Muslim and anti-immigrant rhetoric used by then-candidate Donald Trump. On November 9, 2016, the day after the election, around thirty U.S. mosques received a letter asserting that President Trump "will do to you Muslims what Hitler did to the Jews."[3]

The adoption of Islamophobia at the highest levels of the federal government has led to discriminatory practices such as the exclusion of Muslims most recently seen in the three-part travel ban by the Trump administration. The travel ban includes Executive Orders 13769 and 13780, which suspend entry into the United States for everybody from five majority Muslim countries for certain time periods; all refugees for certain time periods; and Syrian refugees indefinitely. More popularly known as the "Muslim ban," the legality of these Executive Orders has been contested in court over the last eighteen months, but many of these restrictions are currently in force.[4] The biggest fallout of this kind of rhetoric is that it makes Islamophobia seem normal, and it makes discrimination against Muslims an acceptable part of mainstream society.

Similar to other forms of discrimination, Islamophobia disrupts the core values of American civil society—it gives permission to the state to discriminate against Muslim Americans through increased surveillance, profiling, or other ways of undermining their identity. Any overreach by the government on its own citizens threatens the very foundation of democracy. Islamophobic sentiments also result in numerous domestic and foreign policy decisions being based on fear and hatred, rather than the best interests of the nation.[5]

Impact on the Muslim American Community

For the American Muslim population, the impact of Islamophobia is far-reaching and can vary from minor incidents of harassment to violent hate crimes. Broadly speaking, one can classify the negative manifestations of Islamophobia into three categories: violence, discrimination and prejudice, and exclusion.

VIOLENCE

Over the last few years, there have been a number of incidents ranging from hate graffiti and threatening letters sent to mosques, to violent physical attacks on Muslims, persons perceived to be Muslims such as South Asians,[6] and even non-Muslims who try to stand up for and protect Muslims.[7] A report by South Asian Americans Leading Together (SAALT) released in early 2017 stated that the recent hate violence has reached historic levels, mirroring the days after the 9/11 attacks.

DISCRIMINATION AND PREJUDICE

The Council on American-Islamic Relations (CAIR) report titled "The Empowerment of Hate" published in July 2017 indicates that there was a 57 percent increase in anti-Muslim bias incidents in 2016 as compared to 2015. The most prevalent trigger for an anti-Muslim incident was the victim's ethnicity or national origin, and in fact 16 percent of the incidents occurred as a result of a woman wearing a headscarf.

Harassment, defined as a nonviolent or nonthreatening bias incident, accounted for 18 percent of the total number of incidents. Incidents where complainants were questioned by the FBI or otherwise inappropriately targeted by that agency made up 15 percent of the cases. Employment issues—including denial of work, being passed over for promotion, and harassment by a supervisor or other senior staff—were the third largest category, accounting for 13 percent of the incidents. Hate crimes placed fourth, accounting for 12 percent of the cases that CAIR documented. Denials of religious accommodation, such as denying permission to wear a headscarf at work or have a Quran in one's jail cell, was the fifth most frequent occurrence, accounting for 8 percent of anti-Muslim bias incidents.[8] As these incidents demonstrate, discrimination and prejudice impact every aspect of Muslim life in America, from schools to employment, to airports and banks, and, of course, to increased surveillance by the FBI.

EXCLUSION

A 2017 Pew survey of American Muslims indicates that 75 percent of Muslims living in the United States believe there is a lot of discrimination against Muslims, and 62 percent state that they don't believe that Islam is part of mainstream American society.[9] There are very few Muslims holding public office in America today, and it is likely that many people have reservations about electing a Muslim. Muslims in the U.S. Army also face unique cultural challenges, such as bans on wearing beards or not eating pork.[10] Such incidents of institutionalized discrimination and prejudice result in increased exclusion of Muslims from society over time, and this can result in a vicious cycle of marginalization.

Impact on Muslim Children

Muslim children are also acutely affected by Islamophobia and other forms of xenophobia. Children who are perceived to be Muslim based on external signifiers such as the color of their skin, their name, or their clothing also often experience bullying and discrimination. There have been a number of studies on the bullying of children due to their Muslim identity, and in fact, these incidents have become more frequent as Islamophobia has increased in the last few years.

The following are some examples of how anti-Muslim bias has affected children recently:

- In 2015 a young boy, Ahmed Mohamed, was arrested for bringing in a homemade clock to school, because his teacher thought it was a bomb.
- According to a 2015 CAIR report, 55 percent of Muslim students aged 11 to 18 reported being subject to some form of bullying due to their faith.

That is twice the national rate of all students who report being bullied at school.

- In 2016, CAIR recorded 209 incidents of anti-Muslim bias, including harassment, intimidation, and violence that targeted students.
- Following Donald Trump's victory in the U.S. presidential election, a number of direct attacks on students, ranging from verbal harassment to physical violence, were recorded. In the week immediately succeeding the election, CAIR recorded 17 incidents of female students being threatened or attacked and their Muslim attire being touched, pulled, or forcibly removed at a school or on a college campus. In one case, the day after the presidential election, a high school student in Los Angeles was approached by a male student who grabbed her hair and attempted to rip off her headscarf. The attacker said, "You shouldn't be wearing that, you towelhead. You're not American. This isn't America. This isn't what America stands for."
- In May 2017, a student left her dorm in Michigan to go for a run and was accosted by five male students. When she attempted to run away from the group, they surrounded her and took turns shoving and verbally harassing her. Her assailants screamed racial and religious slurs, including, "Arab, go back to your country; you don't belong here."

Needless to say, these Islamophobic incidents impact children in a number of adverse ways. They can result in psychological issues such as lack of self-esteem or feeling unsafe and uncomfortable, and they can result in children not wanting to go to school or not being able to make friends. Sometimes, as a result of these incidents, children drop out of school settings, and may not be able to complete their education.

These incidents also directly impact how Muslim children understand and acknowledge their own identity. Noor Kids' study "From Islamophobia to Identity Crisis: Internalized Oppression among American Muslim Children"[11] found that:

- Over a third of the children interviewed said they don't want anyone to know that they are Muslim.
- Almost 1 in 2 children were confused about the compatibility of their Muslim and American identities.

Such a high incidence of bullying and xenophobic incidents likely results from a lack of awareness about Muslims among other children and a belief among the bullies that such discrimination is implicitly permitted. When children heard President Trump making discriminatory and racist statements, they believed that they too had the liberty to make similar statements.[12]

Key Causes of Islamophobia

In researching the steady growth in Islamophobia over the last thirty years, two main causes emerge:

1. *Ignorance about Muslims:* 55 percent of Americans say they do not know very much (30 percent) or know nothing at all (25 percent) about Islam and its practices.[13] Also, 59 percent of Americans state that they don't personally know a Muslim or have never met a Muslim. Many influential right-wing organizations and individuals actively promote and disseminate Islamophobic views, which further promotes misinformation and ignorance.[14] With such widespread misinformation, Muslims are often viewed as a static and monolithic community that is unresponsive to change. This attitude has been bolstered by prevalent images in the press and popular media.

2. *Negative portrayals of Muslims in the American media:* The media—be it online, print, broadcast, or film—have often presented a narrative of Islam as a primitive, barbaric, and sexist culture. The association of Muslims with violent images of terrorists has led to a skewed and distorted image of all Muslims. Both fictional and nonfictional portrayals of Muslims in the media rely on sensationalist imagery. Often this distorted perspective is reflected in the ways all acts of violence by Muslims are labeled as acts of terrorism, whereas similar acts by others are merely attributed to "gunmen" with unstable mental dispositions. Counter-portrayals of the vast majority of Muslims who condemn acts of violence and reject extremist ideology rarely get a mention in the media. Even mundane things such as the call to prayer and saying Arabic words for "Thank God" or "God willing" have been treated as warnings and have even led to Muslims being evacuated from airplanes as a threat to security.

This widespread ignorance and misinformation reinforced by negative images has many real-life consequences for the Muslim community such as increased hate crimes, acts of violence, and exclusionary policies of the government.

Throughout history, the American people have come together and fought against instances of religious persecution and discrimination in order to maintain a robust civil society. From the civil rights movement to protests against the Vietnam War, to most recently, the Women's March and other protests against racism and discrimination, including NFL players "taking the knee" during the playing of the national anthem at football games,[15] this ability to unite and defend targeted communities showcases the true fabric of American democracy. Using knowledge and critical thinking, we as individuals and as a community can push back against anti-Muslim rhetoric and stem the root causes of Islamophobia.

Notes

1. Wajahat Ali, Eli Clifton, Matthew Duss, Lee Fang, Scott Keyes, and Faiz Shakir, "Fear, Inc.: The Roots of the Islamophobia Network in America," August 2011. https://www.americanprogress.org/issues/religion/reports/2011/08/26/10165/fear-inc/.

2. Runnymede Trust, *Islamophobia: A Challenge for Us All*, iii. See url: https://www.runnymedetrust.org/companies/17/74/Islamophobia-A-Challenge-for-Us-All.html.

3. Council of American-Islamic Relations, "The Empowerment of Hate," 2017 http://islamophobia.org/images/2017CivilRightsReport/2017-Empowerment-of-Fear-Final.pdf.

4. ACLU NorCal Muslim Ban Timeline: https://www.aclunc.org/sites/muslim-ban/.

5. Daniel Burke, "The Secret Costs of Islamophobia," 2016, CNN, https://www.cnn.com/2016/09/23/us/islamerica-secret-costs-islamophobia/index.html.

6. Matt Stevens, "Kansas Man Indicted on Hate Crime Charges in Shooting of Indian Immigrants," 2017, *New York Times*, https://www.nytimes.com/2017/06/09/us/indian-immigrants-kansas-hate-crime.html.

7. Matthew Haag and Jacey Fortin, "Two Killed in Portland While Trying to Stop Anti-Muslim Rant, Police Say," 2016, *New York Times*, https://www.nytimes.com/2017/05/27/us/portland-train-attack-muslim-rant.html.

8. Council of American-Islamic Relations, "The Empowerment of Hate," 2017.

9. "U.S. Muslims Concerned about Their Place in Society, But Continue to Believe in the American Dream," findings from PEW Research Center's 2017 Survey of U.S. Muslims, 2017, www.pewforum.org/2017/07/26/demographic-portrait-of-muslim-americans/.

10. Dave Philips, "Muslims in the Military: The Few, the Proud, the Welcome," 2016, *New York Times*, https://www.nytimes.com/2016/08/03/us/muslims-us-military.html.

11. Noor Kids, "From Islamophobia to Identity Crisis: Internalized Oppression among American Muslim Children," 2016, www.noorkids.com.

12. Albert Samaha, Mike Hayes, and Talal Ansari, "Kids Are Quoting Trump to Bully Their Classmates, and Teachers Don't Know What to Do About It," 2017, Buzzfeed, https://www.buzzfeed.com/albertsamaha/kids-are-quoting-trump-to-bully-their-classmates.

13. Pew Research Center, "Public Remains Conflicted over Islam," 2010, www.pewforum.org/2010/08/24/public-remains-conflicted-over-islam/.

14. Ali et al., "Fear, Inc.: The Roots of the Islamophobia Network in America."

15. Doreen St. Felix, "What Will Taking the Knee Mean Now?" 2017, *New Yorker*, https://www.newyorker.com/culture/annals-of-appearances/what-will-taking-the-knee-mean-now.

Chapter 3

Using Literature to Create Long-Term Systemic Change

W E FELT DEEPLY TROUBLED BY THE GROWING ANTI-MUSLIM prejudice and the vacuum of balanced representation in the media, so we brainstormed on how to facilitate positive engagement to counter the misinformation about Muslims.

As founders of KitaabWorld, a small company focused on diverse children's books, we noticed an acute lack of availability, access to, and awareness of Muslim children's literature. Literature is an integral part of the consciousness of any society, and it is often a reflection of the values and people of that time. Within the United States, Muslim voices have often been marginalized and scattered across the cultural landscape of African American, Arab American, South Asian, and diasporic immigrant literature.[1] Books that often get the most visibility often perpetrate Western narratives and stereotypes. This trend follows through in children's literature as well.

Any introduction to different cultures, especially one designed for younger kids, who are at an age when they are curious and nonjudgmental, goes a long way in developing an appreciation and respect for those cultures. Through common shared experiences, children can develop a deeper and broader understanding of people from other cultures and connect with them. Books that accurately portray multicultural diversity serve as ways to share stories that cross social boundaries and begin dialogues with each other in order to reduce "othering." Yet when we examined classroom and public libraries, we noticed that books featuring Muslim children were either missing, or there were just a handful that got lost in the sea of other books, making them hard to discover. Some that were part of the collections either had stereotypical representations of or misinformation about Muslims. Coupled with the lack of positive images of Muslims in the media, this omission of Muslim stories perpetuates ignorance.

There has been extensive research on how children observe and comprehend race and other differences. Rebecca Bigler's research quoted in the book *NurtureShock* indicates that children as young as three can observe differences in skin color, language, and the foods we eat. Bigler observed that children are most open to learning about new ideas and information when they are aged three to eight, and the learning window tapers off by age ten, as children begin to form concrete ideas of their own identity and the identity of others around them.[2] Children are not born with prejudices, but obviously they acquire prejudices along the way through interactions with family, peers, and what they see and learn at school, as well as the media they are exposed to. Prejudices may be further reinforced by the omission of balanced and accurate information.

Books play an important role in learning for all of us. Children are exposed to books as toddlers; most families encourage reading at home, and reading is a significant part of school instruction as well. The public libraries in the United States with their extensive collections level the playing ground for many families, and create a safe space for children to expand their horizons. Books also provide a wonderful opportunity to expose kids to different worlds, to understand and learn about people who are different from them, and also to see themselves in books.

As we struggled with the growing tensions in the country, we realized that we can use the power of books to create a long-term systemic change in countering Islamophobia. Books show children how different lives are lived. Reading a book can help the reader reflect on the characters' circumstances and frame of mind, rather than external and already formed points of view. Through fictional characters, young readers can be guided to make connections to their own lives, thereby opening them up to a world of possibilities. Books spark discussions with children on many different topics, the illustrations in children's books can help normalize experiences, and of course, the succinct stories can help children understand many different ideas. Learning about our similarities, understanding our differences, and sharing our stories goes a long way towards creating respect for and acceptance of one another.

As Gabriel Greenberg and Peter Gottschalk state in their book *Islamophobia: Making Muslims the Enemy,* "the fact could be recognized that Muslims take part in every aspect of American life as businesspeople, college students, government officials, and neighbors. *Their inclusion in images depicting Americans acting as Americans would help reinforce this notion in the popular mind.*"[3]

American Muslims are integrated into all aspects of American civil society—schools, workplaces, universities, neighborhoods, and governments—and it is imperative that this integration should be reflected in both adult and children's literature. We felt we were uniquely placed to draw these connections, and so we set out to explore depictions of Muslims in children's literature in America.

Reframing the Narrative through Curated Book Lists

There are more than 1.5 billion Muslims around the world, and so there are many stories about them. How do you break down the literature about a 1,400-year-old religion, culture, and a way of life in a way that isn't overwhelming, especially for children?

We began by doing extensive research to explore the kinds of Muslim children's books that already existed. We consciously evaluated books that met the requirements of good literature and cultural authenticity. We narrowed our choices to books with high-quality writing, those which were memorable in exploring the complexity of a theme, were universal in the experiences they depicted, had accurate or believable characters and settings, and were fun books to read and reread. In doing our research, we reviewed a number of books from different publishers all over the world, and we even examined self-published books. We paid particular attention to books written by Muslim authors featuring stories that have their "own voices." With a greater number of Muslim writers telling their stories, multiple points of view have come to the fore. To ensure relevance and easy access, we mostly reviewed books published in the year 2007 and later.

We also spoke to a number of teachers, librarians, and parents and we explored how adults and children choose books to read, the kinds of topics that are universal in curriculums across the country, and the ideas that librarians often use in their storytimes.

Muslims comprise about one percent of the American population and trace their origins to the very founding of America. Some were brought here as slaves, others came here as immigrants and refugees from the Middle East, Asia, Europe, and Africa, and still others converted to Islam. This diversity also extends to the multiple denominations in Islam, as well as the different ethnic, ideological, socioeconomic, and cultural backgrounds of Muslims. With such a vast and sweeping population and its mosaic of languages, dress, food, and traditions, there is no one Muslim voice, no one Muslim identity, so there is no one Muslim story. In attempting to highlight this diversity, our focus was to choose well-researched stories that were timeless in their appeal—we steered clear of books that seemed too religious in their content or that promoted stereotypes.

Based on this research and with the above parameters in mind, we created curated book lists around four different themes, each of which has its own chapter in this book: Muslim Kids as Heroes, Inspiring Muslim Leaders and Thinkers, Celebrating Islam, and Folktales from Islamic Traditions. Examining these four different themes provides multiple opportunities for parents, teachers, and librarians to engage with stories about Muslims and include them in meaningful ways in their curricula throughout the year. The four themes also enable different access points to the varied interests among children—some books reflect traditional folktales, while others are contemporary stories; some showcase the history, art, and leaders who have sought inspiration from Islam; and others are fantasy and adventure stories.

For each book list, we have provided a short introduction on the theme, and categorized books into three categories: Picture Books, Chapter Books and Middle Grade Books, and Young Adult Books. For each book listed in the book list in alphabetical order for each category, we have included an annotation that provides a short review of the book. For picture books, we have included ideas for further engagement that will guide educators towards experiential learning, and for middle grade and young adult books, we have provided discussion starters and quotes for interpretation to enable a deeper discussion. *We have also included a number of activities for experiential learning, and these are denoted with* 🖐. The goal is to facilitate thematic discovery of these books, and provide a toolkit to educators to share these books with children in their communities in an engaging manner.

These books also explore the much-needed idea of "visual diversity" by presenting a wide spectrum of kids of color. Children can also observe how illustrations of everyday items play an integral part in Muslims' daily life. For instance, the books show or mention a wide variety of clothing ranging from *hijabs, kufis, khimars,* and turbans to *shalwar-kameez;* assorted foods including hummus, falafel, *roti,* and kebabs; and distinct pictorial markers such as cooking *tagines,* embroidered cushions, calligraphy on the walls, and henna on women's hands. These varied references can spur conversations that will help inform readers.

The cyclical and interconnected themes identified in this book also offer opportunities for a cross-pollination of insights and ideas. For example, *Escape from Aleppo,* a middle grade novel set in Syria and featured in our "Muslim Kids as Heroes" chapter, showcases the history and contributions of the Arab world. Thus, it will help provide insights into the themes discussed in our second chapter, "Inspiring Muslim Leaders and Thinkers." Similarly, books such as *Amina's Voice* and *Love, Hate and Other Filters* deftly tackle Islamophobic incidents that shape the characters, and they enable readers to understand how discrimination impacts young Muslims. From a peek into the past with books such as *Sophia's Journal,* which imagines the lives of Muslim slaves in Kansas, to present-day stories of anti-immigrant sentiments that mirror our reality in *The Lines We Cross,* these stories open up a complex and nuanced portrayal of Muslims that goes beyond the headlines and humanizes Muslims. And perhaps, just perhaps, they help us reach out and connect to one another.

Each theme presented unique and interesting challenges when it came to curating books. For "Muslim Kids as Heroes," we had an abundance of choice in each of the categories—picture books, middle grade books, and young adult books. For "Inspiring Muslim Leaders and Thinkers," our focus was more on nonfiction, and we struggled to find good young adult choices, but we found a few adult books that crossed over as well. In "Celebrating Islam," our books were fairly balanced in each of the categories. For "Folktales from Islamic

Traditions," we included adult fantasy novels for the young adult selections. The many interesting picture books in the "Folktales" chapter lend themselves to discussion on life lessons and are appropriate for any age.

Overall, our curated book lists provide a cross-section of diverse stories from the landscape of Muslim children's literature that can counter negative associations with Islam and Muslims. These books dip into the past and explore present-day stories to create a balanced representation of a vast culture and its people. With the increasing visibility of Muslim authors and publishers, there are many more stories available now than ever before. We believe that these books will seed new ideas that can help transform how we all see the world.

Notes

1. Mohja Kahf, "Teaching Diasporic Literature: Muslim American Literature as an Emerging Field," 2010, www.jpanafrican.org/docs/v014n02/4.2TeachingDiaspora.pdf.

2. Ashley Merryman and Po Bronson, *NurtureShock: New Thinking about Children* (New York: Twelve, 2011), 45–69.

3. Gabriel Greenberg and Peter Gottschalk, *Islamophobia: Making Muslims the Enemy,* (Lanham, MD: Rowman and Littlefield, 2007), 149.

PART II

Reframing the Narrative through Curated Book Lists and Programming Ideas

Chapter 4

Muslim Kids as Heroes

Connecting across Cultures

MERICA'S UNIQUE BLEND OF PEOPLE FROM ALL CORNERS OF the globe has created a beautiful mosaic of cultures, languages, and identities. One effective way to showcase this diversity to children is through the books they read. Diversity in literature can be reflected in a number of ways: books that feature protagonists with different skin colors or different ethnic or religious backgrounds, stories that examine various family structures and social customs, and more. Initially, the focus of diverse books was primarily to educate people about different traditions and cultures. This "tokenistic" approach led to a number of books on travel, festivals, and folktales. As the discussion on diversity has progressed, the trend now is "casual diversity"—universal stories that feature diverse characters as the protagonists. This approach has the twofold benefit of reaffirming stories of diverse groups of children and providing others a window into their lives. Unfortunately, stories that feature Muslim children as protagonists are few and far between, and form a miniscule percentage of the total number of books published every year.[1]

Our first chapter, "Muslim Kids as Heroes," examines a multitude of stories that depict children in their unique cultural contexts, where their Muslim identity serves as a backdrop to their day-to-day experiences. We use the term hero to identify a Muslim protagonist, empower Muslim children, and emphasize that one need not be extraordinary to be a hero. Whether it is Rubina fighting with her bratty sister in *Big Red Lollipop,* Bilal working to convert his cricket swing to a perfect baseball pitch in *A Long Pitch Home,* or Sophia trying to fit into her high school in *The Girl Who Fell to Earth,* each of their dilemmas echoes in our own daily lives. The heroes in our book list are able to find resilience and beauty in the everyday. In doing so, they shape our sense of wonder, expand our perceptions, and leap from the page to build tangible connections between people.

This chapter also features books that reflect the reality of many Muslim children around the world. From the human cost of war and how it affects Lina and Feroza's friendship in *Four Feet, Two Sandals,* to patriarchal customs that threaten to stymie Razia's education in *Razia's Ray of Hope,* and the unpleasant encounters with racism and xenophobia that Maya experiences in *Love, Hate and Other Filters,* these fictional tales mirror the lived experiences of Muslims. Seen through the lens of universal themes of "justice, survival, conflict, and friendship, readers will be able to make connections across cultures"[2] that help them build empathy and engender respect for their Muslim peers.

The variety of experiences featured in the books in this chapter will also help young readers understand the diversity among Muslims and will help counter the idea of Muslims as a "monolith." The kaleidoscope of African Americans, Arabs, South Asians, Malaysians, Africans, Europeans, and Hispanics of varying ethnic, ideological, and cultural stripes combines to form a multi-hued Muslim community.

Books that feature Muslim protagonists help children affirm their social and cultural identity. These positive stories rooted in an authentic cultural context help Muslim kids develop a healthy self-image. When they see themselves through the looking glass of books, they realize that their stories are important. These stories "normalize" their experiences by showing them characters who face the same joys, fears, challenges, and elation that all kids go through. A Muslim protagonist confronting the cultural conundrums of adhering to Islamically prescribed dietary codes or deciding whether to attend the prom is a familiar friend who is dealing with similar struggles, and is possibly a role model to emulate.

This chapter serves as a well-rounded resource for Muslim children to express pride and a sense of belonging not just within their own ethnic group, but also with their friends and the community at large. The absence of these diverse stories can make others think that those stories are unimportant. When such stories are only presented on multicultural days or traditional holidays, it strengthens the idea of the "other." If children don't understand or acknowledge a significant part of other children's identity, then their stories and their identity are deemed insignificant.

Presenting Muslim kids as heroes helps build common ground with Muslims and creates a sense of inclusion for all children. In these fun tales, the protagonists just happen to be Muslim, but their stories are universal. These youngsters embark on adventures of magic and mystery, and they find love, friends, and healing despite fear, prejudice, and exclusion. In experiencing their own personal transformation, these heroes help readers confront their fears, lift their spirits, and aspire to a better tomorrow.

We believe that reading these relatable stories about the lives and hopes of Muslim kids will help counter prevalent stereotypes and build bridges of understanding. For Muslim kids, we believe it will reflect their reality, create a sense of inclusion, and introduce them to heroes and heroines that inspire them.

Picture Books

Amira's Totally Chocolate World. **J. Samia Mair, ill. by author. Islamic Foundation, 2010. 978–0860374084. 29 pp. Fiction. K–Gr. 3.**

Young Amira wonders what it would be like to live in a world full of chocolate. On the Muslim holiday of Eid, her dream comes true—chocolate grass, chocolate flowers, chocolate rainbows, and rivers full of hot chocolate! However, Amira begins to miss the colors, sights, and smells of her once multi-hued world, and she prays for that world to return just as it was. When she wakes up from her dream, she finds a special surprise waiting for her. This whimsical book with a gentle voice helps us understand and appreciate diversity in the world.

Ideas for Further Engagement

- Use for a storytime whose theme is "Celebrate Diversity."
- Display this book during Ramadan and Eid. (Eid is a lunar-based holiday that moves up every year. It will be around April-June in the coming years.)
- ✋ Dip different fruits in chocolate.

Big Red Lollipop. **Rukhsana Khan, ill. by Sophie Blackall. Viking Books for Young Readers, 2010. 978–0670062874. 40 pp. Fiction. Preschool–Gr.**

Select Awards: 2011 Golden Kite Award Best Picture Book Text, 2011 Charlotte Zolotow Award Best Picture Book Text, Kirkus Reviews Best Children's Books of 2010.

This multiple award-winning book was selected by the New York Public Library as one of the 100 Greatest Books in 100 Years. *Big Red Lollipop* is a simple story about an older sister's reluctance to take her bratty younger sister to her first ever birthday party. Rukhsana Khan's charming story reveals itself as a deep and well-observed tale about immigrants, assimilation, and identity. The book has dynamic and vibrant visuals that complement the delightful story.

Ideas for Further Engagement

- Display this book on Siblings Day (April 10).
- ✋ Look up the word for "Mother" in different languages.
- ✋ Find different birthday songs and traditions from around the world.

Drummer Girl. **Hiba Masood, ill. by Hoda Hadidi. Daybreak, 2016. 978–0990625971. 37 pp. Fiction. Gr. 1–5.**

Select Awards: Literary Classics Best Cultural Book for Early Readers 2017, Literary Classics Best Illustrator 2017.

Young Najma nurses a secret in her little heart. During Ramadan, the Muslim holy month of fasting, she longs to beat the drum that traditional male musaharati drummers use during the wakeup call for the pre-dawn meal. Supported by her loving father, Najma becomes a drummer girl who is loved and admired for her spirit and commitment. This book is all heart and warms the soul, inspiring young people everywhere to push the boundaries of what they can accomplish.

Ideas for Further Engagement
- Display this book on Father's Day and Ramadan/Eid (typically in April-June).
- Discuss issues around empowerment of girls.
- Pair this book with *Drum Dream Girl* by Margarita Engle.
- 🖐 Create a drumming circle with percussion instruments from around the world.

Four Feet, Two Sandals. **Karen Lynn Williams and Khadra Mohammed, ill. by Doug Chayka. Eerdmans, 2007. 978–0802852960. 32 pp. Fiction, Gr. 1–5.**

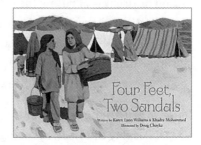

Select Awards: Theologos Award for Best Children's Books 2007; Children's Book Council, Notable Social Studies Trade Books for Young People 2008; Cooperative Children's Book Center, CCBC Choices 2008; International Reading Association, Notable Books for a Global Society 2008; California Young Reader Medal Program, Picture Book for Older Readers Nominee List 2010–2011.

This is a serious yet hopeful story about two girls living in a refugee camp who each find one of a pair of sandals in a pile of used clothing. They decide to share rather than fight over the sandals, and this leads to a lifelong friendship. This story is a sensitive introduction to the refugee crisis around the world, and honors the lives, struggles, and humanity of refugees despite their desperate situation.

Ideas for Further Engagement
- Use for a discussion on friendship and sharing.
- Have the readers make a list of the ten things they would take with them if they had to suddenly leave their home. Follow with a discussion on empathy.

🖐 Trace the journey from Afghanistan to Pakistan, and from Pakistan to the United States.

King for a Day. **Rukhsana Khan, ill. by Christiane Kromer. Lee and Low Books, 2014. 978–1600606595. 32 pp. Fiction. Preschool–Gr. 2.**

Select Awards: Kirkus Reviews Best Books 2014, Picture Books; Center for the Study of Multicultural Children's Literature, Best Multicultural Books 2014.

In this beautifully illustrated book, the textured landscapes of Lahore, Pakistan, come alive to celebrate the spring festival of Basant. Malik, a young disabled boy, has been planning for this day by making a special kite for the kite-flying competition, and he dreams of ruling the skies. The story focuses on Malik and shows his strength of character. He is a thoughtful boy who stands up to a bully, works together with his siblings, and shows kindness to a young girl. Author Rukhsana Khan is an expert at telling great stories about young children while subtly weaving in their cultural contexts.

Ideas for Further Engagement
- Display this book in spring and discuss spring festivals around the world.
- Use for discussion on bullying and kindness.
- 🖐 Create textured art collages mirroring the pages from the book.
- 🖐 Make kites for your own kite-flying contest.

Rukhsana Khan

Stories as Bridges of Understanding

Can you share a little bit about where you grew up, and what inspired you to become a writer?

I love stories, especially children's books, and I wanted to share the stories that grow in my head with other kids. Basically, it comes down to the fact that books helped me survive my childhood.

I grew up in a small town in Canada where my family was the only Pakistani Muslim family in the whole town, so most of the time I was the only brown kid in the class. This was in the 1960s and 1970s, when the white people didn't know much about brown people. They thought we were brown because we were dirty. So I grew up very poor and feeling dirty.

When I read books, I could escape the bullying and the harassment. I could be someone else, I could be somewhere else. Books gave me hope to keep going. They were a respite. And when my eighth-grade teacher told me I was a writer, I thought it would be the coolest thing in the world to grow up and write the kinds of stories that kept me going.

What inspired you to write about Muslim characters in your books?

If you visit any Islamic conference, you'll see instantly that there's a thriving market for Muslim children's books. Parents are desperately snatching up titles that will teach Islamic values to their children. The vast majority of these books are heavy-handed lesson-oriented books that don't translate well for mainstream audiences.

What I really wanted to do was write books that reflect the reality of Muslims here, in North America. I wanted to write the kinds of stories that kids would call "Cool!" or whatever the current hip/slang expression for admiration is.

Muslim children in particular suffer from a sense of insecurity and inferiority—at least I did. While growing up, I felt as though all the bluster of the Muslim leaders in the *masjid* (mosque) arose because they couldn't make it in mainstream circles.

I didn't want to be like that. I wanted to think bigger. I thought, if I'm going to make it, I want to make it in the mainstream because after all, I didn't want to limit myself to writing only for Muslim children. I wanted my stories to be for everyone.

The only ulterior motive I possess is to try to humanize Muslims and create more understanding. But really I just want to write a good story. And because I'm a Muslim and there's still a lack of good books about Muslims, I'm called upon to make sure my stories are about Muslims. It's filling a niche.

Sometimes it's a bit confining. I'm sure one day I'll write about other kinds of characters, but for now it's Muslims.

What is the one thing you would like people to know about Muslims?
Muslims are like any other demographic. The vast majority of us are faithful, law-abiding citizens who are trying to live our best lives while enjoying liberty, all in the pursuit of happiness.

If you had a magic wand, what is the one misconception about Muslims that you would banish forever?
Growing up Muslim in North America was very difficult. The release of each mega-blockbuster depicting Muslims as merciless, bumbling terrorists or ignorant taxi drivers, as well as the fatwa—or death sentence—issued by Iranian leaders against the writer Salman Rushdie in 1989, made Muslims look like a bunch of barbaric idiots.

Especially after September 11, people think Muslims are crazy. And if I can change their minds a little bit, I can open the door and show them, hey, we've got some pretty good stories, and we're really not like that. The vast majority of Muslims, we're not crazy like bin Laden. We would never do something like that.

We're just peaceful, law-abiding people, and we have funny stories, we have sad stories. I try to use stories to build bridges of understanding.

How do we—parents, teachers, and librarians—all of us as a community teach children to respect differences and value diversity?
The best way for parents, teachers, and librarians as a community to teach children to respect differences and value diversity is actually by returning to Islamic principles. When a Christian delegation came to visit Muhammad in Medina, he gave them use of the *masjid* so they could conduct their prayers in peace. He showed utmost respect to all faith groups, but especially to the Christians and the Jews. We have the principles of peaceful coexistence in our Islamic tradition, and we need to return to them as a community. The Quran says there is no compulsion in matters of faith.

If our children mock another faith group or ethnicity, we must stop them, and we, as adults, must set the example. The Quran clearly tells the believers not to mock the beliefs of other people lest they turn around and mock the beliefs we hold dear.

It's all about respect, and living and letting live.

What is your favorite story from Islamic traditions?
The first story that pops into my head is the story of Musa and Khidr in the Quran. I think it's such a beautiful story, and it really makes you look at the things that happen in our lives with a different perspective.

But that said, I also have to mention the story of Yusuf. *Allah subhanahu wata ala* (The Most Glorified, the Most High) says it's the most beautiful story, and it really is! It has it all: treachery, betrayal, lust, romance, dreams and kings and finally ultimate victory. Lately, I keep thinking of how it says that Yusuf's brothers justified their actions by saying, "Oh, we'll do this bad thing to Yusuf and we'll repent (be good) later." It's remarkable how many people live their lives like that.

"We have funny stories, we have sad stories. I try to use stories to build bridges of understanding."

What is your biggest inspiration from Islam?

Islam is just integral.

A while back I came across that hadith about *ihsan*, about living your life as though *Allah subhanahu wata ala* is watching. I think I've been having an internal dialogue with *Allah subhanahu wata ala* since I was about five years old. *Subhan Allah.* He's just always there, at the back of my mind, listening. I talk to Him all the time. And when I'm going to do something bad, I even say "sorry" before I do it and ask forgiveness. And then I make a vow to try not to do it again. And I feel bad.

And when I'm dealing with people and I say something I shouldn't, I cringe inside, and say "sorry" again, and I'm just constantly trying to live up to His expectations for us as Muslims.

I don't always succeed. But I keep trying. I constantly keep trying to improve myself, and sometimes I fall flat on my face. I'll go along for a while thinking, "Hey, I'm doing pretty well," and then something will happen, and I'll do something boneheaded, and I'll have a fall, and I'll realize I was getting arrogant. And I'll feel like the worst person in the world and I'll beg Allah's forgiveness, and then slowly slowly I'll get over it, and keep right on trying.

Each time I fall I don't seem to fall right to the bottom. I'm a little bit higher than I was the last time I fell, so bit by bit I think *insha Allah*, I'm getting better. But I often come across people who are so much better than me. They are so kind, and so sweet and so innocent and so selfless, and I'll look at their example and try to live up to it.

And finally—biryani or kebabs?

Depends on how good the kebabs are. But generally I'm a rice person. MMMMMmmmm. *Biryani!*

Biography

Rukhsana Khan is an award-winning author and storyteller. She was born in Lahore, Pakistan, and immigrated to Canada at the age of three. She grew up in a small town in southern Ontario and was ruthlessly bullied. Drugs and suicide were against her religion, so she turned to books and became hopelessly addicted to the written word.

When an eighth-grade teacher told her she was a writer, she thought the idea was crazy. Writers were white people. They were from England and America. In order to be "sensible," she graduated from college at the top of her class as a biological-chemical technician. When she couldn't get a decent job, she decided to be "unsensible" and become a writer. It took eight years to get her first book published.

Now she has twelve books published, some of which have been published in other countries and in different languages. She has appeared on television and radio many times, and has been featured at conferences and festivals around the world. She's been a corporal in the air cadets, worked on vintage warplanes, composed songs and written stories for children's videos, raised four children, and has ten grandchildren.

She loves reading, writing, storytelling, traveling, gardening, and hiking. She used to like tobogganing, but she broke her wrist while zooming down a slope on one of those little red saucer things. As a result, she no longer likes tobogganing.

She lives in Toronto with her husband and family.

Lost and Found Cat. Doug Kuntz and Amy Shrodes, ill. by Sue Cornelison. Crown's Books for Young Readers, 2017. 978–1524715472. 48 pp. Fiction. Preschool–Gr. 3.

Select Awards: Middle East Book Awards 2017 Winner.

This is a touching story about a refugee family that is forced to flee their home in Mosul, Iraq. Their beloved cat, Kunkush, travels with them on their harrowing journey across land and sea. She goes missing in Greece, and her heartbroken family continues their journey. When relief workers find the cat, a global community comes together to reunite Kunkush with her family. Inspired by a true story, *Lost and Found Cat* is an age-appropriate introduction for discussing ideas of love and loss with younger readers. This bittersweet yet hopeful story of kindness and compassion also shines a light on the plight of refugees.

Ideas for Further Engagement
- Share stories about losing a pet and how you may have found it again.
- Pair this book with *Lost and Found* by Oliver Jeffers.
- Rewrite this story from the cat's perspective.
- Have students volunteer at a pet shelter.

Mirror. Jeannie Baker, ill. by author. Candlewick, 2010. 978–0763648480. 48 pp. Fiction. K–Gr. 4

Select Awards: Horn Book Fanfare, Best Books of 2010, Picture Books; Kirkus Reviews 2010 Best Children's Books; IRA Notable Books for a Global Society 2011; Children's Book Committee, Bank Street College of Education Best Children's Books of the Year 2011, Today, ages 5–9.

This mostly wordless picture book tells a parallel story between two boys, one in Australia and the other in a Moroccan village. It chronicles their daily routines with their families and a trip to the market. The Moroccan boy and his father sell a handwoven rug and they buy a computer at the bazaar, while the Australian family makes a trip to the store, and buys that same handwoven rug. The textured collages depicting the landscape, textiles, and common threads of love and family form mirrors to show in the simplest ways how we are more alike than different.

Ideas for Further Engagement

- Pair this book with *Same Same, But Different* by Jenny Sue Kostecki-Shaw, or with *This Is How We Do It* by Matt Lamothe.
- ✋ Plot the distance between Australia and Morocco on a world map.
- ✋ Start an international pen pal correspondence in your class.
- ✋ Choose a handcrafted object in your home—a rug, a vase—and trace its travel from its place of origin to your home.

***Nusaiba and the 5th Grade Bullies.* Asmaa Hussein, ill. by Zul Lee. Ruqaya's Bookshelf, 2016. 978–0994750136. 44 pp. Fiction. K–Gr. 2.**

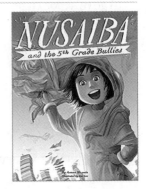

Nusaiba's excitement for show-and-tell at school gets a dampener when she overhears two fifth-graders make a mean comment about her *hijab*-clad mother. Determined to not let it happen again, she walks to school by herself after that. Later, Nusaiba and her best friend Emily accompany her mother on a shopping trip to buy a headscarf. At the store, trying on the scarfs themselves, they imagine themselves in many adventures as deep-sea divers, archaeologists, and even fisherwomen. With a renewed sense of confidence about her identity, Nusaiba confronts the bullies and in a surprising twist, the boys and readers learn the consequences of being too quick to judge.

Ideas for Further Engagement

- Use this book for discussions on standing up for others.
- Pair this book with *One* by Kathryn Otoshi, or with *Never Say a Mean Word Again* by Jacqueline Jules.
- ✋ Organize an anti-bullying activity to showcase the power of words. See examples at http://bullyproofclassroom.com/great-anti-bullying-activities.

***Razia's Ray of Hope: One Girl's Dream of an Educa-tion.* Elizabeth Suneby, ill. by Suana Verelst. Kids Can, 2013. 978–1554538164. 32 pp. Fiction. Gr. 1–5.**

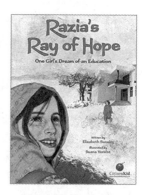

Select Awards: White Ravens Recommended Book, International Children's Library 2014; Children's Book Award, Jane Addams Peace Association 2014; Out-standing International Book, Cooperative Children's Book Center 2014; Social Justice Literature Award 2014; International Reading Association, South Asia Book Award 2014.

This is an inspiring story drawn from a real-life hero—Razia Jan, who runs a girls' school in Afghanistan. Her namesake, a young girl named Razia, yearns to go to school just like her younger brothers. When a new school opens in her remote town, Razia longs to join the other girls, but faces objection from her family. Though her grandfather supports her, her elder brothers believe that girls don't need an education. A determined Razia manages to convince them and show us how one person has the power to make a difference. The mixed-media illustrations bring Razia's world to life and add an extra dimension to this thought-provoking book.

Ideas for Further Engagement

- This advanced picture book is useful for discussions on education as a universal right.
- Make a list of all your chores and compare it to Razia's list of chores.
- When you've really wanted something, how did you go about asking for it?
- ✋ Design a school uniform.

***Saffron Ice Cream.* Rashin Kheiriyeh. Arthur A. Levine Books, 2018. 978–1338150520. 40 pp. Fiction. Pre-K and up.**

A young Iranian girl and her family are excited to make their first trip to the beach at Coney Island. Getting onto the subway, she recalls her trips to the Caspian Sea in Iran—rising early, packing, and enjoying Persian music on the drive with her friend Azadeh. The book moves between her two experiences, one at a gender–segregated beach in Iran where she frolicked in the water and ate saffron ice cream with her friend, and the other where she experienced the sand, sun, and waves at Coney Island. While she is disappointed that the ice cream lady at Coney Island doesn't have her favorite flavor, a new friend urges her to try something different. A sweet tale of the things we leave behind and the new adventures that lay ahead. The bright and happy visuals make this book a treat in itself.

Ideas for Further Engagement

- What is your favorite ice cream flavor? Think of new flavor you would like to try and draw a picture of it.
- Use cotton balls and different colored pom-poms to create your ice cream stand.
- Draw a picture of your favorite things to do at the beach.
- Write about a time when you visited a beach with your family and friends.

***Stepping Stones: A Refugee Family's Journey.* Margriet Ruurs, ill. by Nizar Ali Badr. Orca Book, 2016. 978–1459814905. 28 pp. Fiction, Preschool–Gr. 3.**

Select Awards: Kirkus Reviews Best Books of 2016, Bank Street College of Education Best Children's Books of the Year 2017, CL/R SIG International Reading Association Notable Books for a Global Society 2017, CCBC Best Books starred selection, CA 2017.

Using stone art by the Syrian artist Nizar Ali Badr, the tactile images in this book capture myriad human experiences ranging from a happy childhood to the ravages of war. The story traces young Rama and her family, who live in a peaceful village in Syria. The civil war forces them to flee their homes and take a treacherous journey by foot to safety in a new land. Despite this desperate theme, the faceless stones convey a powerful message of hope and light, as well as spark conversations on world events.

Ideas for Further Engagement

- Pair this book with *The Journey* by Francesca Sanna, *Lost and Found Cat* by Amy Shrodes and Doug Kunt, or with *The Color of Home* by Mary Hoffman.
- Discuss different ways in which a student can make someone new at her school feel welcome.
- ✋ Pair this book with a rock art activity or create stone sculptures.

The Olive Tree. **Elsa Marston, ill. by Claire Ewart. Wisdom Tales, 2014. 978–1937786298. 32 pp. Fiction. Preschool–Gr. 2**

Select Awards: Honorable Mention, Arab American Book Award 2015.

When Sameer's neighbors return to their home after years of war, Sameer is excited to meet them and befriend Muna, a girl his own age. While the family was away, Sameer's family tended to the olive tree that overlooked both homes. Muna, however, doesn't want to play or share the fruits of the tree, and she stakes a claim to the olives as hers alone. One night after a fierce storm, the olive tree is destroyed by lightning. Both families come together to gather the broken branches and slowly overcome their distrust of one another. This is a beautifully illustrated story that shows children how to overcome differences.

Ideas for Further Engagement

- Discuss how an olive branch is often represented as a symbol of peace.
- How can you make new friends?
- Share how you interact with your neighbors.
- Pair this book with *Can You Say Peace?* by Karen Katz, or with *Sitti's Secret* by Naomi Shihab Nye.
- ✋ Look up different symbols of peace and draw them.

Yasmine's Belly Button. **Asmaa Hussein, ill. by Charity Russell. Ruqaya's Bookshelf, 2015. 978–0994750112. 36 pp. Fiction. Preschool–Gr. 1.**

As Yasmine is dressing up for her first day of school, she is anxious and has butterflies in her tummy. Naturally, that means looking at her tummy and finding a little round thingamabob she can't name. Through a lively discussion with her mother, she learns about the special connection that Yasmine had as a baby through her belly button. At school, Yasmine is nervous once again, and her mother reassures her that all will be well once she finds something

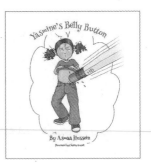

in common with the other kids. With colorful illustrations, a multicultural classroom, and visuals that add to the story, this book will spark many conversations, and a few giggles too.

Ideas for Further Engagement

- Have the students list the things they share in common with a friend.
- Pair this book with *First Day Jitters* by Julie Danneberg and *Judy Love, I Am Too Absolutely Small for School* by Lauren Child, or with *I Am Not a Chair!* by Ross Burach.
- ✋ Look up when school starts for different kids around the world.

Zaid and the Gigantic Cloud. Helal Musleh, ill. by Sabrina Pichardo. Ruqaya's Bookshelf, 2017. 978-0994750198. 36 pp. Fiction. K–Gr. 2.

Zaid's day starts off on a bad note when he learns that his eagerly awaited camping trip is cancelled. Then, things get worse—from the weather, to sitting at the back of the bus, forgetting his lunch and more. As the day progresses, a little gray cloud emerges over Zaid's head and gets bigger and bigger. The author introduces young readers to ideas of frustrations and disappointments. However, by making good choices and taking control of his feelings, Zaid shrinks his gloomy cloud and turns his day around. This is a relatable book full of kind, supporting diverse characters who help children understand and cope with stormy emotions.

Ideas for Further Engagement

- Have the class draw a gloomy cloud and list the things that make them upset.

- Talk about different things you can do to calm down.
- Ask students to share any disappointments they faced recently, and how they got over them.
- Pair this book with *Emily's Tiger* by Miriam Latimer, or with *The Way I Feel* by Janan Cain.

Chapter Books and Middle Grade Books

A Long Pitch Home. **N. D. Lorenzi. Charlesbridge, 2016. 978–1580897136. 256 pp. Fiction. Gr. 2–7.**

Select Awards: South Asia Book Award, 2017 Honor Book.

When Bilal has to move suddenly from Pakistan to America, he encounters many unfamiliar things that confuse him: his ESL course, baseball camp, and how to make new friends. Bilal struggles with a new language and trying to understand foreign customs, and he longs for his home and family. This book is a moving and realistic depiction of the immigrant experience through the eyes of a child. The story effectively weaves in other perspectives: those of a young girl whose father is serving in Afghanistan, Bilal's older cousin and his budding relationship with a girl, and the experiences of Bilal's mom and sister, all in order to talk about the larger issue of assimilating in America.

Discussion Starters

- What are some ways in which Bilal's culture is presented in the book— through food, honorific terms for family members, traditional clothes, and the festivals they celebrate?
- What was difficult for, and what was helpful to Bilal when he first started attending his new school in America?
- How did Bilal make friends? How can you be more empathetic to new kids in the class?
- What were some of the challenges that Bilal faced in getting used to his new life?

- Do you think Bilal was wrong in throwing the ball to Omar Khan in the big game? What would you have done in his place?

Ideas for Further Engagement

- ✋ Ask children to write a short note on the topic "If you had to put your whole life into a suitcase, what would you bring and why?"
- ✋ Research the rules of baseball and cricket, watch short videos of both sports, and compare how they are different.

Quotes for Interpretation

- "Many people are speaking in Urdu, and I overhear some English and Arabic, too. But a few conversations are in languages I've never heard." (24)
- "If I become American, will I still be Pakistani?" (67)
- "It tastes like good memories with friends. It tastes like happiness and holidays. It tastes like home." (148)

A Tale of Highly Unusual Magic. **Lisa Papademetriou. HarperCollins, 2015. 978–0062371218. 320 pp. Fiction. Gr. 3–7.**

Select Awards: South Asia Book Award, Highly Commended Book 2016.

Two girls on opposite sides of the world have a shared adventure through the pages of a magical book. Kai, who is currently visiting her great-aunt in Texas, finds an old book and begins writing in it, and the words magically appear in Leila's copy of the book in Pakistan. As both girls struggle to fit into their worlds—Kai is a loner, and Leila an outsider—they connect with each other through writing, magic, and mystery. This fantasy tale combines issues of belonging and finding oneself with humor and camaraderie.

Discussion Starters

- Have you ever traveled alone to a new place? What was your experience like?

- Why do you think Kai struggled with playing the violin? How did she overcome it?
- Did you empathize with Leila about the goat? What would you have done if you were in Leila's place instead?

Ideas for Further Engagement

🖐 List some family traditions in the various cultures that the children in your classroom belong to, and explore their similarities and differences.

🖐 Design some creative magic teleporting devices that can "talk" to one another.

Quotes for Interpretation

- "Pakistani hospitality is an irresistible force and an immovable object rolled into one." (18)
- "She knew most, but not all, of the dishes on her plate, and she was determined to try everything—even the green stuff. This was part of having 'an authentic cultural experience.'" (40)
- "It was about how, no matter what you did, sometimes things didn't work out." (193)

Amina's Voice. **Hena Khan. Simon and Schuster (Salaam Reads), 2017. 978–1481492065. 208 pp. Fiction. Gr. 3–7.**

Select Awards: Washington Post Best Children's Book of 2017.

Author Hena Khan's first attempt at a middle grade novel showcases the story of Amina, a young Muslim girl growing up in Milwaukee, Wisconsin. Amina struggles with preteen issues of self-confidence, "being cool," and bullying at school, as well as fitting in with her own family. Amina also flounders while juggling the expectations of the two cultures she straddles—her lack of fluency in Arabic, practicing her religion, and balancing the expectations of her extended family. Khan deftly weaves in issues of cultural and religious differences through Amina's interactions with her friends and family.

Discussion Starters

- Why do you think Soojin wanted to change her name? What can you tell about someone by their name?
- What can you do when you come across a name that's hard to pronounce or that you haven't heard before?
- Do you go to any school (other than your middle school) that is like Amina's Sunday school?
- Why do you think the Islamic Cultural Center was damaged? How did it make Amina, her family, and her community feel?

Ideas for Further Engagement

- Write a newspaper article that reports the story of the attack on the mosque.
- Organize a class party to sample Korean and Pakistani food, and write food reviews.

Quotes for Interpretation

- "You know, a lot of Korean people have two names, a Korean one and an English one." (11)
- "If you didn't want American children, you shouldn't have moved here." (18)
- "Muslims have far more friends than enemies in this country." (168)

Escape from Aleppo. **N. H. Senzai. Simon and Schuster/ Paula Wiseman Books, 2018. 978−1481472173. 336 pp. Gr. 3−7.**

Select Awards: Parents Choice Award 2018

Acclaimed author Senzai gently introduces young readers to the Syrian civil war and the fallout on its citizens, especially young children. Suddenly young Nadia's life is transformed from a carefree time of enjoying macaroons, visiting salons, and watching the show *Arab Idol* to a life of fear, hunger, and yearning for her family. Nadia travels through war-torn Syria with an old man, Ammo Mazen, and her pet cat, Mish-Mish, in search of her family. She learns a few tricks of the trade and makes some friends along the way. Senzai creatively weaves in Syrian history, artifacts, and other elements of the country's heritage through flashbacks of Nadia's past.

Discussion Starters

- What are your favorite subjects in school, and why?
- How do you find courage when you're in a difficult situation? What are some helpful thoughts or words you repeat to yourself in order to stay positive?
- Why was it difficult for Nadia to trust the old man?

Ideas for Further Engagement

- ✋ Research the Arab Spring: what caused it and the extent of its impact.
- ✋ Play the BBC's "Syrian Escape Route" smart board interactive activity game (see www.bbc.com/news/world-middle-east-32057601).

Quotes for Interpretation

- "Safe. What does that feel like?" (10)
- "Let's play Assad's army and rebels." (42)
- "Could saving a clay tablet, some books, and coins really preserve five thousand years of history and culture?" (180)

***It Ain't So Awful, Falafel.* Firoozeh Dumas. Houghton Mifflin Harcourt, 2016. 978–0544612310. 384 pp. Historical fiction. Gr. 4–7.**

Select Awards: 2017 Beatty Award Recipient, New York Historical Society's inaugural New Americans Book Prize 2017, Booklist Editors' Choice 2016, Kirkus Best of 2016, Raleigh News & Observer Best of 2016, Time Magazine Best of 2016.

Zomorod Yousafzadeh is a savvy twelve-year-old who struggles with the realities of fitting into middle school and making friends in her newly adopted home in Newport Beach, California. Zomorod, now rechristened as Cindy, expresses dismay at her engineer dad and shy mom for holding on tight to their Iranian roots. Dumas provides a humorous and entertaining autobiographical account of her life

Naheed Senzai
Celebrating Diversity

Can you share a little bit about where you grew up?
When I was four years old I moved to Jubail, Saudi Arabia, from the San Francisco Bay Area, where my father, a civil engineer, was transferred for work. I attended boarding school in London for high school, and then I moved back to the Bay Area when I started college.

Most of my childhood was spent in a Muslim country, Saudi Arabia, within an international community where being Muslim was normative. My transition back to the San Francisco Bay Area was fluid, since it's blessed to have a diverse population representing a variety of ethnic groups, cultures, and religions, and deliciously, a variety of amazing foods!

What inspired you to become a writer?
While growing up, I had access to wonderful librarians and a huge variety of books—both fiction and nonfiction. I was continually amazed at how a bunch of pages could magically transport me to new worlds. I met characters whose shoes I could "walk in," allowing me to visit a marvelous chocolate factory, journey from slavery to freedom, or journey into space to find a long-lost father. As a child, I was fascinated by how authors could produce such wonder simply by stringing words together, and one day I hoped to write a book myself.

What is the one thing that you would like people to know about Muslims?
Muslims are not a monolithic, homogeneous group, especially in the United States—they represent different races and ethnicities, speak different languages, and follow different interpretations of Islam. At the most basic level, we are individuals with our own personalities, strengths, weakness, backgrounds, and goals in life.

What inspired you to write about Muslim characters?
Growing up, the only contemporary American novel I came across with a Muslim character was Harry, in *Sport*, by Louise Fitzhugh. He was black, proud, and smart as a whip—finally reflecting someone who was similar to me—a minority and a Muslim.

As a writer, I first wanted to create similar "mirrors" for Muslim kids—to see valued characters, in stories that reflected their life experiences. And for kids who had never met a Muslim, my goal was to build "windows" where they could "walk in" the shoes of others and befriend people, encounter places and lifestyles different from their own, and hopefully realize that they were more similar than different.

If you had a magic wand, what is the one misconception about Muslims that you would banish forever?

The word *Islam* is derived from the root word *salaam*, which means "peace" and "safety." Today, sadly, Islam is hardly linked to either word. Islam and Muslims, particularly after 9/11, have been portrayed in the public eye, media, films, and literature as a people prone to violence.

In a vicious cycle, those fearing Muslims have turned to violence themselves, as Islamophobia is on the rise. At the root of this fear is ignorance; with my magic wand, I would erase ignorance and encourage a safe place in which to build peace.

What is your favorite story from Islamic traditions?

As a child, I was fascinated by the story of Lailat al Miraj, where the Prophet Muhammad is visited by the angel Gabriel, who provides him with a winged steed, the Buraq. Flying upon its back, the prophet goes on a miraculous night journey, which is both physical and spiritual.

From Mecca, the prophet traveled to Jerusalem, and then into the heavens, where he prays with the prophets that came before him—Abraham, Moses, John the Baptist, and Jesus. The story evoked great magic and imagery for me, engendering a cosmic connection between the earth and the heavens. It also initiated a love of fantasy and science fiction.

How do we—parents, teachers, and librarians—all of us as a community teach children to respect differences and value diversity?

Every religion follows a common "golden rule"—the ethics of reciprocity. It's a simple statement, but if we instill it in our young people (and in adults who seem to have forgotten about it), the world would be a much better place.

> In Islam it is: "None of you [truly] believes until he wishes for his brother what he wishes for himself." Number 13 of Imam "Al-Nawawi's Forty Hadiths."
>
> In Buddhism: "Hurt not others in ways that you yourself would find hurtful." Udana-Varga 5:18
>
> In Christianity: "And as ye would that men should do to you, do ye also to them likewise." Luke 6:31, King James Version.
>
> And in Confucianism: "What I do not wish men to do to me, I also wish not to do to men." Analects 15:23

What is your biggest inspiration from Islam?

While studying American history, the photographs of immigrants arriving at Ellis Island have stayed with me—they came from all corners of the world, and still do, to find their American dream, reminding me of a verse from the Quran:

> O mankind! We created you from a single (pair) of a male and a female, and made you into nations and tribes, that ye may know each other (not that ye may despise each other). Verily the most honored of you in the sight of Allah is (he who is) the most righteous of you.

America is a grand experiment, unique in its composition—except for the Native Americans, we are all from somewhere else. Looking at the hopeful faces from Italy, Ireland, Russia, and Lebanon, I'm inspired by what the verse asks us to do— embrace and celebrate diversity, learn from one another, eat others' delicious foods, and not turn against one another. As I look around the current political landscape, there is much to be done to live by the ideals of the verse.

And finally—biryani or kebabs?

Biryani all the way!

Biography

N. H. Senzai is the author of the award-winning book *Shooting Kabul*, which was chosen by the Asian Pacific Librarians Association as their Young Adult Literature winner and was an NPR Backseat Book Club pick. She is also the author of the Edgar Award nominee *Saving Kabul Corner* and the YALSA pick *Ticket to India*. She spent her childhood in San Francisco and in Jubail, Saudi Arabia, and she attended high school in London, where she was voted "most likely to lead a literary revolution" due to her ability to get away with reading comic books in class. Her upcoming novel is *Escape from Aleppo*, about a girl fleeing Syria when the Arab Spring triggers a civil war there. Visit Senzai online at **www.nhsenzai.com.**

growing up in the United States in the 1980s. The book also shows how the political turmoil in Iran in the late 1970s, and the American hostage crisis in 1980, impact Cindy and her family in America.

Discussion Starters

- Why would Zomorod's life have been easier if her dad named her Sara?
- Did changing Zomorod's name to Cindy help her to fit in?
- What are some questions others ask you when you meet them for the first time?
- How did Cindy struggle to adapt to her new life and school? What could have helped her fit in more easily?

Ideas for Further Engagement

- ✋ Organize a Middle Eastern-themed party with falafel, kebabs, and hummus, or organize a cooking demonstration.
- ✋ Learn about Nowruz, the Persian New Year, and re-create a haft-seen tablescape.
- ✋ Create a list of unique names from different cultures and their meanings.

Quotes for Interpretation

- "So I chose the most normal American name I know, Cindy. Like Cindy Brady from *The Brady Bunch*." (15)
- "All my friends are in books." (16–17)
- "Did you like, bring your camel with you?" (61)

Nine, Ten: A September 11 Story. N. R. Baskin.
Atheneum Books for Young Readers, 2016.
978–1442485068. 197 pp. Fiction. Gr. 3–7.

Select Awards: Bank Street Best Books of the Year 2016,
CBC/NCSS Notable Social Studies Trade Book 2016,
Chicago Public Library's Best of the Best 2016.

This is an insightful look at the intersecting lives
of four kids across America and how 9/11 impacted
their lives. The story reflects on the theme of inter-
connectivity in our society, in particular between children. It is told from
four different perspectives: Naheed, who is struggling with her religious
identity; Sergio, who lives with his grandmother in Brooklyn; Aimee from
California, whose mother is flying to New York; and Will, who recently lost
his father. Despite their different lives, each of them explores the boundaries
of friendship in their day-to-day lives. The description of the events of 9/11 is
age-appropriate while delicately addressing the issues behind the act. The
book ends on an optimistic note where many stand up for a Muslim family
that is being harassed for expressing their solidarity and concern for the victims of 9/11.

Discussion Starters
- What do you know about the 9/11 attacks? Do you know anyone who
  was impacted?
- Was Naheed a good friend to Eliza? Why or why not? What could she
  have done differently to not hurt Eliza's feelings?
- What values did Will learn from his father? How are they reflected in
  his actions?
- How were Naheed and her family impacted after 9/11? Was it fair to
  them?
- How do you think Naheed feels about her hijab? Does she like wearing it
  or not? How has it affected her identity?

Ideas for Further Engagement
- ✋ Show pictures of the 9/11 memorial, discuss the importance of memorials, and ask students about the memorials they have visited. Tie this

into current events with a discussion on the recent removal of the Confederate memorials.

🖐 Design a memorial for the 9/11 victims.

Quotes for Interpretation

- "Sometimes I wish I didn't have to be Naheed the Muslim girl. I wish I could just be Naheed." (107)
- "They did, in a way. Maybe in that way white people think black people all look similar." (134)
- "We are Americans, and no one is going to take that away from us." (180)

Power Forward. **Hena Khan. Simon and Schuster (Salaam Reads), 2018. 978–1534411982. 144 pp. Fiction. Gr. 2–5.**

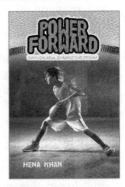

Zayd Saleem is your average fourth grader who loves to play basketball, gets annoyed by his sister, Zara, and tries to walk the fine line between meeting his parents' expectations while also chasing his own dreams. However, things come to a standstill when his mom finds out that he's been missing his violin lessons to practice basketball. Zayd's uncle, Jamal Mamoo, is going through this own tribulations in an arranged marriage. The first in the forthcoming series Zayd Saleem, Chasing the Dream, *Power Forward* provides a light-hearted story with insightful everyday cultural details about a Muslim American household (and their quirks) along with life lessons on standing up for yourself and working hard to achieve your dreams.

Discussion Starters

- How would you describe Zayd's relationship with his parents and extended family? Is it similar to the relationships you have with your own family or different? In what way?
- Why do you think Zayd hesitates to talk to his parents about his waning interest in violin lessons? Have you ever given up a hobby you started?
- How does his journal help him discover his anxiety? What are some strategies you use to figure out something that is bothering you?

Ideas for Further Engagement

- ✋ Write a short story about a time when you had the courage to ask your parents for something you really wanted.
- ✋ Read the sequel *On Point* to find out if Zayd makes the basketball team.

Quotes for Interpretation

- "It's a statement. Like she knows the future. Naano kind of speaks like Yoda." (13)
- "The only thing she's more obsessed with than the perfect cup of chai is how to fatten up 'skinny mouse.' That's her nickname for me."(14)
- "I wouldn't trade these people for anything. Okay, maybe just Zara. But only for a starting spot on the Wizards." (126)

The Breadwinner. Deborah Ellis. Groundwood Books, 2000. 978–1554987658. 176 pp. Fiction. Gr. 3–9.

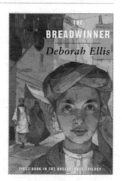

Select Awards: Middle East Book Award 2002, Peter Pan Prize 2003.

A compelling account of a young girl's life during the Taliban rule in Afghanistan, *The Breadwinner* is highly recommended for ages eight and up. It provides a window into the lives of an educated Afghan family, the struggles they face, and their attempts to stand up to the Taliban. The story focuses on the experiences of a young girl, Parvana, who is forced to "become" a boy (*bachaposh*) to earn money for her family after her father is arrested. A sequel titled *Parvana's Journey* continues the story of her difficult journey to find her mother and the rest of her family.

Discussion Starters

- What do you have in common with Parvana?
- What examples can you find in the book which showcase women resisting the Taliban rule and standing up for themselves as best they could?
- Though Shazia and Parvana were not good friends in school, how did they become good friends in the story?
- How do you think Parvana's parents helped her to be brave and courageous?

- Pair this book with the graphic novel *The Breadwinner* and discuss the similarities and differences between the original story and the graphic novel.

Ideas for Further Engagement

-  Organize a screening of the movie *The Breadwinner* by Nora Twomey, and compare it with the book.
- Show short videos or postcards on Afghanistan for children to understand the cultural setting of the story.

Quotes for Interpretation

- "You are all brave women. You are all inheritors of the courage of Malali." (29)
- "Up until then, she had seen Talibs only as men who beat women and arrested her father. Could they have feelings of sorrow, like other human beings?" (80)
- "I just want to be an ordinary kid again." (128)

The Green Bicycle. **Haifaa Al Mansour. Puffin Books, 2016. 978–0147515032. 368 pp. Fiction. Gr. 4–8.**

Select Awards: Amelia Bloomer List, Middle Grade Fiction, 2016; Notable Social Studies Trade Books for Young People, 6–8, 2016.

Mansour spins a relatable story of Wadjda, a determined young girl who finds herself in a society and place where she doesn't belong. She struggles to follow school rules, and dreams of getting her own shiny new bicycle one day. She is industrious and resourceful and sells bracelets, mixtapes, and anything else she can to fund her bicycle. The lure of money leads her into some unfortunate circumstances, but resilient Wadjda tries to fix them by signing up for the Religious Club and the Quran Recitation Contest. Can she memorize the long verses of the Quran to win the 1,000-riyal prize and fulfill her dream? This book addresses many issues of priorities, honesty, expectations, and friendship in an age-appropriate and heartwarming way.

Discussion Starters

- Did Wadjda fit in her school? Why or why not?
- Why was Wadjda so keen on getting a bicycle? How did she go about getting it?
- Has there been anything you really wanted but could not have? What did you do about it?
- What did you think of Wadjda's relationship with her mother? Was it similar or different from your relationship with your mother?

Ideas for Further Engagement

- 🖐 Watch the film *Wadjda,* and compare it to the book.
- 🖐 Screen the documentary *A Stranger in Her Own City* by Khadija al-Salami and compare the characters of Wadjda and Najmia.

Quotes for Interpretation

- "Something troubling was happening between her parents, but she didn't like to think about it. Thinking about it made it real." (18)
- "... A bicycle! Have you ever seen a girl riding a bicycle?" (80)
- "Her abayah flowing behind her like a true superhero's cape, she rode in circles through the empty lot." (273)

***The Gauntlet.* Karuna Riazi. Simon and Schuster (Salaam Reads), 2017. 978–1481486965. 304 pp. Fiction. Gr. 3–7.**

Farah Mirza is a smart girl who is ready to take up the gauntlet for a good cause anytime. Still, she never imagined she would ever have to do so to protect her little brother, Ahmad. Author Karuna Riazi spins an invigorating tale in which twelve-year-old Farah and her two friends are transported into an ancient game called the Gauntlet. They must use every ounce of ingenuity, presence of mind, and courage to protect themselves and save Ahmad or risk being imprisoned in the game forever. This fantasy thriller will captivate the attention of young and old readers alike, and expose them to various everyday objects, concepts, and references to

Muslim culture and heritage such as souks, *sandesh*, saris, *chai*, *pahelis*, and *samosas* that form part of the subtext.

Discussion Starters

- What's your favorite board game and why?
- What religion does Farah practice? How can you tell?
- How were Farah, Alex, and Essie different from each other? Which of their individual skills helped them in the Gauntlet game?
- Can you describe some traits of Farah's character that you admire? Did you notice the sense of pride Farah has for her family?

Ideas for Further Engagement

✋ Find words in English that were derived from Arabic. For example: captain is from al-kaptan, and so long is from salaam.

✋ Design a board game around the book.

Quotes for Interpretation

- "As in many families, every once in a while, Farah was expected to lose a game or two to her younger sibling." (1)
- "She didn't do sweets, not even the Bangladeshi kind that the rest of her family devoured. She liked to think of herself as a bit of a rebel, at least in this small way." (3–4)
- "It was jinn almost every time. There weren't the sweet, wish-granting genies that Disney had turned them into. These jinn ranged from mischievous to . . . vengeful." (20)

The Red Pencil. **Andrea Davis Pinkney, ill. by Shane W. Evans. Little, Brown Books for Young Readers, reprint edition, 2015. 978–0316247825. 368 pp. Fiction. Gr. 4 and up.**

Select Awards: SLJ Best Books 2014, Middle Grade; Kirkus Reviews Best Books of 2014, Middle-Grade Books; Booklist Lasting Connections 2014, Language Arts; Center for the Study of Multicultural Children's Literature, Best Multicultural Books of 2014; Winner, IRA Notable Books for a Global Society 2015; *Booklist* Top 10 Multicultural Fiction for Youth 2015; ALA Notable

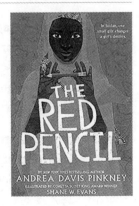

Books for Children 2015, Middle Readers; 2015 Amelia Bloomer Project List, Middle Grade, Fiction; New York Times Notable Children's Books of 2014, Middle Grade; Capitol Choices 2015.

This book offers an insightful perspective on gender issues. It is narrated by twelve-year-old Amira, who is eager to go to school, despite the insurmountable obstacles in both her personal life and the turmoil in her country. Set in Sudan during the war, the story details the impact on Amira's life when the Janjaweed attack her village. She has to muster the courage and resilience to walk to a neighboring refugee camp and reestablish her life. At the refugee camp, she is given a red pencil which empowers her in more ways than one. The book's vivid hand-drawn illustrations and poetic verses bring her story to life and entice readers to identify and empathize with her. This book exquisitely explores powerful ideas of friendship, aspirations, and life and death against a backdrop of turmoil and instability.

Discussion Starters

- What is special about Amira's twelfth birthday? Are there any traditions in your family that are based on a certain age?
- Why do wars occur? What are some major wars that you are familiar with? How can we reduce the possibility of more wars?
- Amira and her mother disagree on the value of education. What are the benefits of education? Why do you think so many girls around the world are unable to get an education?
- What are some games, toys, and ideas that Amira uses to remain optimistic and cheerful as she goes about her life?

Ideas for Further Engagement

- ✋ Write a poem or draw a picture of something that inspired you from the book.
- ✋ Find out the name of the ingredient used in ice cream and gummy bears that is found in large quantities in Sudan.

Quotes for Interpretation

"'Schooling costs money we do not have,' she says."

"What they teach from those books is useless to you, Amira."

"We need you here, to milk our cows, to pick okra and melons, to rake."
(48)

"Everywhere bodies:
Mix-and-match
Cultures,
Clashing,
Smashing
Against
One another.
All so different,
But also the same." (155)

"Here is the problem:
So many thousands of nomads + bellies +
souls + hearts + wandering + torn
+ hungry + aching + longing =
Too many
Tragedies
To count." (233)

The Refugee. Alan Gratz. Scholastic, 2017. 978–0545880831. 352 pp. Fiction. Gr. 4–7.

Select Awards: 2018 NCTE Charlotte Huck Outstanding Fiction for Children Honor Book, New York Public Library Top 100 Best Books for Kids 2017, *Publishers Weekly* Best Books of 2017, ABC Best Books for Young Readers 2017, Texas Bluebonnet Award Nominee 2018–2019, Junior Library Guild Selection.

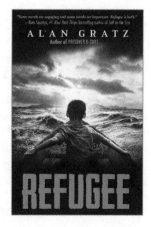

Drawing on parallels between the lives of three children during three different times of political turmoil (in Germany, Cuba, and Syria), Gratz showcases the resilience, courage, humility, empathy, and resourcefulness of children in exquisite ways. The stories in this book are best suited for older middle grade children, or even young adult readers, and they will fuel numerous discussions on war, discrimination, humility, kindness, difficult decision-making, and character-building.

Discussion Starters

- Can you find examples of how Josef, Mahmoud, and Isabel were coura- geous?
- Which character did you identify with and why?
- What were the commonalities between the three characters?

Ideas for Further Engagement

- Examine the histories of persecution in Germany, Cuba, and Syria.
- Identify a local organization that supports refugees, and have the stu- dents participate in a fund-raising project or help refugees in any other appropriate manner.

Quotes for Interpretation

- "Suddenly, Josef was the man of the family—the only adult in the fam- ily—whether he wanted to be or not." (167)
- "All his life he'd practiced being hidden. Unnoticed. Now, at last, when he most needed to be seen, he was truly invisible." (192)
- "The refugees had stopped to get down on their knees and pray, and these people watching them didn't do that. Didn't understand. Now the refugees looked foreign again, alien. Like they didn't belong." (302)

The Turtle of Oman. **Naomi Shihab Nye. HarperCollins, 2014. 978–0062019721. 304 pp. Fiction. Gr. 3–7.**

Select Awards: Kirkus Reviews Best Books of 2014, Mid- dle-Grade Books; Winner, IRA Notable Books for a Global Society 2015; 2015 NCTE Charlotte Huck Award for Out- standing Fiction for Children, Recommended Title; ALA Notable Books for Children 2015, Middle Readers; *Horn Book* Fanfare List: Best Books of 2014, Fiction.

Many of us have experienced the hardship of moving from our homes. Through this story, Nye deftly shares the thoughts and feel- ings of Aref, a twelve-year-old boy preparing for his move from Muscat to Michigan. The story explores Aref's relationship with his grandfather, his pet cat, his cousins who stay behind, and his love and familiarity for his home and country. Nye weaves many Arabic words and customs into the story in a natural way, giving readers a genuine exposure to and understanding of Aref's life in Oman, which in many ways is similar to life in America.

Discussion Starters

- Have you ever moved to a new place? How did you feel about it?
- What did you miss about the place you moved away from?
- Does your family have a motto? What is it?
- What did you enjoy about Aref's relationship with his grandfather, Sidi?

Ideas for Further Engagement

✋ Write about a move that your family made and how it made you feel. If you have not moved, think about where you would like to move to, and why.

✋ Look up an animal that Oman is famous for.

Quotes for Interpretation

- "I can't fit any good things into it. Just stupid things, like underpants." (96)
- "You weren't sure who lived in any of them, but you felt you could knock on any door and the people inside might know some of the same things you knew or welcome you in—just because you all belonged there." (117)
- "What if they make fun of my hat?" (236)

The Sky at Our Feet. **Nadia Hashimi. Harper Collins, 2018. 978–0062421937. 304 pp. Fiction. Gr. 2–7.**

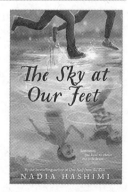

This is a gripping story about a young boy, Jason Shah, whose mother had come to America from Afghanistan with Jason in her belly, but ended up overstaying her visa. Jason is fearful when his mother is taken away by two police officers just days after she has told him that she is an illegal immigrant in the United States. Seeking solace with his sole acquaintance in Manhattan, he decides to make the arduous journey from New Jersey to Manhattan on his own. His journey turns into a series of adventures resulting in a trip to the emergency room, making a new genius friend, a visit to the Central Park Zoo, and even meeting a famous movie star. Hashimi weaves in funny riddles along the way to entertain younger middle grade readers.

Discussion Starters

- What did you enjoy most about this story?
- Did you feel sorry for Jason or proud of him?
- Why was Jason's mother taken away by the police officers, but Jason wasn't?
- How do you think Max and Jason were similar? How were they different?

Ideas for Further Engagement

- ✋ With a map of New Jersey and Manhattan, trace Jason's path from his home to his aunt's house.
- ✋ Research immigration laws in the United States, and trace the history of how people of various nationalities came to live in America.

Quotes for Interpretation

- "But you're from another country, so it's different for you. I bet you eat different foods and speak a different language and all that. You're not plain old American." (79)
- "My second grade teacher used to tell the kids to be extra nice to me because I was a brave and special girl—as if I couldn't tell what kind of *special* she meant." (154)
- "Can I be American and Afghan? I may not have been born in that country, but I'm hiding in a truck right now because of what happened there. The food I eat is Afghan, the music we listen to is Afghan, the gift-filled holiday I look forward to is Eid, not Christmas or Hanukkah." (252)

The *Vine Basket*. Josanna La Valley. Clarion Books, 2013. 978–0547848013. 256 pp. Fiction. Gr. 5–9.

This is a haunting story about loss, struggle, and the power of hope. The northwestern region of China is home to the Uyghur, an ethnic and religious minority persecuted by the Chinese government. Fourteen-year-old Mehrigul has been pulled out of school to work on the family farm. Her family has fallen on hard times: a brother has absconded due to political turmoil, her father has taken to drinking and gambling, her mother is depressed, and even the unforgiving landscape outlines a bleak future. Yet, Mehrigul strives to change her fortunes with her talent at basket-weaving. She is encouraged in this endeavor by her grandfather, and driven by her own desire for change. This engaging and realistic portrayal of the Uyghur spotlights the political, social, cultural, and familial tensions that are at the heart of the survival of an ancient culture in modern times.

Discussion Starters
- How does Mehrigul feel about being taken out of school to help with her family's farm?
- How is Mehrigul's family different from her friends Pati and Hasinja?
- What were the different Uyghur crafts mentioned in the book?
- Do Mehrigul's parents treat her differently from her brother Mehmet? Why or why not?
- What are Mehrigul's motivations to continue her basket-weaving? What changes do you see in her as the book progresses?

Ideas for Further Engagement
- ✋ Write a postcard to the author of the book or address it to one of the characters from the book.
- ✋ Watch the short film *Dream from the Heart* about young Uyghur soccer players.

Quotes for Interpretation

- "Mehrigul wanted to be the person telling visitors that her Uyghur ancestors had been here greeting people during the golden age of the old Silk Road." (46)
- "Is it wrong for a girl to make baskets? Ata said it's only the men who are craftsmen." (48)
- "She rattled on in English that had no meaning for Mehrigul but was surely meant to make her feel inferior." (101)

Young Adult Books

A Bottle in the Gaza Sea. **Valerie Zenatti. Bloomsbury US Childrens', 2014. 978–1599902005. 160 pp. Fiction. Young adult.**

Naim and Tal are on opposite sides of the Palestine-Israeli conflict. Though Tal believes in a peaceful resolution, she is shaken by a recent terrorist attack. Seeking answers to the many questions that haunt her, she asks her brother, an Israeli soldier, to throw her letter in a bottle out to sea. Naim finds the letter and begins to correspond with Tal through e-mail. Initially wary of each other's positions, Tal and Naim slowly open up to one another and exchange their views on fear, hate, and their circumscribed lives. Within the safe confines of the Internet, both teenagers begin to express themselves honestly. They are able to replace their anger, confusion, exhaustion, and cynicism with hope. Told with nuance, Tal and Naim's eye-opening story brings alive their desire for freedom, and ends on a note for peace.

Discussion Starters

- Why does Tal continue to write to Naim despite his hostile responses? What is she trying to understand about him and by extension Palestine?
- What are the differences in Tal and Naim's worldviews? Is this difference a result of their class backgrounds?

- Why do you think both Tal and Naim keep their correspondence a secret from their family and friends?
- What changes do both of them undergo as a result of communicating with one another?
- Pair this book with *Habibi* by Naomi Shihab Nye.

Ideas for Further Engagement

✍ Watch the film *A Bottle in the Gaza Sea* and compare the film and the book. Does the film have more information about the supporting characters? Why do you think this is so?

✍ Write a short note on the quote "Dreams are what get us somewhere," and what it means to you.

Quotes for Interpretation

- "... streets where a donkey could bump into a man without wondering whether he was a Jew, Christian, or a Muslim. Several thousand good, pious people watched over the sacred sites of three religions, thinking they were the last to remember them." (8)
- "I imagine you are the same age as me, but I don't know whether, at seventeen, you feel very old or very young." (16)
- "... if people like you and me try to get to know each other, the future might have a chance of turning out some other color than the red of spilled blood and the black of hate." (25)

***An Ember in the Ashes.* Sabaa Tahir. Razorbill (imprint of Penguin Random House), 2015. 978–1595148049. 480 pp. Fiction. Young adult.**

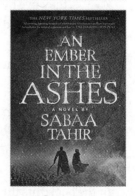

Select Awards: New York Times Bestseller list 2015; Winner Favorite Fantasy, People's Choice Award 2015.

Inspired by ancient Rome, this evocative fantasy novel questions ideas of heroism, the hunger of power, and the price of freedom. Laia lives with her brother and grandparents, learned Scholars who now avoid the prying eyes of the Empire. However, when her brother gets arrested for treason, Laia reaches out to the Resistance for help. She ends up bartering her freedom in order to become a slave and a spy within the Empire's imperial academy that trains its ruthless soldiers. Elias is one such soldier with a plan to change the Empire's ways if he can become Emperor through a deadly contest. With a fast-paced narrative, oppressive violence, and allegorical references to the world today, Tahir's impressive debut novel warns us against the dangers of history repeating itself and the power of knowledge to effect change.

Discussion Starters

- How do you think slavery has affected the Scholars and other communities? How are the slaves treated by the Martials?
- What can you infer about the value of military might over knowledge?
- What is the growth arc of Laia's character in the book?
- What are Elias's and Laia's feelings towards their parents?
- What parallels can you draw from the story to our world today?
- Pair the book with the sequels: *A Torch against the Night* and *A Reaper at the Gates.*

Ideas for Further Engagement

- Think back to one moment in your life that has significantly impacted your life. Write a short essay about that moment and its impact.
- Create an ad or billboard for the book.

Quotes for Interpretation

- "... they live by Izzat, a code of honor as old as the Scholar people." (23)
- "If you or I had been born to different parents, we might be in her shoes instead of our own." (244)
- "Seeing the enemy as human. A general's ultimate nightmare." (367)

A Girl Like That. **Tanaz Bhathena. Farrar, Straus & Giroux, 2018. 978–0374305444. 384 pp. Fiction. Young adult.**

Set in Jeddah, Saudi Arabia, this remarkable debut novel begins with the tragic death of the two main protagonists, Zarin and Porus. The remainder of the book flits through the past and the present and threads interweaving narratives of Zarin, Porus, Mishal, Abdullah, and Farhan, to stitch together a portrait of a misunderstood teenager. Zarin Wadia, a headstrong orphan, adopts a devil-may-care attitude to block out the physical abuse she suffers at home and the bullying she experiences at school. Porus Dumasia is her closest friend and confidante and perhaps something more, while the others form part of her school universe. The well-realized characters allow readers to examine how the nuances of their backstories shape them. This book also provides an insider perspective on a mostly unknown culture where "segregation in

Saudi Arabia wasn't limited to gender alone." The book sensitively tackles complex issues of bullying, abuse, rape culture, and peer pressure. The prevailing sense of claustrophobia in the lives of the female characters is particularly affecting. In reflecting on the tragedy of Zarin's death, Mishal finds the strength to alter the course of her predestined life. Heartbreaking in its honesty, the lingering power of Bhathena's prose unsettles long after you're done with the book.

Discussion Starters

- How was Zarin seen by her peers at school?
- Why did Zarin break up with Abdullah? Do you think she handled the situation well?
- What were the differences in the expectations and treatment of Mishal and Abdullah?
- How did Zarin and Mishal feel constrained in their own homes?
- Why was Zarin afraid to open up to Porus? Why couldn't she reach out to her teacher Mrs. Khan, or to Dr. Thomas?
- What are the different kinds of peer pressure that kids face today?
- Discuss how gender plays a role in the story.

Ideas for Further Engagement

- ✋ Write a short note on an event that has taken place which has made a significant impact on your life so far.
- ✋ Organize an anti-bullying awareness campaign in your high school with explanations of how bullying can take different forms, and what a person being bullied can do.

Quotes for Interpretation
- "What are you? Hindu, Muslim, Christian, or Jew?" (36)
- " . . . for a second I wasn't Zarin Wadia everyone knew, but a girl, a normal schoolgirl who had won something and was proud of it." (185)
- "Our roots are often a source of pride for us; mine were a constant source of shame." (308)

Arab of the Future: A Childhood in the Middle East, **1978–1984: A Graphic Memoir. Riad Sattouf, ill. by author. Metropolitan Books, 2015. 978–1627793445. 160 pp. Fiction. Young adult.**

Select Awards: Los Angeles Times Book Prize 2015.

This is an incredibly honest, quirky, and deeply personal account of the author Riad Sattouf's childhood. Sattouf is the son of a Syrian professor and a French mother, and his childhood straddled two cultures, three continents, and multiple viewpoints. His father's work took him to Tripoli, Libya, under the dictatorship of Muammar Gaddafi and then to Homs, Syria, under Hafez al-Assad, where the young Sattouf proves to be a fly on the wall who makes detailed observations on such issues as the scarcity of food, casual racism, and how political changes affect the common man. Follow his story in *Arab of the Future 2.*

Discussion Starters
- Why do you think the author was embarrassed to speak Arabic in France?
- How does the author's perspective change in each of his new surroundings?

Ideas for Further Engagement
- Research the Arab Spring and the events leading up to it. Also, research the role that the United States played in it.
- Create your own graphic novel about key cultural influences in your life.

Quotes for Interpretation

- "You must LOVE your family, love them more than yourself." (128)
- "In Arabic, there are lots of sounds that don't exist in French. To me, it sounded like a person throwing up . . . So I was embarrassed to speak Arabic in front of strangers." (148)
- "You have to be tough with them. You have to force them to get an education, make them go to school . . . If they decide for themselves, they do nothing. They're lazy-ass bigots, even though they have the same potential as everyone else." (150)

***Love, Hate and Other Filters.* Samira Ahmed. Soho Teen, 2018. 978–1616958473. 288 pp. Fiction. Young adult.**

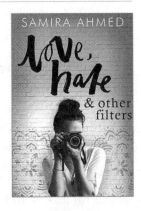

In this memorable coming-of-age story of a young Muslim teen, author Samira Ahmed deftly weaves her protagonist's search for her own identity against the larger backdrop of political issues simmering in America today. Seventeen-year-old Maya Aziz keeps her film school dreams firmly shuttered from her parents. She struggles to toe the conventional line of the "good daughter" who must accept the mantle of parental expectation, marry the man of their dreams, and live the life they have charted out for her. Maya attempts to balance her identity with trying to fit in as "a normal teenager." To complicate matters, she is in the blushes of a first love. While Maya is engrossed in her own battles and is testing the waters to make it on her own, a sinister crime committed miles away impacts her life in profound ways that force her to forge her own path. With cleverly interspersed vignettes that point to the bias and discrimination that Muslims face in America, *Love, Hate and Other Filters* calls out the hypocrisy of law enforcement, the media, and mainstream society. As Maya's character matures, you end up rooting for her to chase her dreams even if it means letting go of the people she loves.

Discussion Starters

- How does Maya perceive herself? Are her experiences growing up in America similar to Kareem's?
- How does Maya react to Kareem's drinking wine? Does she expect him to be a certain kind of Muslim? What does it tell us about the many ways people follow their faith?
- How do Phil and Maya feel about their parents' expectations of them? Why do they both hesitate to tell their parents their own aspirations?
- How does Maya envision assimilation in America?
- In the aftermath of the terrorist attack, are law officials and the media quick to jump to conclusions about the perpetrator? What does this say about the attitudes prevalent in mainstream American society?

Ideas for Further Engagement

- ✋ Look up newspaper and magazine articles related to the issues discussed in the book, and examine them to determine the perspective they have been written from.
- ✋ Pair this book with *The Hate You Give* by Angie Thomas and compare the turning points for the protagonists in both books.

Quotes for Interpretation

- "Listen to you. We raised you with too much American independence. Talking back to your elders. And all this privacy business. Who needs privacy from their parents?" (69)
- "We share an unspoken understanding, two people from similar backgrounds raised in similar ways in America. I never have to explain so many basic things to him." (115)
- "And we can help make it better by being here and living our lives and being happy. We can be . . . We are American and Indian and Muslim." (249)

Ms. Marvel: No Normal. G. Willow Wilson. Marvel, 2014. 978–0785190219. 120 pp. Fiction. Young adult.

Select Awards: 2015 Hugo Award, Best Graphic Story.

A true-blue (okay, brown) teenage Muslim super-hero in a comic book? Bring her on! Kamala Khan feels like she is failing at being an average New Jersey teen—she is not blonde or popular enough to fit in. Her multiple identities—teenager, Jersey girl, daughter of Pakistani-immigrant parents, Muslim—pull her in different directions. Though she morphs into Ms. Marvel and is endowed with extraordinary powers, she struggles to gain control over her powers. Kamala must look inward to her own strengths, and outward to the values imparted by her parents and by religious teachings, to come to her own realizations about duty and responsibility. This comic-book series ends on a cliff-hanger to see if the newly minted Ms. Marvel will use her powers to help herself and her community. Kamala's cultural and religious background, as well as her domestic dilemmas, provide a fertile, angsty ground for this teenager at a crossroads, but this story of a gutsy, nontraditional heroine is buoyed by strong writing, visually popping graphics, and did we mention a cape?

Discussion Starters
- Are Kamala's struggles with culture and discovering her own identity similar to those of all American teenagers?
- Do Kamala's expectations of what a hero looks like and does change during the course of the comic?
- Why do you think people from diverse cultural, ethnic, and religious backgrounds find it difficult to fit in?
- Read the additional volumes of *Ms. Marvel* to follow Kamala's story.

Ideas for Further Engagement
- ✋ Divide students into groups and ask them to create a superhero/heroine and brainstorm her character traits, superpowers, and related characteristics.

🖐 List out some aspects of cultural folklore that have shaped your identity and continue to inspire and inform your choices.

Quotes for Interpretation
- "Aren't I allowed to do anything my way? Just once?" (7)
- "Why am I the only one signed out of health class? Why do I have to bring pakoras to school for lunch? Why am I stuck with the weird holidays? Everybody else gets to be normal." (7)
- "You and Baba want me to be a perfect little Muslim girl . . . straight As, Med school, no boys, no booze, then some handpicked rich husband from Karachi and a billion babies." (90)

***Rebels by Accident.* Patricia Dunn. Francis Sourcebooks Fire, 2014. 978–1492601388. 320 pp. Fiction. Young adult.**

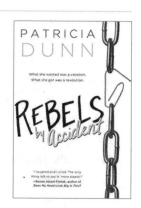

Select Awards: Middle East Book Awards 2015, Honorable Mention.

When Mariam and Deanna's one act of bravado—sneaking out of their homes to a high school party—gets them busted by the cops, their parents are furious. Mariam's traditional Egyptian parents pack her off to Cairo to live with her grandmother, or *sittu*. They hope that the grandmother's well-known "iron fist" will provide the discipline and structure that Mariam needs. Deanna's mother sends her along too, and both girls embark on a journey where they experience a revolution that is both political and personal. Mariam's notorious grandmother turns out to be a fount of wisdom and love, and soon both friends discover her secrets amid the civic unrest that follows. This is an engaging and fast-paced read that packs everything from history, sightseeing, teenage fights, and political protests to teenage crushes and marriage proposals. Dunn offers a whirlwind view of life as an Egyptian American and the transformative power of events that are larger than us.

Discussion Starters
- How are Mariam and Deanna bullied at school? How do their reactions differ from one another?

- What does Mariam think of her Egyptian heritage, and how do her feelings change as the book progresses?
- How do the female characters in the book challenge the stereotypical notions of being a Muslim woman?
- If you were traveling abroad, what resources would you use to plan the trip? What can you do to be culturally aware of and sensitive to the places you visit?

Ideas for Further Engagement

- ✍ Write a personal note about one of your grandparents and how they inspired you or shaped you into who you are today.
- ✍ Divide the class into groups and have each group share information about different periods of Egyptian history.

Quotes for Interpretation

- "Their favorite insults were that my dad was in Al-Qaeda and my mom was only one of his many wives." (2)
- "I don't want to look like I'm Egyptian. I don't want to walk like one or talk like one or be one. I just want to be what I am: American." (73)
- "Look, I act all tough because I got tired of being bullied." (176)

Ten Things I Hate about Me. **Randa Abdel-Fattah. Orchard Books, 2010. 978–0545050562. 304 pp. Fiction. Young adult.**

Select Awards: Kathleen Mitchell Award 2008, CBC/NCSS Notable Social Studies Trade Book for Young People 2010.

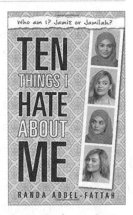

Jamilah Towfeek has been hiding her Lebanese Muslim background at her Australian high school for the last ten years. Dying her hair blonde and wearing blue contact lenses is all she needs to transform into "Jamie" and avoid the racial slurs targeted at the more ethnic students. At home, she is a dutiful daughter who is at the mercy of the rules of her "Stone Age" widowed dad, who monitors her friends and curfew like a hawk. Her happy place is her weekly outing to the Arabic school, where she is the drummer of the band. While Jamilah can't invite her friends over and avoids going to parties, she realizes that her search for acceptance among her peers comes at a price. She manages to fly under the radar, though, until a popular boy in school takes an interest in her. The constant pressure of being someone else forces Jamilah to turn to an online forum, and she opens up to an anonymous boy who in turn questions her secrets and lies. This book about a young teenager searching for her identity is told with humor and grace. In the end, Jamilah learns to find her voice and figure out for herself how to blend her two selves into one.

Discussion Starters
- Why does Jamilah feel she needs to hide her true identity to be accepted? Why does this become a bigger issue when a boy is interested in her?
- Does Jamie's father have a different set of rules for her brother Bilal? Why do you think this is?
- Why is Jamie more comfortable opening up to John online? What do you think prevents her from being honest about herself in real life?
- Are there times when you have hidden something about yourself for fear of how you will be judged?

Ideas for Further Engagement
- Listen to the Layaali Arabic Music Ensemble and the way they incorporate traditional Arab musical instruments.
- Write a short piece on how to interpret this quote: "I am not a headline or a walking stereotype. I'm just me."
- Organize a training or discussion on the dos and don'ts of social media etiquette.

Quotes for Interpretation
- "I am not a headline or a walking stereotype. I'm just me." (30)
- "At my school if you speak two languages, or have dark skin or don't celebrate Christmas, you're never really accepted as an equal." (75)
- "He's a bigot and a bully, but he's popular because he provides entertainment value." (116)

Randa Abdel-Fattah
The Personal and Political

Can you tell us a little about where you grew up and what inspired you to be a writer?

I grew up in Melbourne, Australia. I'm a child of the 1980s (Kylie Minogue, Madonna, *The Goonies*, roller skates, and *The Baby-Sitters Club*) and a teen of the 1990s (Michael Jackson, making dua that Allah would send me the equivalent of Colin Firth in BBC's *Pride and Prejudice*, *X-Men* comic books, antiracism activism, chips in white buttered rolls). I've loved writing stories ever since I was a child. Reading a good book was always my best muse. It made me passionate about wanting to try to create my own stories, worlds, and characters.

What inspired you to write about Muslim characters?

I came of age at the time of the first Gulf War. Suddenly, being Arab and Muslim was no longer an identity but an accusation. Australian Arabs and Muslims were cast as the fifth column, the threatening "other." At age fifteen, I wanted to write a story from the point of view of a teenage Muslim girl negotiating her identity in such a climate, and so I wrote the first draft of what was later published as *Does My Head Look Big in This?*

Your books don't shy away from touching on a lot of political issues—white supremacy, identity politics, political debates surrounding the hijab. How do you balance different points of view on these issues?

Political issues such as racism shouldn't be confined to academic or media discussions. It is a lived experience, a funda-mental part of many people's everyday lives, something they negotiate and struggle against. And I think it's so important that young people have their stories validated and that those who are born into the privilege of whiteness understand that privilege and what it means for their life chances and experiences compared to racialized minorities. I balance these points of view by remembering first and foremost that what drives my writing are my characters, not some bigger "message." I am just as interested in the backstory, life-world, mindset, and social-ization of a racist character, for example, as I am in the story of my "heroes." The intersections between these characters are what count the most to me.

What is the one thing that you would like people to know about Muslims?

That there is no "one thing." That Muslims do not constitute a fixed category or monolith. There is diversity in knowledge, experience, understanding, observance of Islam, and in Muslim identity. Every facet of the human condition is present among "Muslims" too.

But okay, if I have to say one thing: remember where you leave your shoes when you visit a mosque, because the chances are you will lose them.

If you had a magic wand, what is the one misconception about Muslims that you would banish forever?
That the Muslim world is in turmoil because Muslims are "uncivilized/don't get along/only understand violence." I have sat through interviews with so-called educated journalists who act as though the only thing stopping Muslims from living lives of peace and stability is Islam and/or the "lack of a Reformation/Enlightenment."

We need a radical shift in educating people about the history of the Muslim world, how it is fundamentally inter-twined with the rise of "the West," and how the West has intervened, interfered, exploited, and abused the Muslim world and has a massive part to play in the state we are in today. Maybe I'm being too ambitious. How about we just start with two words: Sykes-Picot, and work our way from there!

How do we—parents, teachers, and librarians—all of us as a community teach children to respect differences and value diversity?
Reading! Reading fiction, nonfiction, poetry. I sincerely believe that it is through opening our hearts and minds to stories that we build understanding and empathy. We start to appreciate who we are, how and why we got here, and what we can do to learn from our mistakes. When we read we are engaged in suspending our own beliefs, values, personalities, and judgments, and we're surrendering ourselves to somebody else's point of view. It demands empathy. It demands that you open yourself to another person's perspective.

What is your favorite story from Islamic traditions?
There are so many! But one story that always makes my heart melt is when an old senile woman wanted to speak to Muhammad and he sat with her patiently, letting her talk and talk as he listened until she was finished. Such a simple, generous, tender act of compassion and patience.

What is your biggest inspiration from Islam?
To be conscientious and humble, invest my life with purpose, and remember that every atom's worth of goodwill must be accounted for.

Finally, biryani or kebabs?
Biryani. And I'm Arab. Go figure. Thanks— now I'm hungry!

Biography

Randa Abdel-Fattah is the award-winning author of 11 novels that have been published in more than 15 countries. She has worked as a lawyer, human rights advocate, and community volunteer with different human rights and migrant and refugee resource organizations. She has a PhD in sociology and is a researcher on Islamophobia, racism, and everyday multiculturalism in Australia. Abdel-Fattah is currently working on the feature film adaptation of *Does My Head Look Big in This?* In 2017 her novel *Where the Streets Had a Name* was adapted to the stage by Australia's leading children's theatrical company. Abdel-Fattah is a regular guest at schools around Australia, where she addresses students about her books and the social justice issues they raise. She is a regular guest at writer's festivals and is regularly sought for comment in the media. She lives in Sydney with her husband and children.

That Thing We Call a Heart. **Sheba Karim. HarperTeen, 2017. 978–0062445704. 288 pp. Fiction. Young adult.**

Shabnam, a young Pakistani American teen, is listless at the start of her last summer before college, when a chance meet-up with Jamie turns her summer of boredom into a summer of love. Working at Jamie's aunt's pie shack, she is quick to experience the first blushes of romance. Though Shabnam is bursting to tell her best friend Farah, she must first patch up a friendship gone awry. Shabnam and Farah began to drift apart when Farah starts wearing the hijab. Shabnam, who kisses boys, drinks, and now finds herself head over heels in love with a white boy, finds herself distinctly uncomfortable with Farah's more conservative approach to Islam. In trying to voice her intense love for Jamie, Shabnam indirectly connects with her father through his love for Urdu poetry. This realistic portrayal of young love serves as the backdrop to rebuilding the friendship between the two girls. The contrast between the two is also drawn out to explore the different ways of being Muslim. Farah as a weed-smoking punk hijabi girl doesn't fit into the traditional image of a conservative Muslim. Her full control of her identity and path in life serves as a foil to Shabnam's more bumbling approach to desire and finding herself. The title of the book, a lovely translation of a mellifluous Urdu phrase, takes on the various stages of love—from a summer romance to the deeper and more lasting ties of friendship and family.

Discussion Starters

- In what ways did Shabnam and Farah feel like misfits—at school and in the community?
- What were Shabnam's expectations of her relationship with Jamie? Was she able to share them with him?
- Why did Shabnam and Farah drift apart? Do you think they could have cleared up their misunderstanding earlier?
- How did Shabnam and Farah differ in their approach to being Muslim? What are some of the stereotypes that the author challenges with both these characters?

Ideas for Further Engagement

✋ Look up the poems of Faiz Ahmed Faiz.

✋ Conduct an identity exercise where each student lists ten things to explain their individual identity in terms of race, gender, class, privileges, sexual orientation, religious preferences, and so on.

Quotes for Interpretation

- "She prayed every day, didn't drink, wouldn't date, fasted during Ramadan. She also swore a lot, listened to punk music, wore combat boots outside of school, and wanted to pierce her lip." (99–100)
- "It's so weird to see you smoke pot in hijab." (132)
- "I'm too Muslim for the non-Muslims, but not Muslim enough for the Muslims." (134)

The Complete Persepolis. **Marjane Satrapi. Pantheon, 2007. 978–0375714832. 341 pp. Fiction. Young adult.**

Select Awards: 2004 ALA Alex Award winner, 2004 *Booklist* Editor's Choice for Young, Adults, 2004 New York Public Library Books for the Teenage, 2004 *School Library Journal* Adult Books for Young Adults, 2004 YALSA Best Books for Young Adults.

The personal is political. Nowhere is this more evident than in Marjane Satrapi's award-winning memoir of growing up in Iran at a time of political and cultural upheaval. Told with observant humor and an absurd and relatable childlike perspective, Satrapi's graphic novel is a lesson in the lives of ordinary Iranians. The book traces the developments and repercussions of the ouster of the shah, the takeover by a totalitarian Islamic regime, the torture and persecution of communists, and the Iran-Iraq War. As a nine-year-old trying to make sense of her world, Marji (Marjane) turns to the adults in her life to explain the changes—going from a co-ed to a gender-segregated school, and going from miniskirts to being fully veiled. Her outspoken ways and fear for her safety prompt her parents to send her to Austria at age fourteen. After a self-imposed exile, she moves back to Iran for college, married life, and her final release. The expressionist quality of the book's black-and-white art perfectly captures moments of light and darkness. From Marji's adolescent adventures in Vienna underlined by a feeling of never belonging, to her finally finding herself, Satrapi's book is searing in its honesty and is an essential read to understand the human condition.

Discussion Starters

- How did Marji and her friends show their resistance to the theocratic Islamic regime?
- During her childhood, how do Marji and her friends make sense of their political situation in Iran?
- What were the different social and political divides that Marji highlights? What informs her own political and religious leanings?
- Why did her parents decide to send Marji to Austria? Why did she decide to return? Did she feel a version of survivor's guilt during her time there?
- Who were Marji's heroes? Were they the same as the government's venerated heroes? How do her ideas of being heroic change?

Ideas for Further Engagement

- 🖐 Watch the animated film *Persepolis.*
- 🖐 Have a weeklong book reading of graphic novels such as *Dare to Disappoint: Growing Up in Turkey* by Ozge Samanci, *A Game for Swallows* by Zeina Abirsched, *Arab of the Future* by Riad Sattouf, and *Palestine* by Joe Sacco, along with *The Complete Maus* by Art Spiegelman, in order to discuss growing up in a time of war.

Quotes for Interpretation

- "The harder I tried to assimilate, the more I felt that I was distancing myself from my culture, betraying my parents and my origins, that I was playing a game by someone else's rules." (193)
- "Now, as soon as they learn our nationality, they go through everything, as though we were all terrorists." (203)
- "I was a Westerner in Iran, an Iranian in the West. I had no identity." (272)

The Girl Who Fell to Earth: A Memoir. **Sophia Al-Maria.**
Harper Perennial, 2012. 978–0061999758. 288 pp.
Fiction. Young adult.

Select Awards: Middle East Book Awards 2013.

As a young Arab American growing up on her
grandmother's farm in the rainy Pacific Northwest,
Sophia Al-Maria is more than a little curious about
her Bedouin father who lives in the parched lands of
the Middle East. Through her personal story of oscil-
lating between two cultures, Al-Maria's quest for self-discovery is punctu-
ated by observations of the similarities between these disparate places and
people. In Doha, she is mesmerized by the lights and the constant construc-
tion as she is excited to discover a new family with multiple cousins, aunts,
and uncles. Back in the United States, she struggles to find herself, and is also
witness to the various forms of prejudice against Arab Muslims. Al-Maria's
original voice seeps through and opens up the still mostly unknown lives
within the Gulf Arab countries. Her experiences of "cultural whiplash" are
laden with humor and honest explorations that defy most of our expectations of a conservative culture. She tackles the many stereotypes of Gulf
Arabs and the changes in the lives of one of the oldest nomadic tribes in the
Middle East. Her access to and experience of the interior spaces of girls and
women is full of life, freedom, and joy. Her complex journey continues on to
Cairo, where the political backdrop not only colors how others see her, but
also how she sees herself.

Discussion Starters
- Where did Matar and his friends get a lot of their information about
  America from? What did he find most fascinating about America? How
  was his experience different from his daughter's?
- What were the similarities that Sophia found between her families in
  Puyallup and Doha?
- From both Gale and Safya's experiences—how did people react to them
  wearing the hijab and the abaya? How do you think girls and women
  who wear the hijab are treated differently?
- What were the instances of prejudice that Sophia experienced as an

Arab American in her middle school in Seattle? What were the challenges she faced at her American school in Doha?

- What image did people in Cairo have of Gulf Arabs? How did Sophia reconcile all of her identities and learn to be true to herself?

Ideas for Further Engagement

 Watch the film *Theeb* by Naji Abu Nowar. Discuss how modernity affected the Arab nomadic way of life with examples from the film and this book.

 Organize a class debate on the value of family in one's life and the factors that impact it.

Quotes for Interpretation

- "I'm not from outer space, I promise." (59)
- "Now that we're too old for jump rope, we compared the tone of our skin, measured ourselves back-to-back, and grinned stupidly at one another." (126)
- "I'd jumped the trap of needing to belong to my tribe in Qatar, but now there was a new kind of tribalism to figure out: middle-school cliques." (168)

The Lines We Cross. **Randa Abdel-Fattah. Orchard Books, 2017. 978–1338118667. 400 pp. Fiction. Young adult.**

Select Awards: Booklist Top 10 Books for Youth 2017.

This is a timely and well-written book that tackles many difficult issues on both a local and global scale. Michael and Mina are two teens from the opposite sides of an ideological divide. Michael and his family are anti-immigrant, while Mina's immigrant family is trying to rebuild their lives in their new home in Australia. They both meet at a private school to which Mina transfers on a scholarship. Each of them firmly defends their position—Michael stands behind the rhetoric that immigrants are welcome if they leave their culture behind, while Mina holds her own and refuses to do the "refugee-myth-busting" thing. Through

Michael and Mina's budding relationship, author Randa Abdel-Fattah shows us how hate passes down to our children, and she breaks down misconceptions surrounding Muslim immigrants. Abdel-Fattah writes with nuance on issues of racism, xenophobia, and Islamophobia without demonizing any of her characters. Her book is an engaging and compelling read that mirrors the story of our times and the work we all need to do to unpack privilege and our own internal biases.

Discussion Starters

- How did Mina feel about moving from her public school to a private school? What were some of the differences she experienced from her old neighborhood?
- How did Michael, his family, and their organization perceive Muslims? Do Mina and her family fit into their notions of "economic refugees"? How do Mina and her family define their experience as refugees?
- How do Michael and Mina both feel on discovering their shared interests in music and books?
- Have you ever had to change your identity to fit in?
- Have you been in a situation where you've had to deal with people who have opposing views? How can you best handle such a situation?

Ideas for Further Engagement

- 🖐 Watch *Where do you come from—no, really, where do you originally come from?* a lecture-performance by Tintin Wulia.
- 🖐 Create a class project on immigration and how it has influenced the growth of America.
- 🖐 Write a letter to the president of the United States outlining the benefits of immigration to the United States.

Quotes for Interpretation

- "She's the one person I would least expect to have anything in common with. But our encounters have left me intrigued." (66)
- "You want me to make it easier for you to confront your privilege because God knows, even antiracism has to be done in a way that makes the majority comfortable?" (219)
- "It's hard to accept that nice people can be racist too." (226)

Watched. **Marina Budhos. Wendy Lamb Books, 2016. 978-0553534184. 272 pp. Fiction. Young adult.**

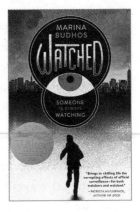

Select Awards: 2016–2017 Asian/Pacific American Award for Literature, YALSA 2017 Best Fiction for Young Adults, 2017 Notable Books for a Global Society, YALSA 2017 Quick Picks for Reluctant Young Adult Readers, Fiction, 2017 Walter Dean Myers Award, Honor Book.

Naeem, a young Bangladeshi boy growing up in Queens, New York, tries to live up to his parents' expectations. But his fall from a treasured firstborn son to a failing and adrift teenager is swift. He is a charming protagonist who can talk his way out of any problem, but the problems keep on piling up. When he gets caught on the wrong side of the law, the police offer to drop the charges in exchange for his turning informer: he is free to walk as long as he spies on his neighbors. While Naeem sees himself as a hero at first, that ideal quickly crumbles in the face of ethical and moral questions that plague him. In a realistic and gripping story which blurs the boundaries between fact and fiction, author Marina Budhos examines racial profiling and the police surveillance of Muslim communities after 9/11. She explores these larger sociopolitical issues from the perspective of a teenager discovering his identity, values, and place in the world. Naeem's conflicted experiences give a visceral feel to being hyper-visible in the eyes of the law and show how Islamophobia is a present force in the daily lives of Muslims. This edgy and gritty story shows the darker side of power and entrapment, teases out the nuances of diverse immigrant communities, and portrays the burden on immigrant children to succeed and the hard choices they are forced to make.

Discussion Starters

- Why did Naeem not reach out to his drama teacher when things got tough at school?
- Why did Naeem feel compelled to accept the officers' deal?
- What was Naeem's relationship with his parents and brother like?
- How did Naeem's experiences of spying on his community change during the course of the book?
- At what point did Naeem reach out for help?

Ideas for Further Engagement

🖐 Watch *Punching in the Sun* by Tanuj Chopra, which is about young teenagers growing up in Queens after 9/11.

🖐 Research the various methods of digital surveillance that are used
today. Organize a debate on the benefits and concerns of such surveillance.

🖐 Ask students to write a persuasive note on maintaining the fine balance
between privacy while protecting national interests by conducting
digital surveillance.

Quotes for Interpretation

- "The thing about being a superhero is that you have to be okay with
lying." (116)
- "Why is it whenever there is a terrorist attack, we have to explain ourselves?" (152)
- "That's all we want. All everyone wants. To be normal." (251)

Notes

1. Cooperative Children's Book Center, School of Education, University of Wiscon-
sin-Madison, Publishing Statistics on Children's Books about People of Color and First/
Native Nations and by People of Color and First/Native Nations Authors and Illustrators, https://ccbc.education.wisc.edu/books/pcstats.asp.

2. Craft Al-Hazza, Tami and T. Bucher, Katherine. (2008). *Building Arab Americans' Cultural Identity and Acceptance with Children's Literature*. The Reading Teacher International Reading Association. 62. 210-219. 10.1598/RT.62.3.3. See url: https://www.jstor
.org/stable/20143932?mag=importance-publshing-more-muslim-children-books&
seq=1#page_scan_tab_contents.

Chapter 5

Inspiring Muslim Leaders and Thinkers

Showcasing Current and Historical Contributions

MARTIN LUTHER KING JR. ONCE SAID, "WE'RE NOT MAKers of history, we are made by history." Historical narratives play a critical role in shaping our understanding of the world, and are often repeated and shared with children of different ages. Both in schools and at home, young children learn about inspiring personalities, the challenges they faced, and how they created change. Children in middle grade and high school are introduced to the rise and fall of ancient civilizations, world history, and how economic and geopolitical factors have influenced the balance of power between modern nation-states. But while the facts of history may be indisputable, the stories are always colored by the perspective of the storyteller. One such story that is troubling in the context of Muslims is the idea that Islam is backward and Muslims have not contributed to modern society.[1] Often this idea is posited as a clash between East and West, with the underlying assumption that Western civilization is and has always been superior to all others.

The theme for this chapter challenges these assumptions through books that showcase the long and complex history of the Islamic world; describe the contributions made by scholars, inventors, and philosophers of Muslim heritage; and provide stories of contemporary Muslim visionaries. Books on the sciences, art, music, and literature and those addressing pressing social issues of poverty, race, and self-determination can help young people to better understand the histories of and connections between cultures and people.

The Islamic Golden Age (which lasted approximately from the seventh to the thirteenth century) was a period of significant global achievements in architecture, education, the arts, literature, mathematics, and medicine. Driven by the Quranic decree to seek knowledge, Muslims traveled around the world with a desire to learn. This led to the growth and expansion of trade and the rise of great cities along the routes of the Islamic empire. Travelers and traders from the Middle East went as far as Spain in the west and China in the east. The cities of Cairo, Córdoba, and Baghdad were famed centers of learning and innovation where institutions such as libraries, hospitals, and universities first emerged. Arabic was the language of learning, culture, and intellectual progress of all scholars, regardless of ethnicity or religion throughout the Middle East and the Mediterranean. From the ninth to the twelfth century, there were more philosophical, medical, historical, religious, astronomical, and geographical works written in Arabic than in any other human tongue.[2]

This Golden Age adapted and built upon the wisdom of the Chinese, Hindu, Greek, and Roman civilizations. It was also an extraordinary time of cultural and intellectual exchange, cross-fertilization, and the sharing of ideas. Based in the House of Wisdom in Baghdad, Al-Khwarizmi, one of the leading Muslim scientists, worked on translating Greek and Indian mathematics and astronomy texts into Arabic. He was primarily responsible for the spread of algebra and the Hindu-Arabic numeral system to Europe in the late Middle Ages. Many other commonplace items such as the orange juice on the breakfast table, clocks, toothpaste, the guitar, and the first flying machine were introduced by Muslim thinkers, inventors, and scientists. Contemporary books such as *1001 Inventions and Awesome Facts from Muslim Civilization* (2012) and *Lost History* (2007) by Michael Hamilton Morgan showcase the enduring history and accomplishments of Muslim civilization.

While the Western world was engulfed in the Dark Ages, Muslim scholars preserved and translated a number of ancient Greek and Roman classical texts which formed the basis of the Western canon. These texts, ideas, and innovations paved the way for the Renaissance. For instance, the renowned Persian physician Ibn Sina (better known in the West as Avicenna) *al-Qanun Fi al-Tibb*

(*The Canon of Medicine*) was translated into Latin and served as the seminal reference text for medical studies in Europe for several centuries.[3]

Learning about these achievements at an early age encourages children to rely on their own fact-based knowledge rooted in history, rather than being swayed by rhetoric. This awareness of the contributions made by people of Muslim heritage gives Muslim children a sense of pride in their own identity and counters the idea of the backwardness of Islam. It also supports the idea that Islam spread through trade and knowledge and not just "by the sword." Teaching young children about inspiring Muslim personalities, and how their ideas contributed to society, serves as a critical springboard for children to shape their own identities.

Biographies are often used to teach children about visionaries who were resilient, courageous, and resourceful when faced with adversity. In this chapter, we have curated biographies of various Muslims leaders and thinkers who have made significant contributions to the world. We have featured books on historical pioneers such as Ibn Battuta, whose travels surpassed those of Marco Polo, and Ibn Sina (Avicenna) whose method of treating fractured bones is still in use today, as well as more contemporary trailblazers. Mohammed Yunus spearheaded the microcredit movement to help break the cycle of poverty, architect Zaha Hadid pushed the boundaries for Arab women, and the young Malala Yousafzai's courage and unbreakable sense of justice have spotlighted girls' education with renewed vigor. These leaders continue to work to find solutions for national and global issues. Learning about their stories, especially in classrooms, will enable a deeper discussion of issues of war and conflict, economics and poverty, and race and gender inequality.

Rather than a "clash of the East and West," the books curated in this chapter bring out a nuanced perspective of the richly intertwined histories of the East and the West. The ideas and information in these books will help examine and question deep-seated prejudices which often ignore the accomplishments of Muslims and people from Islamic nations.

By spotlighting books that present an accurate account of the contributions of Muslims to modern-day society, we hope to encourage the development of critical thinking and open up different versions of history. Knowledge and understanding of this interdependent history are imperative if we are to tackle interconnected global issues of environmental degradation, poverty, and justice for all.

Picture Books

Journey through Islamic Art. Na'ima bint Robert, ill. by Diana Mayo. Mantra Lingua, 2005. 978–1844443505. 30 pp. Nonfiction. Pre-K–Gr. 4.

Select Awards: UK National Literacy Association WOW! Award 2005 for Best Children's Title.

Written in verse, this engaging book follows a dreamlike sequence of a young girl as she settles in for the night. In the course of her journey across time and space to faraway places from "Samarkand to Baghdad," she shares the contributions of Islamic art, architecture, aesthetics, and inventions from around the world. These "silken threads of history" will pique curious young readers to explore more on their own. The book is available in multiple dual-language editions such as Arabic, Bengali, Cantonese, Croatian, Farsi, French, German, Hindi, Italian, Kurdish, Somali, Vietnamese, and others.

Ideas for Further Engagement
- Trace the route from Cordoba through Seljuk, Baghdad, Samarkand, and Agra on the map.
- Create your own design on ceramic tiles.

The Librarian of Basra. Jeanette Winter, ill. by author. HMH Books for Young Readers, 2005. 978–0152054458. 32 pp. Nonfiction. Pre-K–Gr. 3.

Select Awards: Flora Stieglitz Straus Award 2005.

Winter reminds the world of the immeasurable contribution of Alia Muhammad Baker, who saved 30,000 books in the Al-Basrah Central Library from destruction during the Iraq War in 2003. Baker's personal inspiration is the quote, "In the Koran the first thing God said to Mohammed was 'Read.'" She risked her life to protect the books, among which was a biography of Muhammad dating from about 1300. *The Librarian of Basra* is a timely reminder of the human cost of war, its impact on civilians, and its destruction of history and culture.

Ideas for Further Engagement

- Pair this book with *Hands around the Library* by Karen Leggett Abouraya, which tells of a similar story that took place in Egypt.
- Discuss the power of libraries, and how they help create a sense of community.
- 🖐 Have students volunteer in their local library and assist with age-appropriate tasks.

Malala's Magic Pencil. **Malala Yousafzai, ill. by Kerascoëts. Little Brown, Books for Young Readers, 2017. 978–0316319577. 48 pp.
Fiction. Preschool–Gr. 3.**

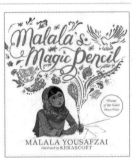

This is the inspiring story of Malala Yousafzai, told in her own words. Malala connects her childlike dreams of finding a magic pencil that would "erase the smell of garbage" and get her an extra hour of sleep in the morning with her desire for equality and justice for all. She pins her hopes on these small fantasies while dealing with the reality of girls who are barred from going to school in her hometown in the Swat Valley in northwest Pakistan. Despite the many challenges Malala faces, she maintains a hopeful and optimistic tone that celebrates the magic that lies within us all to make a difference in the world. While still a young girl, Malala Yousafzai became active in efforts to advance female education in Pakistan and survived an attempt by the Taliban to assassinate her in 2012. In 2014, she was co-awarded the Nobel Prize for Peace, becoming the youngest Nobel laureate.

Ideas for Further Engagement

- Display this book with *Malala: A Brave Girl from Pakistan / Iqbal: A Brave Boy from Pakistan: Two Stories of Bravery* by Jeanette Winter, and *Malala: Activist for Girls' Education* by Raphaele Frier.

- Pair this book with *Ruby's Wish* by Shirin Yim Bridges.
- Display this book on July 12 every year to commemorate Malala Day.
- Lead a discussion with children on the value of education and working to ensure the universal right to education for children all over the world.
- ✋ Draw your own magic pencil and what powers it would have.

Malcolm Little: The Boy Who Grew Up to Become Malcolm X. **Elizabeth Mann and Alan Witschon-ke, ill. by Alan Witschonke. Mikaya, 2008. 978–1931414203. 48 pp. Picture book/Nonfiction. Gr. 3–8.**

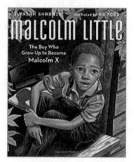

Select Awards: Eureka Nonfiction Honor Book 2009, MSTA Reading Circle List 2009, Wisconsin State Reading Association's Reading List 2009.

Written by his daughter, this inspiring book shares a story from Malcolm X's childhood. Malcolm X was one of America's most influential African American leaders, and this book celebrates his vision of freedom and justice. When confronted with intolerance and a series of tragedies, Malcolm's optimism and faith were shaken, but he learned how to be strong and hold on to his individuality. This lyrical story carries a powerful message that still reso-nates today—for all of us to live to our highest potential.

Ideas for Further Engagement

- Display this book on May 19 every year to commemorate Malcolm X's birthday.
- Get the Malcolm X stamp and commemorative stamps of other famous people from the post office, and lead a discussion with the students about these people.
- ✋ Find out why Malcolm X adopted an X as his last name.

Muhammad Ali: A Champion Is Born. **Gene Barretta, ill. by Frank Morrison. Katherine Tegen Books, 2017. 978–0062430168. 40 pp. Nonfiction. Pre-K–Gr. 4.**

This is a well-written and vibrantly illustrated picture book about the greatest

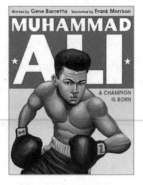

heavyweight boxer of our time. This book recounts the story of Ali as a young boy racing down the streets on his favorite bike. When it gets stolen, he vows to get it back and won't back down without a fight. The book touches on important issues such as racism and the value of hard work and determination to achieve your dreams. Muhammad Ali was a high-profile American Muslim, and the detailed information in the book's afterword shows how his faith informed his career as a boxer.

Ideas for Further Engagement

- Lead a discussion with children about different forms of unfair or discriminatory treatment, and how they can be addressed.
- 🖐 Research famous African Americans who have represented the United States at the Olympics.

Raza's Bindu. Vanita Pai and Ritu Khoda, ill. by S. H. Raza. Art1st Publications, 2015. 978–8193287804. 62 pp. Art book. Gr. K–4.

Select Awards: Finalist, Printed Children's Book of the Year, Publishing Next Industry Awards 2015.

This hands-on art book is a look at the life, inspirations, and artwork of one of India's leading artists, S. H. Raza. As an art student in Paris, Raza was inspired by the abstract painter Wassily Kandinsky's work, which informed his trademark dot or bindu. The book shares the unique backstory about the bindu, and the interactive worksheets will inspire young artists to create ideas of their own.

Ideas for Further Engagement

- Have the children share a story that inspired them to create a poem, painting, or any other work of art.
- 🖐 Re-create a Kandinsky and a Raza painting. Spot the similarities and differences between these two artists' work side by side.

Rumi: Whirling Dervish. **Demi, ill. by author. Marshall Cavendish, 2009. 978–0761455271. 48 pp. Nonfiction. Gr. 4–7.**

Rumi was born in Afghanistan in the thirteenth century and spent most of his life in what is now Turkey. He wrote most of his poetry in the Persian language. Rumi is considered to be one of the greatest mystical poets that ever lived, and his poetry and its innate philosophy remain popular and relevant even today. Illustrated in Demi's signature gold artwork, the book shares Rumi's biography and contributions in an engaging and accessible way for children. Demi weaves in snippets of poetry, stories, the significant role that various teachers played in Rumi's life, and many of the poet's key ideas.

Ideas for Further Engagement

- Discuss some of the poetry in the book and encourage children to find inspiration from the poetry.
- Pair with other poetry books.
- 🖐 Look up the whirling dervishes' ceremony and how it is connected to Rumi.

Silent Music: A Story of Baghdad. **James Rumford, ill. by the author. Roaring Book, 2008. 978–1596432765. 32 pp. Fiction. Preschool–Gr. 3.**

Select Awards: 2008 Middle East Book Award Winner.

This visually stunning book is a wonderful introduction to the art of Arabic calligraphy. Ali, a young boy from Baghdad, loves soccer, "parent-rattling music," and dance. But what he loves above all else is to practice calligraphy. The loops, swirls, and dots of Ali's writing introduce us to his warm and intimate family. The book's mixed-media illustrations showcase textured collages and geometric designs, and they incorporate contemporary imagery of stamps and postcards into the ancient art form of Arabic calligraphy. Ali also mentions the conflict in Iraq, and he finds refuge in his secret hero, the thirteenth-century calligrapher Yakut, who wrote "letters of rhyme and grace" throughout the Mongols' destruction of Baghdad in 1258. Ali makes a simple observation on how the Arabic word for "war" glides off his pen with ease, while the word for peace, "salaam," is far trickier.

Ideas for Further Engagement

- Compare Arabic, Chinese, and Japanese calligraphy.
- Find volunteers in your community who are conversant in Arabic, and have them write each child's name in Arabic. Have the children trace and decorate their names.
- Listen to the *maqam* style of music from Iraq.

The Amazing Discoveries of Ibn Battuta. **Fatima Sharafeddine, ill. by Intelaq Mohammed Ali. Groundwood Books, 2014. 978–1554984800. 32 pp. Picture book/Fiction. Gr. 1–4.**

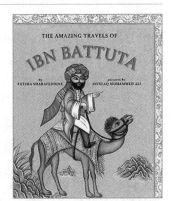

Do you ever wonder what it was like to travel hundreds of years ago, in the days long before cars and airplanes? Ibn Battuta, a great traveler from the fourteenth century, paved the way for the modern age of discovery. He traveled for thirty years from North Africa through India, Sri Lanka, and Southeast Asia to China, surpassing the travels of Marco Polo and encountering lands rare for travelers at the time. This book traces his travels gleaned from Ibn Battuta's own account of his journeys, *Rihla (The Travels)*, which was compiled from his diaries. This work has timeless appeal for his remarkable observations and deep understanding of different societies and his appreciation for the richness and diversity of the world.

Ideas for Further Engagement

- Do you like to travel? What's your favorite place to travel?
- Compare Ibn Battuta's travel routes with Marco Polo's routes.

Fatima Sharafeddine

The Importance of History for the Present

Can you tell us a little about where you grew up and what inspired you to be a writer?

I grew up in Lebanon in the 1970s and 1980s, during the time of the civil war. Depending on the situation, my family had to change cities, residences, and schools for us, the children. I have always been an observer rather than an inter-actor. I think I was born a writer, taking mental notes since early childhood about what is going on around me and how it made me feel.

What is the one thing that you would like people to know about Muslims?

It is very important to understand that Muslims in the world are a wide variety of peoples. For example, not all Muslims are Arabs, and not all Arabs are Muslims.

What made you decide to write about these Muslim leaders? Why do you think it is important to know about these leaders from the past?

The polymath leaders about whom I am writing in the series entitled Do You Know Who I Am? are scientists whose discoveries helped form the bases of all science and technology in the twenty-first century. Their discoveries in the fields of medicine, pharmaceutics, astronomy, architecture, chemistry, and mathematics contributed to all of humanity. I decided to write about these personalities in order for the new generations worldwide to be aware of this extremely important history. In particular, I want people in the Arab world to be proud of this heritage and to look up to these examples in order to build a better future.

If you had a magic wand, what is the one misconception about Muslims that you would banish forever?

I would banish forever the misconcep-tion that all Muslims are Arabs and that all Arabs are Muslims. The millions of Muslims around the world come from dif-ferent continents and cultures and have different languages and histories.

How do we—parents, teachers, and librarians—all of us as a community teach children to respect differences and value diversity?

We can only do that by setting the exam-ple for it. We need to respect differences so that our children learn to do the same. We need to show our young children how we value diversity by highlighting the positive aspects of others and by valuing the richness that diversity brings to our communities.

Biography

Fatima Sharafeddine is a writer and translator for children and young adults. She is the winner of several awards, including the Bologna Ragazzi New Horizons Award for her book *Tongue Twisters* and the Etisala Award for the best young adult book of 2017 for *Cappuccino*. Several of her Arabic-language books have been widely translated into various European and other languages. Sharafeddine has written and published over 120 books, and she participates in various book fairs and conferences focusing on children's literature. She also offers workshops for aspiring writers. More information can be found on her website: **www.fatimasharafeddine.com.**

What is your favorite story from Islamic traditions?

The Prophet Muhammad received an *abaya* (a cloak) as a gift from a believer who thought he needed a replacement for his old ragged one. One day, a poor man knocked at the door asking for a donation. The Prophet told his wife Aisha to give him the *abaya.* The poor man, full of joy, took it to the market to sell it, where he started yelling: "Who wants to buy the Prophet's abaya? It is the Prophet's! It is the Prophet's!" People gathered around him very interested. A blind man who heard the yelling ordered his slave boy: "Go and try to buy it for me regardless of its price. If you succeed, I will set you free." The slave boy went and bought it for his blind master, who then held the *abaya* tight and prayed: "Allah, for the sake of the Prophet's blessed *abaya* between my arms, give me back my sight." As soon as the man finished his prayer, his sight returned to him.

He ran to the house of the Prophet and told him: "Oh our Prophet, I can see again. Here is your *abaya*, a gift from me to you." The man told the story of how he returned the abaya to the Prophet. The Prophet laughed a lot, then told his wife Aisha: "Look at this abaya, Aisha; it made a poor man rich, it set free a slave, and it returned the sight to a blind man, then it came back to us."

What is your biggest inspiration from Islam?

The peacefulness and tolerance in this religion.

Finally, biryani or kebabs?

Neither. I am vegetarian.

***The Amazing Discoveries of Ibn Sina.* Fatima Sharafeddine, ill. by Intelaq Mohammed Ali. Groundwood Books, 2015. 978–1554987115. 32 pp. Picture book/Nonfiction. Gr. 1–4.**

Ibn Sina, or Avicenna, as he is better known in the West, was born in Persia more than a thousand years ago. As a child prodigy he had memorized the Quran by age ten, and he finished his medical studies by the time he was sixteen. His contributions and innovative ideas in the fields of medicine, chemistry, astronomy, physics, and philosophy live on to this day, such as the observation that light travels at a definite speed, and the use of anesthesia. His most famous work, the *Canon of Medicine*, was a standard text on medicine in the Islamic world and Europe until the eighteenth century.

Ideas for Further Engagement

- Pair this book with *1001 Inventions and Awesome Facts from Muslim Civilization* by National Geographic.
- ✋ Research famous medical inventions that took place from the thirteenth to the nineteenth centuries. Lead a discussion with children on which invention is the most fascinating one for them.

***The Story of Hurry.* Emma Williams, ill. by Ibrahim Quraishi. Triangle Square, 2014. 978–1609805890. 36 pp. Fiction. Pre-K–Gr. 2.**

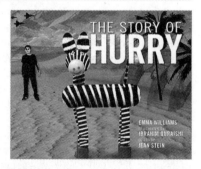

Select Awards: 2015 Middle East Book Award Honorable Mention.

Inspired by the true story of Mahmoud Barghout, this book captures the spirit of hope. Barghout set up Happy Land Zoo in the heavily militarized Gaza Strip to give children a reprieve from the never-ending war. Some of the animals died of hunger, thirst, and injury, and the war created immense daily challenges to running the zoo. So Barghout converted donkeys to zebras by painting them in black and white stripes. Kids get up close and personal, and even ride these "zebras." This book is a reminder for all of us to find joy, beauty, and ingenuity in the everyday.

Ideas for Further Engagement

- ✋ Have you ever heard of a liger or a cama? Create a list of hybrid animals.
- ✋ Draw your own hybrid animal.

***The World Is Not a Rectangle: A Portrait of Zaha Hadid.* Jeanette Winter, ill. by Author. Beach Lane Books, 2017. 978–1481446693. 56 pp. Nonfiction. K–Gr. 5.**

Select Awards: 2017 Parents' Choice Award Winner: Nonfiction, Recommended; *Publishers Weekly*'s Best Books of 2017.

Winter fills a much-needed gap about stories of accomplished Muslim women with her book about the Iraqi-born, British-educated architect Zaha Hadid. The story brings to life Hadid's struggles to break into a male-dominated profession and gain recognition for the buildings she designed. Winter's trademark folk-inspired illustrations and simple text bring this powerful story to life. The book traces her childhood when Hadid, inspired by the "river and marshes and dunes and ruins" of her native Iraq, designed unconventional buildings that incorporate nature. Despite being rejected numerous times, she persisted and never lost sight of her creative vision. Zaha Hadid's iron will and her passion can inspire all readers to think outside the box.

Ideas for Further Engagement
- Design your own building inspired by nature.
- Research biographies of women architects from all over the world.

Jeannette Winter
Finding Commonality

Can you share a little bit about what inspired you to become an author and an illustrator, and your path to get there?

I always loved to draw, to make pictures, to tell stories with my pictures. Being an artist was my goal from as far back as I can remember. I studied art at the Art Institute of Chicago in high school, and in college I knew that I wanted to be a children's book illustrator, to tell stories with my pictures. I pursued this goal intensely, and illustrated my first book when I was in my late twenties.

In particular, what inspired you to create picture book biographies?

After a number of years illustrating stories that were written by others, I made the leap to writing my own stories. My first nonfiction book was *Follow the Drinking Gourd*, about the Underground Railroad, and I found that true stories were what engaged me the most. My first biography, *Diego*, told a true story about the artist Diego Rivera, and about Mexico. The possibilities, after this book, seemed limitless.

You've written about people across cultures with sensitivity. How do you ensure that you are authentic in your representation—of the person, the culture they come from—both in the text and your illustrations?

I admire the people I write about. I often find my initial inspiration in newspaper stories about these people. Luis, Wangari, and Alia Baker, the librarian from Basra,

all began with an article in the newspaper. I read everything I can about my subjects, look at many, many pictures of their environment, read what they have written themselves (very important), and listen to music from the countries I am writing about. The music makes me feel present in their lives.

We're thrilled to see that you have written so many amazing stories featuring Muslim characters. What inspired you to write about so many Muslim characters—Nasreen, Malala, Iqbal, Alia Muhammad Baker, and Zaha Hadid?

I was so taken with their stories, and I wanted children here to learn about their lives, their bravery, courage, and vision. And yes, to give a human face to what we see of war footage on TV. And to encourage children to identify with people in other parts of the world, living very different lives—to find a commonality.

What is the one thing that you would like people to know about Muslims?
I would like people to know what I have discovered through my work—that Muslims are a strong link in the unbroken chain of humanity. We are all as one in our hearts, if we open our hearts.

If you had a magic wand, what is the one misconception about Muslims that you would banish forever?
If I could wave my magic wand, it would be to erase the misconception that Islam is a breeding ground for terrorism, and instead, that it be seen as one of the great religions of the world. Those who use religion for political and criminal purposes are not people of true faith. I would hope people would realize this when they demonize a religion, and its followers.

In "Nasreen's Secret School," the illustrations of the doorways and windows, which seem confining in the beginning, later seem to open up Nasreen's world and her imagination. Did you consciously seek to convey this transformation through the illustrations?
Yes, that is what I was hoping to convey. In a picture book, the pictures tell the part of the story that the words do not. Ideally, the words and pictures will come together and join in the mind, to make the story whole.

Your book on Malala and Iqbal is very inspiring to us. We love that it showcases stories of two children from Pakistan who faced difficult circumstances and chose to speak up against them. What is the key takeaway you would want children to learn from this book?
First of all, I would hope that children would see how brave Malala and Iqbal were. And that they would be able to identify with them. In their determination to make their world better, these two children had the courage to speak up, and speak out, about injustices in their world. And they both helped to bring about change.

Change begins with one person, even a child. Children are brave, and smart, and can recognize injustice.

How can parents, teachers, librarians, and all of us as a community teach children to respect differences and value diversity?
Parents, teachers, and librarians can tell their children stories about people in other parts of the world who have different customs, ways of life, and languages, and through this show the connection we all have with each other through our humanity. We're all in this together. We need this now, more than ever.

Since not all children live in diverse communities, or go to schools with a diverse student body, stories remain the best way for children to inhabit the minds and hearts of people of different backgrounds, religions, and color. Teaching through stories has been happening since the beginning, for good reason—it works.

Biography

Renowned author-illustrator Jeanette Winter finds inspiration in real-life stories. Her picture books introduce young readers to people around the world who are making a difference in their communities. Her books *Zaha Hadid: The World Is Not a Rectangle, Malala: A Brave Girl from Pakistan / Iqbal: A Brave Boy from Pakistan, Nasreen's Secret School,* and *The Librarian of Basra* tackle the fallout as well as the human face of war.

Advanced Picture Books

Al-Ghazali. Demi, ill. by the author. Fons Vitae, 2015. 978–1941610121. 48 pp. Picture book/Nonfiction. Gr. 3–7.

With beautiful miniature paintings by Demi, this advanced picture book introduces young and old readers to Al-Ghazali, an exemplary tenth-century philosopher, theologian, and thinker of the Islamic world who was also known as the "Proof of Islam." He spent years searching for the truth and harmony between the inner and outer aspects of Islam, and he is credited with making Sufism (Islamic mysticism) an integral part of Islam. Al-Ghazali's critiques of Arabic philosophy, logic, and physics encouraged critical thinking. His writings emphasized living in harmony with all beings, seen and unseen, humans, animals, and plants—a value we could all learn from today.

Discussion Starters

- What does it mean to be a "philosopher"?
- What do the following quotes mean to you: "He who knows himself is truly happy" (Al-Ghazali), "The whole is more than the sum of its parts" (Aristotle), and "I hear and I forget. I see and I remember. I do and I understand" (Confucius).

Ideas for Further Engagement

✋ Research famous scholars from different religions, and the role they played in helping people understand those religions.

Quotes for Interpretation

- "He said that our hearts, or souls, are like mirrors that get covered by dust and become rusty when we do bad deeds. We need to polish our hearts because getting into heaven depends on the state of our hearts." (17)
- "During this period, he began to write his greatest work, The Revival of the Religious Sciences, which is made up of forty books . . . He also emphasized that the way people deal with each other is important." (23)

- "Although Imam al-Ghazali did not meet Western thinkers in person, he influenced them through his books. Some of the leading Christian and Jewish thinkers such as Thomas Aquinas and Moses Maimonides read his books." (26)

Mansa Musa: The Lion of Mali. **Kephra Burns, ill. by Leo and Diane Dillon. Gulliver Books, 2001. 978–0152003753. 56 pp. Nonfiction. Gr. 5–7.**

This is a coming-of-age story about a young boy who is destined to become the king of Mali. Kankan Musa gathers to celebrate, welcome, and listen to the stories of the mysterious traveler from the Tuareg tribe. Fate, however, has other plans for him when a band of slave raiders abducts him from the village. He ends up traveling the world with his mentor and guide until a revelation takes him back to his home and people. This book invokes the feel of magic realism in its mixture of historical fact and myth, and the stunning illustrations paint a colorful and vibrant picture of ancient Africa. The detailed notes showcase the riches of the Mali empire and its importance as a trade route in historical times.

Discussion Starters

- Pair this book with *Sundiata: Lion King of Mali* by David Wisniewski for a history of the Mali empire, or with *Mansa Musa: The Richest Man in History* by Mike McCraw.
- What commodities was Mali most famous for?

Ideas for Further Engagement

- Look up the origin of the phrase "as far away as Timbuktu."
- Listen to the music of Salif Keita, an internationally renowned Malian musician and one of Mansa Musa's descendants.

Quotes for Interpretation

- "Tariq al-Aya talked of the ways of the nomadic Tuareg, Wodaabe, and Bedouin. He told of the origins of the Dogon who built their villages on the sheer face of cliffs; of Taghaza, a city built entirely of salt; and another city, Baladu, built entirely of copper." (22)

- "Al-Kemia was a land of many prophets, Kankan discovered, and some were shared by Muslims, Christians and Jews alike." (31)
- "Kankan Musa, now Mansa Musa, expanded the empire to the north and east, where he gained control of the all-important cities of the Sahara, the copper mines of Takedda, and the world-renowned learning centers of Timbuktu and Gao." (47)

Taj Mahal: A Story of Love and Empire. **Elizabeth Mann and Alan Witschonke, ill. by Alan Witschonke. Mikaya, 2008. 978–1931414203. 48 pp. Picture book/Nonfiction. Gr. 3–8.**

The reign of Shah Jahan, the fifth Mughal emperor of India, was a golden period for Mughal architecture in India. He commissioned the building of the Red Fort and the Jama Masjid in Delhi, and most famously, he built the Taj Mahal, a lavish tomb in honor of his beloved wife Mumtaz Mahal. The Taj Mahal, a harmonious integration of Indian, Persian, and Islamic influences, is considered "the jewel of Muslim art in India" and was described by Nobel laureate Rabindranath Tagore as "a teardrop on the cheek of time." This book looks at the artistic contributions of the Mughal Empire in architecture, literature, and painting and is a story of love and loss.

Discussion Starters

- Lead a discussion on the role of symmetry in the Taj Mahal and the use of water features in Islamic architecture.
- What do you think the Taj Mahal represents?

Ideas for Further Engagement

- Create a replica of the Taj Mahal.
- Look up memorial sites from around the world such as the Egyptian pyramids and the Parthenon in Athens, and discuss how these reflect the values of the cultures in that time in history.

Quotes for Interpretation
- "The Mughals were not about to let religious differences interfere with building an empire. They appointed Hindus to important government positions and adopted Hindu traditions. They married Hindu wives and hired Hindu artists and workers." (10)
- "Mughals could be very generous . . . Jahangirnama young Prince Khurram (who later became Shah Jahan) is seated on one side of a scale; bags of gold and silver are stacked on the other side. When the scales balanced, Jahangir gave away his son's weight in gold and silver to the poor." (16)
- "The idea of his wife's tomb began as a simple expression of love and grief, but in true Mughal fashion it became very large and grand." (19)

Twenty-Two Cents: Mohammed Yunus and the Village Bank. **Paula Yoo, ill. by Jamel Akib. Lee and Low Books, 2014. 978–1600606588. 40 pp. Nonfiction. K–Gr. 5.**

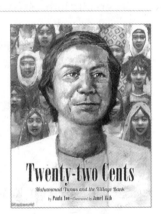

Select Awards: Center for the Study of Multicultural Children's Literature, Best Multicultural Books of 2014; Winner, IRA Notable Books for a Global Society 2015; VOYA's Nonfiction Honor List 2014.

This picture-book biography of Muhammad Yunus, the 2006 Nobel Peace Prize winner and founder of the microcredit lender Grameen Bank, is an inspiring tale of empowerment. The story begins with his childhood and includes background information about the political and economic situations of the time. This is a great book for introducing kids to ideas of economics and how to break free from the cycle of poverty, along with an inspirational message of how one person can improve the world. Readers of this book will be encouraged to ask their own hard questions and perhaps find their own solutions to current and future problems.

Discussion Starters
- What is Bangladesh best known for?
- What different kinds of jobs do women have around the world? Which of these are higher-paying ones?

- Why was education so important to Muhammad's parents? What sort of learning did Muhammad's father value most?

Ideas for Further Engagement

✋ Re-create the Bangladeshi flag and discuss the significance of the colors in the flag.

✋ Create a jute wall hanging.

Quotes for Interpretation

- "Muhammad noticed how just a few coins could buy enough rice to feed a family for an entire week." (11)

- "While in America, he witnessed college students holding peace rallies to show their opposition to the Vietnam War. . . . Muhammad was greatly impressed by the students' belief that they could make a difference." (13)

- "He could easily give Sufiya twenty-two cents she needed to buy more bamboo. Then she wouldn't owe the mahajon anything and could keep all the profits to herself. But Muhammad hesitated. If he gave Sufiya the money, she would always be dependent on strangers for charity. Giving her the twenty-two cents would not solve her problems in the long run." (22–23)

Chapter Books and Middle Grade Books

1001 Inventions and Awesome Facts from Muslim Civilization. **National Geographic Kids, 2012. 978–1426312588. 96 pp. Nonfiction. Gr. 3–7.**

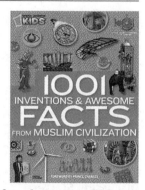

This is an informative and visually delightful book that traces the contributions of Muslim scholars, philosophers, artists, scientists, and more. The book uses a mix of facts, photos, and fun to bring history to life. It celebrates an underappreciated time when people from different countries, cultures, religions, and backgrounds worked together for a better world. Muslim scholars' practice of translating Arabic books into Latin and preserving ancient Greek texts was the foundation for Europe's Renaissance. From mapping over 160 stars, to sailing the high seas, to developing cosmetics, the world's first hang glider, and cafe bookshops, there were many inventions from the Muslim civilization which are used to this day.

Discussion Starters

- Which invention in this book was the most fascinating to you and why?
- Pair this book with *Arts and Culture in the Early Islamic World* by Lizann Flatt for a greater understanding of the arts, architecture, and crafts of the time.

Ideas for Further Engagement

- Research the history of the hang glider and create your own model.
- Choose your favorite constellation and write about the myths around it.
- Design and create a windmill of your own.

Quotes for Interpretation

- "Seven hundred years ago, people in the Muslim civilization designed clever clocks that were powered by water." (38)
- "Many cities gave their names to the famous goods they produced: muslin from Mosul, Iraq; gauze from Gaza; and damask cloth from Damascus, Syria." (69)
- "Five hundred years before windmills appeared in Europe, they were a common sight in Asian Muslim lands. You can still see the remains of ancient vertical windmills in Afghanistan." (84)

A Kid's Guide to Arab American History.
Yvonne Wakim Dennis and Maha Addasi.
Chicago Review, 2013. 978–1613740170.
224 pp. Nonfiction. Gr. 2–4.

Select Awards: 2014 Arab American Book Award, Children/Young Adult Category.

This book paints a kaleidoscope of the diverse group of Arab Americans—Lebanese, Syrians, Jordanians, Egyptians, Iraqis, and Yemenis—and broadens our understanding of Arabs and their culture. From the book's vignettes of famous and ordinary Arab Americans, we see how their lives and contributions have shaped America, both in the past and the present. This book is sure to keep readers of all ages engaged by the fun hands-on activities it offers, such as playing a game of *senet,* making hummus, learning traditional dances, and counting in Kurdish.

Discussion Starters

- The old saying "A friend is found at the time of hardship" originated in Yemen. Can you think of a similar saying that is popular in the United States?
- How is the Kuwaiti festival of Gigian similar to Halloween?
- Do you know who Ernest Hamwi is? What invention that you eat often was invented by him?

Ideas for Further Engagement

- Research similar words in the different dialects of Arabic: Jordanian, Egyptian, Tunisian, Moroccan, and Yemeni.
- Research the origins of the modern game of checkers and its connection to the game of *el-quirkat* or alqueque.

Quotes for Interpretation

- "More than four million Americans have ancestors from Arab countries." (2)
- "Columbus is thought to have used the early Arab maps to chart his trip, and records indicate that there were Arab crew members on his vessels." (141)
- "Anakin Skywalker's home is in Tunisia! The building used to portray young Anakin's home in *Star Wars* movies is a *ksar,* an ancient grain storage castle in southern Tunisia." (154)

Alia's Mission: Saving the Book of Iraq. **Mark Alan Stamaty. Dragonfly Books, 2004. 978–0375857638. 32 pp. Nonfiction graphic novel. K–Gr. 3.**

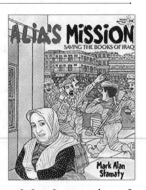

Select Awards: 2005 Middle East Book Award, Honorable Mention.

The heroic efforts of Alia Muhammad Baker to save over 30,000 titles from the library of Basra is a multifaceted tale about the human cost of war. Iraq was a center of learning during the Golden Age of Islam and the destruction of these books and the library is an irreplaceable loss of history and culture of a nation. Illustrated in black and white, with different shades of gray in between, the story dramatically conveys the impending doom, while also highlighting one person's commitment to save "the collective memory of her people."

Discussion Starters
- What is the value of books and libraries? How can books serve as windows and mirrors to other places, peoples, and cultures?
- How can you engage within your community, and take action? How can one child make a difference around her?
- What would you have done if you were in Baker's situation?

Ideas for Further Engagement
- Watch the film *Bekas* by Karzan Kader.
- Volunteer at your local library.

Quotes for Interpretation
- "It is based on true events in the life of a real person who shows us it's not necessary to see through walls or fly or have any superpowers at all to be a real-life superhero." (1)
- "Ever since Alia was a little girl, books had been a source of happiness and adventure for her." (2)
- "All the records of our culture, our history . . . the irreplaceable collective memory of our people, our ancestors, our place in the world." (8)

Arts and Culture in the Early Islamic World. **Lizann Flatt. Crabtree, 2011. 978-0778721741. 48 pp. Nonfiction. Gr. 5–8.**

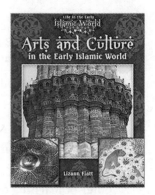

This book is a good follow-up to *1001 Inventions and Awesome Facts from Muslim Civilization*, and it gives more detailed information on the contributions to art and culture made by the Islamic world. The book has chapters dedicated to each art form such as calligraphy, pottery, glassware, books, music, and architecture, and history buffs will enjoy tracing how these works came to be. The book's illustrations, maps, paintings, and beautiful photographs emphasize the value that art plays in the daily life of Muslim communities. Short biographies of historical figures at the end also add to the depth of information presented.

Discussion Starters

- Pair this book with *1001 Inventions and Awesome Facts from Muslim Civilization* by National Geographic, or with *Science, Medicine and Math in the Early Islamic World* by Trudee Romanek.
- Why was art an important part of the economy of the Islamic world in these early times? How have art forms evolved over the years?

Ideas for Further Engagement

- 🖐 List popular industries in the seventeenth and eighteenth centuries.
- 🖐 Trace the origins of the use of drums, cymbals, and trumpets in military bands.
- 🖐 Create your own tessellation pattern on poster board.

Quotes for Interpretation

- "Much of Islamic art is 'decorative,' which means it is useful as well as beautiful, such as a painted pot, an illustrated book, or a carved table." (4)
- "Water was precious and a symbol of Paradise, so water became an important feature of Islamic architecture." (12)
- "Rulers collected books and valued them greatly. They gave books as gifts to other rulers and also set up public libraries." (33)

Ibn al-Haytham: The Man Who Discovered How We See. Libby Romero. National Geographic Children's Books, 2016. 978–1426325007. 48 pp. Nonfiction. Gr. 1–4.

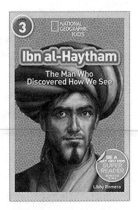

This is an informative and engaging book for young children to learn more about Ibn al-Haytham, a leading Muslim scholar who discovered how we see. Ibn al-Haytham, also known as Alhazen, was a pioneer in the field of optics and vision who correctly proposed that we see by means of light bouncing off objects and entering our eyes. Al-Haytham was also an early advocate of the "scientific method" that was rediscovered by European scientists 500 years later in the Renaissance. This book's colorful illustrations and fact boxes help create a picture of al-Haytham's time and tell us many interesting details about his life as well. This is an important book that links history to the present.

Discussion Starters
- What is a scientist? Do you enjoy being a scientist?
- How many craters are there on the moon? How are they named?

Ideas for Further Engagement
- Make a pinhole camera with a cereal box.
- List ten inventions that were invented during the Islamic Golden Age.
- Look up the "1001 Inventions and the World of Ibn al-Haytham" campaign that includes interactive exhibits, workshops, live shows, and a twelve-minute film starring Omar Sharif in his final film role before his death.

Quotes for Interpretation
- "Ibn al-Haytham is sometimes called the Father of Modern Optics. Because of his methods for testing ideas, many people even consider him to be the first scientist." (31)
- "The Alhazen crater on the Moon is named after Ibn al-Haytham. So is the asteroid 59239 Alhazen." (32)
- "Newton studied Ibn al-Haytham's ideas about forces." (43)

***Jannah Jewels Book 1: The Treasure of Timbuktu.*
Umm Nura, ill. by Nayzak Al-Hilali. Gentle Breeze
Books, 2010. 978-0986720802. 69 pp. Historical
fiction. Gr. 1–5.**

This twelve-book historical fiction series features
four *hijabi* girls: Hidayah, Iman, Jade, and Sarah,
who are selected to save the world by finding
twelve missing artifacts in time. In each book, they
are transported back in time to recover artifacts
from different countries which have had Muslim
rulers or populations. In the first book, the girls
visit Timbuktu in Mali where they discover that someone has stolen a price-
less manuscript and that they must work together and race against time to
find the manuscript and return it to its rightful owner. Subsequent books in
the series involve adventures in China, Egypt, India, Uzbekistan, and even
the United States of America. Engaging and informative, this book series has
a tinge of the popular Magic Tree House series, and is sure to appeal to all
children.

Discussion Starters
- What did you learn about Mali through this book?
- Where should a historical artifact be housed: in the country of origin
  or the place where it was subsequently taken to?

Ideas for Further Engagement
- ✋ Research the history of Mali and the famous king, Mansa Musa.
- ✋ Listen to a lineup of songs from Festival Au Desert, an annual concert
  in Mali, and learn more about the historical origins of this tradition.
- ✋ Watch Bino and Fino's animated adventure about the Ancient Manu-
  scripts of Timbuktu in Mali.

Quotes for Interpretation
- "I was just reading here that a man named Ibn Battuta travelled for
  almost 23 years and he came to Mali, too. He was known as a world
  traveler and wrote a book called the Rihla." (33)
- "The knowledge in these manuscripts is worth more than any other
  thing here, even food." (40)

- "You're—you're Mansa Musa! You are one of the greatest kings! You have one of the widest kingdoms and the largest armies." (45)

***Proud: Living My American Dream.* Ibtihaj Muham-mad. Little, Brown Books for Young Readers; Young Readers edition, 2018. 978-0316477000. 304 pp. Nonfiction. Gr. 3–8.**

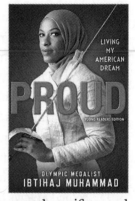

Growing up in a middle class family in New Jersey, Ibtihaj Muhammad dreamt of fame and success in an unlikely sport—fencing. Muhammad soon found that she was one of the few women of color and the only Muslim woman in a hijab in what is often seen as an elite sport. Her honest portrayal of her strug-gles, as well as her grit and determination and the personal sacrifices and obstacles that came her way, make for a compelling read. Though she encoun-tered discrimination and social pressure at every stage, her faith made her stronger. The desire to represent her country at the Olympics and to be an influential role model for African American and Muslim Americans became her clarion call to succeed. Ibtihaj Muhammad's inspirational memoir is one of succeeding despite daunting odds, and persevering against stereotypes and negativity.

Discussion Starters
- How do you think Ibtihaj felt when she first walked into the cafeteria for fencing tryouts alone?
- What were her parents rules about taking on a sport? Do your parents have rules about sport or other extracurricular activities that you want to pursue?
- What helped Ibtihaj persist in the face of social pressure from friends and family who "thought I was crazy for choosing a sport like fencing, and then crazier for sticking with it."?
- Have you ever felt as if you were the odd person out at a sporting or other event? How do you try to fit in?

Ideas for Further Engagement
- ✋ Trace the origins of the sport of fencing.

✋ Look up some female fencing athletes.

✋ Name some of your favorite sports personalities and write about how their stories inspire you.

Quotes for Interpretation

- "The way I identify myself has been even more confusing to them: Black but Muslim. Muslim but American. A hijab-wearing athlete. I've walked into many rooms and stood on stages where it was clear people didn't know what to make of me." (10)

- "We trained as a team, we won and lost as a team. Everyone was treated equally, and you got out of the sport what you put in. We weren't black or white or Muslim or Christian; we were athletes. Even though I was the only Muslim on the team and one of only a handful of people of color, I always felt safe and like I was exactly where I belonged." (54)

- "All the people who'd made me feel like I'd never succeed because of my race or my religion should be ashamed of themselves. I'd defied the odds. My success wasn't measured only by wins on the fencing strip, but also by the number of people I was able to inspire by sharing my story of triumph." (189)

Razia and the Pesky Presents. **Natasha Sharma. Duckbill, 2015. 978-9383331208. 80 pp. Historical fiction. Gr. 1–5.**

Select Awards: 2016 South Asia Book Award, Honor Book.

Razia Sultan ruled the Delhi sultanate in the thir-teenth century, and was its only female ruler. Against this backdrop of history, and using her own spar-kling wit and humor, Natasha Sharma takes you back to Razia's reign. Some-one who is upset about a female ruler leading the Delhi sultanate is sending Razia pesky presents which challenge her throne and authority. How does Razia find the sender of these pesky presents and understand what they want? This book is a fun historical twist and a great introduction to the brave leader and warrior Razia Sultan for early readers. The author's note at the end provides more information about Razia Sultan, along with commonly used words and references from that time period.

Discussion Starters

- Do you think female rulers have a more difficult time than male rulers?
- Name some countries with women heads of state.

Ideas for Further Engagement

- ✍ Have your own "pesky present" treasure hunt.
- ✍ Research brave queens around the world who fought for their kingdoms.

Quotes for Interpretation

- "I'm no Sultana! I am the Sultan—as much a Sultan as any man who has ruled!" (5)
- "For the third anniversary of your rule. A dress would be best. Better than pants and the rest." (33)
- "A grim-faced Sultan Razia entered, fiddling with her body armor—her head under a steel cap with a chain link covering her neck, shield in one hand and sword in another. She leapt onto the back of her horse, also covered in armor, and turned to face her army. The fiddling stopped. Everyone stiffened in attention." (44)

Respecting the Contributions of Muslim Americans. **Sloan MacRae. Power Kids, 2013. 978–1448874446. 24 pp. Nonfiction. Gr. 2–4.**

This is a simple but direct book that provides facts about Islam, describes how Muslims came to America, and profiles some famous Muslim Americans such as Muhammad Ali, Ahmed Zawail, Fareed Zakaria, and Keith Ellison. This book would be a useful and easy reference book for libraries to include in their collection.

Discussion Starters

- When did the first Muslims come to America and how?
- What are some of the challenges immigrants face when they move to a new country?

Ideas for Further Engagement

- 🖐 Research a famous Muslim American and write a short biography of him or her.
- 🖐 Research the breakup of the population of the United States, and explore the origins of the American population.
- 🖐 Watch the short film *American Muslims: Facts vs. Fiction.*

Quotes for Interpretation

- "The United States has more people of the different branches of Islam living together than any other country in the world." (8)
- "Like other families, Muslim American families balance embracing everyday American life with teaching their children about their religious and cultural traditions." (11)
- "Records also show that there were soldiers with Muslim names on the lists of people who fought in the American Revolution." (13)

Saladin: The Muslim Warrior Who Defended His People. **Flora Geyer. National Geographic, 2006. 978–0792255364. 64 pp. Nonfiction. Gr. 3–7.**

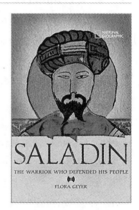

With a good blend of images and text, this chapter book provides a perfect introduction to the great Muslim warrior Saladin. The book chronicles his life from his birth, his upbringing, how he came to power, won wars and suffered some defeats, and became the first sultan of Egypt. In addition to sharing the significant facts of his life, the book examines Saladin's personal attributes and behavior and emphasizes how his kindness and generosity helped him become one of the greatest Muslim rulers of the time. A helpful time line of the key events during Saladin's life trails the bottom of each page to put the events in context.

Discussion Starters

- Discuss different forms of government: monarchy, democracy, and military rule.
- What attributes make a person a good king?

Ideas for Further Engagement

 ✋ Look up which countries of the world still have kings.

 ✋ Watch the film *The Sultan and the Saint* by Alex Kronemer, narrated by Jeremy Irons.

Quotes for Interpretation

- "By the time Saladin was born in 1138, Muslim lands stretched from southern Spain and North Africa to China and India." (16)
- "Muslim scholars also carefully preserved discoveries made by past civilizations, especially the ancient Greeks and Egyptians, and used these to improve their own skills in science, medicine, astronomy, and math." (16)
- "Later reports praised Saladin for treating his Christian enemies with fairness and mercy during the siege of Alexandria." (36)

The Silk Road: Explore the World's Most Famous Trade Route with 20 Projects. **Kathy Ceceri, ill. by the author. Nomad, 2011. 978-1934670620. 128 pp. Nonfiction. Gr. 3–7.**

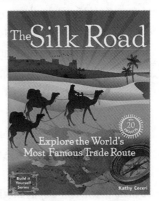

Before the days of cars, airplanes, and the Internet, ideas and information were exchanged through travelers who journeyed by foot and caravans over long distances. The Silk Road was a series of east-west routes which connected the Middle East with Central Asia and all the way to China. It was a vital trade route, and it also spread technology, mathematics, science, arts, and languages between the East and West. This engaging and well-written book provides interesting facts and fun hands-on activities to help children understand the relevance and contributions of the Silk Road.

Discussion Starters

- Explore UNESCO's World Heritage List of Silk Road cities.
- When and where was glassblowing invented?

Ideas for Further Engagement

 ✋ Look up places in the United States where Central Asians reside. For instance, the Queens neighborhood of Rego Park is home to Jews from

Bukhara, while many Mongolians are settled in New Jersey and Richmond, California.

- 🖐 Learn more about the music and arts of the Silk Road through the Silk Road Project.
- 🖐 Listen to the music by the Silk Road Ensemble, which combines old and new music from both Eastern and Western traditions.
- 🖐 A piaza was a passport or badge used along the Silk Road that allowed people access to food, shelter, horses, and guides. Create your own piaza with a design.
- 🖐 Create your own Turkish good luck charm to ward off the evil eye.
- 🖐 Find the origin of the term Silk Road.

Quotes for Interpretation

- "The Epic of Manas from Kyrgyzstan is 20 times longer than the Iliad and the Odyssey combined." (61)
- "Pants were invented in the Silk Road region to make it possible to sit comfortably on a horse." (70)
- "The earliest written version of the story of Cinderella comes from China about 850 CE. There are at least 300 other variations from places like Persia, Italy, Greece, and the Middle East." (107)

Young Adult Books

Arabic Graffiti. **Pascal Zoghbi and Don "Stone" Karl. From Here to Fame, 2011. 978–3937946269. Nonfiction. All ages.**

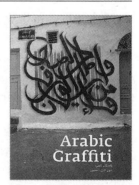

This exquisite book provides a detailed introduction to the Arabic alphabet and calligraphy, it showcases graffiti from all over the Middle East (primarily in Lebanon, Tehran, and Palestine), and it provides essays by many accomplished graffiti artists and calligraphers. The authors also interweave the sociopolitical messages contained in graffiti that are written on walls, shops, trucks, and public places, often during difficult times of war and political turmoil. Beautiful pictures of Arabic script, Islamic art, and graffiti bring this book to life and provide an authentic window into contemporary Arabic culture.

Discussion Starters

- Are graffiti and calligraphy the same? How are they different?
- Compare Arabic graffiti with murals in San Francisco and examine the similarities or differences between the messages conveyed by these art forms.
- Compare with the works of Banksy and other famous graffiti artists, and examine if any of them were influenced by Arabic graffiti or Islamic art.

Ideas for Further Engagement

- 🖐 Look up the origin and influence of the Arabic language, and its impact on art.
- 🖐 Watch the film *Microphone* by Ahmad Abdalla about the underground art scene in Alexandria, Egypt.

Quotes for Interpretation

- "A thousand years ago, a man who lived in Baghdad, Ibn Muqlah (886–940), designed and developed many of the calligraphy styles that we know today as the Six Pens Styles." (23)
- "Is the spray can mightier than the sword?" (65)
- "Developing from the traditions of neocolonialism, Arab and Muslim voices are stifled by dominating stereotypes which are often unconsciously absorbed. The creation of art, especially highly visible street art, takes back this voice through authentic expressions of identity and culture." (103)

Art of the Middle East: Modern and Contemporary Art from the Arab World and Iran. **Saeb Eigner, foreword by Zaha Hadid. Merrell, 2015. 978–1858946283. Nonfiction. All ages.**

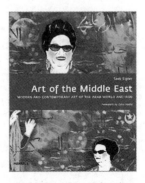

A foreword by the renowned architect Zaha Hadid celebrates this book, with its comprehensive look at over 300 artists from the Arab world including the Middle East, North Africa, and Iran. A glimpse of "future possibilities, yet derived from rich cultural traditions and timeless history," the book is a stunning compilation of modern artists from 1945 to the present. It explores themes of nature, portraiture, politics, conflict, and war as well as art inspired by literature, music, and performance. The multitude of styles, mediums, and art forms showcase the diversity within modern Islamic art, and the artist biographies and detailed notes in the introduction and for each artwork make this a rewarding visual treat.

Discussion Starters

- How does the use of arabesque designs and the repetition of geometric patterns reflect spirituality?
- Examine how elements of Islamic art inspired Western artists such as M. C. Escher.

Ideas for Further Engagement

- ✋ Look up works of art that are inspired by literature and music.
- ✋ Listen to National Public Radio's *Muslim Artists, Now* series for a look at creative contemporary Muslim artists from around the world.

Quotes for Interpretation

- "Despite the emphasis on calligraphy, natural and human forms have appeared in the art of Islamic countries for many centuries." (18)
- "Painter and calligraphers have combined modernist Western forms with a reverence for the written word that remains a characteristic of the Middle East and Arab world." (66)
- "The *Shahnameh (Book of Kings)* has remained an important source of inspiration for Iranian artists up to the present day." (187)

Becoming Kareem: Growing Up On and Off the Court. **Kareem Abdul-Jaffar and Raymond Obstfeld. Little Brown Books for Young Readers, 2017. 978–0316555388. 304 pp. Nonfiction. Gr. 5 and up.**

Select Awards: School Library Journal's Best Books of 2017.

Kareem Abdul-Jabbar, the NBA's all-time leading scorer, has been inducted into the Basketball Hall of Fame and was awarded the Presidential Medal of Freedom by President Obama in 2016. This book is an honest and compelling account of his life: his childhood as Lewis Alcindor, how he got into basketball, his friendship with Muhammad Ali, his decision to convert to Islam, and the racism and anti-Islamic prejudice that he experienced during the course of his life. A lot of context and explanation is provided around Jabbar's decision to change his name and religion, which were significant moments in his life. Young readers will be inspired by the numerous influences of people, books, and movies that shaped Jabbar into one of the greatest basketball players in the history of the sport.

Discussion Starters

- Explore your own racial identity. Have you ever experienced racism in your life?
- How can we reduce racist actions and feelings in our society?
- Think of one person in your life who has been a significant positive influence and write some words of gratitude for him or her.
- How was Jabbar influenced by Martin Luther King Jr. and Muhammad Ali?
- Pair this book with *X: A Novel* by Ilyasah Shahbazz and Kekla Magoon.

Ideas for Further Engagement

- Research examples where famous athletes have become embroiled in issues of politics and social justice.
- Create a poster board of key moments in your favorite athlete's life.

Quotes for Interpretation

- "To many, by changing my religion and name, I was no longer the *typical* American kid playing a *typical* American sport embodying *typical* American values." (ix)
- "Lew Alcindor carried the name and religion of the white slaveholder who had exploited, humiliated and abused my ancestors." (ix)
- "His [Muhammad Ali's] explanation of how Islam helped him find his true self, and gave him the strength not only to face hostile reactions from both black and white critics, but also to fight for social justice, led me to study the Quran." (216)

I Am Malala: The Girl Who Stood Up for Education and Was Shot by the Taliban. **Malala Yousafzai and Christina Lamb. Back Bay Books, 2013. 978–0316322409. 368 pp. Nonfiction. Young adults.**

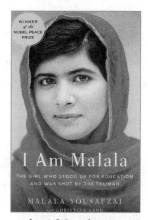

Select Awards: Non-Fiction Book of the Year, National Book Awards 2013.

Malala Yousafzai's extraordinary story recounts the lives and struggles of ordinary people during a time of conflict. She talks about her childhood growing up in the Swat Valley in northwestern Pakistan, a place of pristine beauty marred by the war in Afghanistan and controlled by traditional tribal factions. While Malala's father, the founder of a school, encouraged her to pursue her education as well as use her voice to champion the rights of all girls, he was an exception to the growing Islamic radicalization of the valley. Malala's family refused to succumb to the pressure from the Taliban, and one fateful day, Malala was shot point-blank by them on her way back home from school. Her miraculous recovery strengthened her fiery spirit and her resolve to continue her fight for girls' education on an international level. Malala's mature and eloquent voice comes through in her writing, while Christina Lamb's historical and political commentary provides the context for understanding the sociopolitical climate in Pakistan. Malala's story is a powerful tale that will inspire empathy and understanding for the cause of universal access to education for all.

Discussion Starters
- Pair this book with *Girls Rising: Changing the World One Girl at a Time* by Tanya Lee Stone, or with *Because I Was a Girl: True Stories of Girls of All Ages* by Melissa de la Cruz.
- How does gender affect access to education, leadership, and other aspects of life?

Ideas for Further Engagement
- Listen to Malala's Nobel Peace Prize acceptance speech.
- Watch *Girls Rising* by Richard E. Robbins and narrated by Meryl Streep, Kerry Washington, Anne Hathaway, and others.

Quotes for Interpretation

- "I am Malala, a girl like any other—although I do have my special talents." (11)
- "As I looked at the TV, a tiny voice in my heart whispered to me: 'Why don't you go there and fight for women's rights? Fight to make Pakistan a better place?'" (55)
- "One child, one teacher, one book and one pen can change the world." (192)

Islamic Art. **Luca Mozzatti. Prestel, 2010. 978–3791344553. 320 pp. Nonfiction. All ages.**

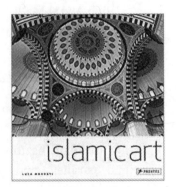

A magnificent encyclopedia that features various forms of Islamic art in architecture, painting, calligraphy, ceramics, glass, and carpets, this book will appeal to all ages and is a visual feast for its readers. It explains the basic principles of Islamic art, the forms of Islamic architecture, and it also provides a detailed history of Islamic rulers from the Umayyads to the Indian subcontinent, and how they influenced the art of their times. Engaging explanations are provided about how geometry was rooted in Islamic principles and reflected in Islamic architecture, how Islamic architecture was designed, and the importance and thought behind the development of calligraphy, pottery, and other forms of art and architecture.

Discussion Starters

- Visit a neighborhood museum or Islamic center where you can view different forms of Islamic art.
- Is there an indigenous style of architecture where you live?
- What are some of the features of Western architecture inspired by Islamic architecture?

Ideas for Further Engagement

- 🖐 Look up the history of Persian miniature paintings.
- 🖐 Watch the documentary *Islamic Art: Mirror of the Invisible World* by Robert Gardner, narrated by Susan Sarandon.

Quotes for Interpretation

- "The circle represents a complete unity that reflects the 'perfect and not perfectible' unity of the starting point . . . Having neither beginning nor end, it represents eternity." (24)
- "Architecture in Islamic lands tends to face inwards, perhaps in conformity to a typology harking back to the traditional Mediterranean house, protected by blind walls and, wherever possible, furnished with an inner courtyard." (31)
- "The birth of Islamic architecture came about through the efforts of Caliph Abd al-Malik, who erected the Dome of the Rock in Jerusalem, and al-Walid, who built the Great Mosque at Damascus." (66)

***Lost History: The Enduring Legacy of Muslim Scientists, Thinkers and Artists.* Michael H. Morgan. National Geographic, 2007. 978–1426200922. 320 pp. Nonfiction. Adults.**

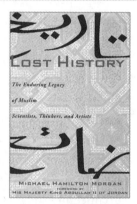

As the title explains, this informative book draws unique parallels and teases out connections between our world today and the contributions of Muslim civilization in its Golden Age in the fields of mathematics, astronomy, medicine, music, literature, and civic development. Through his fictional narratives, Morgan connects the past to the present not just for the people, but also to show us how the flow of knowledge has crossed cultures and borders and extended over great spans of time.

Discussion Starters

- Discuss how geometry made its way into Islamic architecture and decorative objects.
- Who was the first scientist to prove that the Earth revolves around the Sun?

Ideas for Further Engagement

- ✋ Look up how the history of the mass production of paper led to mass literacy.

🖐 Research how Arabic music notations from the ninth and tenth centuries influenced Italian musical notation.

🖐 Trace the origins of the guitar, mandolin, and lute and explore their connection to the *'ud*, or oud.

🖐 Who built the world's first teaching hospital, university, and library?

🖐 Research the contributions of Al-Zahrawi to the medical field.

🖐 Watch the documentary *Cities of Light: The Rise and Fall of Islamic Spain* by Rob Gardner.

Quotes for Interpretation

- "At its peak in the 11th century, Cordoba will be the most advanced city in Europe with a population of half a million, boasting some 300 baths, 300 mosques, 50 hospitals, and a high public literacy expressed in libraries, public and private, with more books than in all the rest of Europe." (69)

- "In 1079 in an astonishing feat of computation without computers, Omar Khayyam will calculate the length of the year to be 365.24219858156 days. In the 21st century, using the Hubble telescope, atomic clocks, and computers, the year will be calculated to be 365.242190 days." (112)

- "Ibn Sina will eventually be proven right in his belief that tuberculosis is infectious, though the Europeans will reject his theory for about 400 years." (195–96)

Michael Hamilton Morgan

Intertwined Histories

What inspired you to write about Muslim civilization?
There were many factors. First, I was totally intrigued with and infatuated with old, intricate, layered cultures, and Muslim cultures fit the bill. My interest was further piqued by political issues in the West in terms of dealing with extremism and so many misunderstandings and misconceptions. As I did my initial research, I realized that this thousand-year-old culture was one that was built in large part on knowledge and intellect. As a student of history, I know of no case in human history where there was such a sustained, long-term religious loyalty to knowledge. This was a period of invention and creativity coupled with ideas of tolerance and coexistence, so for all these reasons I wanted to explore more about Muslim civilization.

Why do you think this period is, as you say, "Lost History"?
All cultures, nations, and big organizations that exist over time are driven by the reality that nothing in the physical world lasts forever. One of the fatal flaws of historical Muslim civilization was that there was never a political decision at the top to promote mass education. No one else was doing it at that time; it only started to happen in Europe in the sixteenth century. However, if Muslim cultures had made this a priority earlier, then the outcome would have been different. Also, there was a real cleavage between the elites and everyone else in terms of edu-

cation. The masses had no appreciation for the phenomenal things being done by Muslim-supported thinkers, and this trend continues even today. You can even see it in the United States in some ways, where the great mass of people doesn't know much about what's going on, and this creates a tension that was played out in the Muslim world a thousand years ago and is now being played out in the United States today.

What were the most fascinating inventions or discoveries that you uncovered?
There were so many, and my new book deals with more things that haven't made it out to the mainstream. I would have to say that mathematical discoveries, mainly algebra and algorithms, which were not totally Muslim but drew from the work of mathematicians in India and China, were the most important. Algorithms developed by Al-Khwarizmi are today the basis of current digital software and analyzing data. In the West, we worship great mathematicians, but not in quite the same way

as the thinkers in Baghdad did—there was more of an exchange and building on information. The Hindu thinkers in India worked on the concept of the zero and the decimal system which the Arabs and Persians then made standard. The great thing about Muslim cultures was that they were so open to finding the best ideas no matter where they came from.

What is the biggest misconception about Muslims that you believe it is important to change?
The biggest misconception about Muslims is that Islam is a religion of domination and conquest. That Muslims created

Why do you think it is important for people to know about this era of lost history?
History has a way of showing us how we are all connected. Not just in the present day, but with ties that take us back into the past. Knowing about this era is part of the narrative of being connected. Today, we have some really nefarious political voices that thrive on creating perceptions of division, alienation, and subversion, but if we can show the fabric of how we live, how we make our money, how our medicine works, and show that it was not just created by white men sitting in Paris, it brings together a different narrative. It

"... If we can show the fabric of how we live, how we make our money, how our medicine works, and show that it was not just created by white men sitting in Paris, it brings together a different narrative. It challenges the nationalism rising in the West."

nothing of their own and took things from Greek, Persians, and others. The common mainstream perception is that Islam is based on those values, which is not true.

You begin each chapter of your book in the modern day, and you integrate discoveries from the past into the present. What made you choose this format?
Personally, the idea of the book was not to reach an academic audience but a mass audience. How would an average person confronted with history relate to it in the context of today? They are likely to ask; how does it affect me? So, this format showed people how it affects their modern day-to-day life, in order to make it relevant for them.

challenges the nationalism rising in the West. Still, it is a tough sell for people to turn away from the sensationalist news, but a look back at our interconnected histories is the only way to combat this intellectual dishonesty that is going on.

What were the relations between Muslims, Christians, and Jews during this time?
It really depended on where you lived at that time. There were very few Jews in the Gulf, but there were many more Jews in Central Asia at the time of the rise of Islam, and there were certainly Christian communities in Iraq, but not so much in Persia. It was also a time of tolerance of people of different faiths, as well as an age of learning that lasted a long time.

This sense of intense and sustained religious division was only promoted more recently, say in the last 50–60 years. Of course, it wasn't a love fest all of the time. In Spain, Christians were sometimes militantly opposed and somewhat disgruntled with a sense of having lost something. In places such as Moorish Spain, Muslims and Jews were more prominent than Christians. But people moved to intellectual centers and were able to live alongside each other in these different communities.

Do you have any advice for educators and all of us as a community on how to teach children to respect differences and value diversity?
Educational curricula the world over are so politically sensitive that it is a challenge to introduce concepts that are based on fact rather than promoting a particular ideology. This is true not just in the United States but also in countries such as Pakistan, Jordan, Egypt, and so on, so for me the best way to address that was to write this book. Even in this cluttered digital landscape, books never die with a thinking audience.

Biography

Michael Morgan is an international speaker, business advisor, and award-winning former U.S. diplomat who currently advises companies in the United States, Europe, Latin America, Africa, and Asia-Pacific that are seeking capital and partnerships—in industries like energy, infrastructure, telecom, pharmaceuticals, entertainment, sports, and real estate.

Morgan has appeared on ABC's *Good Morning America*, Al Jazeera (Arabic and English services), the BBC, *CBS Evening News*, CSpan, Public Radio International, Voice of America TV, and elsewhere. His op-eds and advertorials have appeared in the *New York Times*, *Time*, the *Washington Post*, and the *Wall Street Journal*.

Rúmí: Poet and Mystic, Selections from His Writings. Reynold A. Nicholson. One World, 2012. 978–1851680962. 190 pp. Nonfiction. All ages.

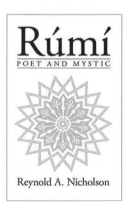

Nicholson provides a translated version of selected poems by the renowned mystic poet Rúmí from his magnum opus, *Masnavi*, complete with notes to provide additional context. Rúmí's poetry provides a unique reflection on one's relationship with God, life, and love, which is relevant even now, after the lapse of almost a thousand years since it was first written.

Discussion Starters
- Discuss the poetry styles of famous poets, and explore which one is more appealing and why.
- Which one was your favorite Rúmí poem?

Ideas for Further Engagement
- Explore writing a short poem of your own.
- Watch *Rumi–Turning Ecstatic* by Tina Petrova and Stephen Roloff.

Quotes for Interpretation
- "Oh, music is the meat of all who love,
  Music uplifts the soul to realms above.
  The ashes glow, the latent fires increase:
  We listen and are fed with joy and peace." (32)
- "The faint-hearted merchant neither gains nor loses; nay he loses: one must take fire in order to get light." (55)
- "I died as a mineral and became a plant,
  I died as a plant and rose to animal,
  I died as animal and I was Man.
  Why should I fear? When was I less by dying?" (103)

Significant Figures: The Lives and Work of Great Mathematicians. **Ian Stewart. Basic Books, 2017. 978–0465096121. 282 pp. Nonfiction. All ages.**

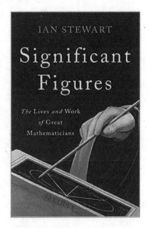

This is an informative book that provides concise and interesting biographies of a hand-picked group of twenty-five different mathematicians ranging from Archimedes to Benoit Mandelbrot. Stewart has been careful in his selection and has included both men and women mathematicians from both the West and East. He shares personable stories about how they became mathematicians, their major contributions to the field of mathematics, and their quirky personalities. Muhammad ibn Musa al-Khwarizmi, a Persian mathematician who gave us the words *algorithm* and *algebra*, is featured as one of these twenty-five significant figures.

Discussion Starters
- Discuss how all of modern-day computing originates from algorithms.
- What do you think was al-Khwarizmi's primary contribution to the field of mathematics?

Ideas for Further Engagement

- ✍ Trace the geographical development of mathematics over the centuries and how the East and West built upon each other's work.
- ✍ Watch the documentary *Al-Khwarizmi: The Father of Algebra*, on Al-Jazeera.

Quotes for Interpretation

- "In mathematics, we move on, but we don't discard our history." (1)
- "His *al-Kitab al-mukhtasar fi hisab al-jabr wa-1 -muqabala (The Compendious Book on Calculation by Completion and Balancing)*, written around 830, was translated into Latin in the twelfth century by Robert of Chester as *Liber Algebrae et Almucabola*. As a result, *al-jabr*, Latinized to "algebra," became a word in its own right." (30)
- "Alongside the mathematicians of ancient China and India, al-Khwarizmi's achievements add to the weight of evidence that during the Middle Ages, when Europe's science mostly stagnated, the center of scientific and mathematical advances moved to the Far and Middle East." (36)

***The Ultimate Ambition in the Arts of Erudition: A Compendium of Knowledge from the Classical Islamic World.* Shihab al-Din al-Nuwayri and Elias Muhanna. Penguin Classics, 2016. 978–0143107484. 352 pp. Nonfiction. Adults.**

Select Awards: NPR: Best Books of the Year 2016, *The Guardian*: Best Books of the Year 2016.

This is a quirky catalog of the Muslim world in the fourteenth century as recorded by Shihab al-Din al-Nuwayri, a scholar and bureaucrat who served the Mamluk dynasty in Egypt. Condensed from thirty volumes and translated by Elias Muhanna, this collection is "a view into the kaleidoscopic and multifarious intellectual traditions of the classical Islamic world." It includes poetry, proverbs, information on science, history, and governance, and interesting observations on other places around the world, from the wildlife in India to the curios in China and the never-ending rains in England. This is a fascinating look at the past and a totally engrossing fun read for the present. *The book does have some sexual content in its (probably unreproducible) recipes for aphrodisiacs.*

Discussion Starters

- Discuss how the etymology of the word "human" or *insan* in Arabic is similar to the idea that man is a social animal.
- Why do you think early astronomers describe the seven planets as confused stars? How does this match up with what we know of the planets today?

Ideas for Further Engagement

- ✋ Compare the book's discussions about the phases of the moon to contemporary facts.
- ✋ Look up the different names that Bedouin Arabs have for the night and compare these to the names in *The Girl Who Fell to Earth.*
- ✋ Tally how the book's description of the growth of a fetus compares with what we know today.

Quotes for Interpretation

- "The night is divided into twelve hours, each with its own name given to it by Bedouin Arabs." (24)
- "In Egypt many of the sciences were born that made the world civilized and prosperous such as Greek medicine, astronomy, mensuration, geometry, alchemy, and others." (37)
- "As for the seasons of the year, the body has four humors whose natures mirror the nature of the four seasons." (51)

Notes

1. For example, see this sentence: "Malala is the best thing to come out of the Muslim world in a thousand years," in https://www.samharris.org/blog/item/no-ordinary -violence, implying that Muslims have not contributed to anything else.

2. Phillip K. Hitti, *The Arabs: A Short History* (Washington, DC: Princeton University Press, 1996).

3. Michael Hamilton Morgan, *Lost History: The Enduring Legacy of Muslim Scientists, Thinkers and Artists* (Washington, DC: National Geographic, 2007).

Chapter 6

Celebrating Islam

Understanding Religious Practices and Traditions

I
N THE EARLY DAYS OF CHILDREN'S LITERATURE, CHILDREN'S books were mainly instructional, and many of them focused on explaining religion.[1] Led by none other than "the father of children's literature," John Newbery, the trend gradually shifted to publishing more books with a focus on entertaining children, rather than mere instruction.[2] Today the landscape is much broader, with children's books ranging from purely religious ones to a great variety of fiction and nonfiction texts. In a reflection of today's pluralistic society, children's literature is gradually becoming more inclusive and is featuring books that showcase ethnic, linguistic, and religious diversity. Many publishers cleverly combine details of various religions with the plot and characters in a children's book to provide an entertaining story for all children.[3] This approach facilitates early exposure to other religions in a secular way that allows for greater understanding of the common moral beliefs across faiths, and it promotes tolerance, respect, and solidarity. Unfortunately, there are many misconceptions about Islam that exist today, and few children's books accurately portray the traditions and practices of Muslims.

This chapter, "Celebrating Islam," showcases engaging books that introduce children to the tenets, celebrations, and values of Islam. Islam is the second largest religion in the world, with over a billion followers. Along with Judaism and Christianity, it is one of the three monotheistic religions that believe in one God.

Many people believe that the Five Pillars of Islam are similar to the Ten Commandments in Judaism and Christianity. Islam also recognizes the prophets and teachings of the Old and New Testaments. Islam shares a common moral code with the world's major religions with its call to provide for the less fortunate, respect elders, search for the truth, look out for one's neighbors, and be just and kind.

All religions emerge from complex histories of social, cultural, and philosophical engagement with myriad belief systems, traditions, and practices that are constantly evolving. These belief systems shape how we perceive and navigate life. Depending on the degree of adherence, religious practices often impact one's social and cultural identity in significant ways. Religion can influence everything from ceremonies at birth and death, food, holidays, personal etiquette and conduct, and dress and wedding celebrations, to prayer and charity.

Books such as *Mabrook! A World of Muslim Weddings* and *Growing Up Muslim* show various Muslim traditions around weddings and food. An effective and relatable way for young children to explore religion is by experiencing celebrations around different festivals. Eid and Ramadan are the two main Muslim holidays, and books such as *It's Ramadan, Curious George, Lailah's Lunchbox,* and *Moon Watchers* introduce students to the histories, traditions, and festivities of Islam. Pairing these books with art and craft activities serves to create hands-on learning in classrooms and libraries in order to explore Muslim culture and traditions. Through these engaging experiences, children can become more open to recognizing similarities and more tolerant and respectful of differences.

While some aspects of Islam are the same everywhere, religious expressions and practices vary widely within the religion from region to region: for example, Indonesian Muslims practice Islam differently from Arab Muslims, and the history of Islam and traditions within the African American community differ extensively from those of South Asian Muslims. In this chapter, we have consciously curated books that expose readers to the diversity within Islam and examine the idea of many different Islams. For example, Ausma Khan's book *Ramadan: The Holy Month of Fasting* shares the traditions of Muslims in Bosnia, China, Turkey, India, and Indonesia, to mention just a few places. This ability to contextualize Islam as a global religion shaped by many social factors also expands on the idea that different cultures influence religion and are in turn influenced by it.

Widespread religious illiteracy is known to fuel prejudice and bigotry, and these in turn can motivate violence towards people of another faith. History is rife with instances of anti-Semitism, religious persecution, and more recently, equating Islam with terrorism, which has led to increased hate crimes and discrimination against Muslims. Interfaith awareness is a useful tool for addressing these misconceptions and stereotypes, as well as fostering a collaborative culture in which people of different backgrounds, beliefs, and points of view are able to work together. Books such as *The Grand Mosque of Paris*, about Muslims who helped Jews escape during the Holocaust, and *Many Windows*, a story of five children from different faiths coming together to help their community, are excellent examples of interfaith books. An increased awareness of all our cross-cultural and interreligious differences helps promote a respect for diversity of beliefs, peaceful coexistence, and the hope for a better future.

We intentionally highlight "own voices" books so readers can learn about the authentic experiences of Muslim authors and how they engage with their religion. These books often counter Western perspectives of Islam as a restrictive religion, provide the social and cultural context for contemporary Islam, and offer nuanced perspectives on many Islamic religious practices. For example, books such as *The Hijab Boutique* and *Does My Head Look Big in This?* explain how the *hijab* (the headscarf) is often a personal choice, and is viewed as a symbol of maturity. Other books such as the *Bestest Ramadan Ever* and *Saints and Misfits* share the perspectives of Muslim teens and their struggles to balance their Muslim beliefs with their need to fit in socially.

We hope the books reviewed in this chapter will foster a spirit of inquiry among children about world religions, help affirm their own religious identity, and encourage them to seek common ground. In the long run, we believe that this exposure will counter prevalent negative stereotypes about Islam, and will help readers recognize that the beliefs of a few extremist Muslims are not a reflection of *all* Muslims.

Picture Books

Bismillah Soup. **Asmaa Hussein, ill. by Amina Khan. Ruqaya's Bookshelf, 2015. 978–0994750105. 40 pp. Fiction. K–Gr. 2.**

Inspired by the classic story "Stone Soup," this book situates the story in Somalia, where young Hasan has an idea to cook a delicious feast for his mother. She sends him to the mosque to ask the *imam* (a priest who leads the prayers at the mosque) for a bag of rice, and Hasan's idea turns into a more elaborate plan. Encouraged by the imam to put his trust in God, Hasan sets up some water to boil for his special pot of *bismillah* soup and invites everyone to the feast. The market vendors, baker, spice merchant, farmers, and the entire community generously donate their wares and are eager to share this communal meal. The cultural details add flavor to the story, and the reader will discover the spirit of kindness, sharing with the community, and the rewards of putting one's trust in God.

Ideas for Further Engagement

- Pair this book with any version of the "Stone Soup" story.
- Have each child bring in extra art and craft supplies from home. Place these in a "creativity box" and encourage the children to create something together, such as a tree of life.

Deep in the Sahara. **Kelly Cunnane, ill. by Hoda Hadidi. Schwartz and Wade, 2013. 978–0375870347. 40 pp. Fiction. Pre-K–Gr. 3.**

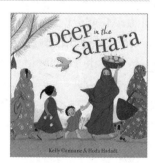

Select Awards: Kirkus Reviews Best Children's Books of 2013; ALA 2014 Notable Children's Books, Younger Readers; Booklist 2014 Top 10 Books for Youth, Religion and Spirituality; Winner, NCSS/CBC Notable Children's Trade Books in the Field of Social Studies, 2014.

With prose that flows like poetry and spellbinding illustrations, this story looks at a little girl's fascination with the *malafa*—a long, colorful cloth worn by the women of Mauritania. In this coming-of-age story, Laila asks every woman she interacts with to allow her to wear the *malafa*. Each of them gently guides her to make her own choice. This is a warm and positive story about Islam and personal choice.

Ideas for Further Engagement

- Pair this book with *Mommy's Khimar* by Jamilah Thompkins-Bigelow.
- Discuss religious head coverings that people of different faiths wear such as turbans, *hijabs*, and yarmulkes.

Crescent Moons and Pointed Minarets: A Muslim Book of Shapes. **Hena Khan, ill. by Mehrdokht Amini, Chronicle Books, 2018. 978–1452155418. 32 pp. Fiction. Preschool–K.**

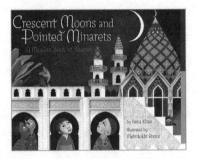

This beautiful and creative picture book has luminous illustrations and lyrical verses that celebrate the beauty of shapes seen in the crescent of the moon, hexagonal tiles, and the arches of the pulpit in mosques. The book celebrates the beauty of faith in everyday objects such as patterned doors and fountains. This is a fun way to learn about new shapes and ways to spot them everywhere around us.

Ideas for Further Engagement

- Pair this book with *Golden Domes and Silver Lanterns* by Hena Khan.
- Draw your favorite shape and create objects with it.

Hena Khan
Countering the Narrative

Where did you grow up, and what inspired you to become a writer?
I was born and raised in Maryland, in a Washington, DC suburb, to Pakistani immigrants. I loved reading and writing as a kid, and I wrote epic poems and silly plays and a family newspaper called "The Khanicles" for fun. As I got older, I continued to gravitate toward writing. I wrote for my high school newspaper, and went on to work in international health communications, where I focused on editing and sharing information with others. A lot of my work centered around making technical reports and data accessible to a variety of audiences, so I had to learn to write clearly and simply. My children's writing career started with Scholastic Book Clubs, where I got to publish books on a variety of exciting themes like space and spies and "how to be good at anything." The kid in me who wrote for fun never imagined in a million years that she'd be writing children's books one day.

What inspired you to write about Islam?
Being a mother, and reading multicultural books to my young son that celebrated other cultures and traditions in a beautiful way, made me want to see books like that about Islam and Muslims. But when we went back to the same public library I grew up in, I couldn't find books that reflected our heritage, culture, or faith. Most books about Islam were nonfiction, published overseas, and they made Islam seem "foreign." It was and remains important to me for my kids and other American Muslims to see themselves in the books they read, and for stories to reflect their experience. I also want all kids to be able to learn about our culture and traditions through fun, lighthearted, and appealing books, and to see that we have more in common than they might realize.

What is the one thing that you would like people to know about Muslims?
Muslims are regular Americans who care about the same things as anyone else—their families, their communities, their security, their country—and we have contributed an enormous amount to our nation. There's a common misperception that Muslims are new to America, when in fact we have been here since colonial times; and there's another misperception that Muslim values are incompatible with American values, which is honestly offensive.

If you had a magic wand, what is the one misconception about Muslims that you would banish forever?

It would sadly have to be that the quarter of the world's population that is Muslim, is part of a faith that promotes violence. No faith promotes violence or condones the heinous acts committed by extremists. They, like others, subscribe to a perverted and evil interpretation of Islam. And until I find that magic wand, we all have to do what we can to counter that narrative.

What is your favorite story from Islamic traditions?

Probably the story of Bilal ibn Rabah, whom the Prophet Muhammad freed from slavery and made a beloved companion. Bilal refused to renounce the Muslim faith, even when he was tortured, and he became the first Muslim to give the call to prayer. My husband and I named our firstborn Bilal in honor of his story of courage and unwavering faith.

What can parents, teachers, and librarians do to mitigate these issues, and raise children who respect and value diversity?

Stories are powerful tools for fostering acceptance and understanding, and highlighting diverse stories can expose children early on to people who are different from them. Inviting children into the lives of Muslim characters helps to demystify a community that is often misunderstood and misrepresented. This notion was a huge reason why I wrote *Amina's Voice*.

I wanted people to get to know a Muslim child and family and to offer a window into her family, home, and religious community; I did this through a story about a Muslim American girl who is dealing with relatable middle-school challenges. Any child, from any background, can identify with Amina and the feelings and changes she is forced to confront. I tried to weave in practices that are often part of Muslim life without overemphasizing them. Like all my books dealing with Muslim themes, I introduce the idea that we all have a lot more in common than it may seem, and that we share the core values of community, family, and charity. Parents and educators can do their part to help drive home this message as well.

What is your biggest inspiration from Islam?

The fact that Muslims are encouraged to seek knowledge and to learn, even through travel, and to think and reason, is an aspect of our tradition that inspires and motivates me. Muslim thinkers, scholars, and artists have made such incredible contributions to the world, and they continue to do so today.

And finally—biryani or kebabs?

Kebabs! I'm a big carnivore and love a good tikka or seekh kebab, and steaks and burgers too!

Biography

Like so many other writers, Hena Khan grew up with her nose in a book. She still thinks of the characters and stories she absorbed years ago. That's why she loves writing for kids—in the hope that something she writes will help shape them. Hena explores her Pakistani American and Muslim culture in her writing, along with outer space, spies, and other themes. Her award-winning multicultural books include the middle grade novel *Amina's Voice* and the chapter book series *Zayd Saleem, Chasing the Dream*, along with the picture books *Golden Domes and Silver Lanterns*, *Crescent Moons and Pointed Minarets*, *Night of the Moon*, and *It's Ramadan, Curious George*.

Going to Mecca. **Nai'ma Robert, ill. by Valentina Cavallini. Frances Lincoln Children's Books, 2014. 978–1847804907. 32 pp. Fiction. K–Gr. 4.**

With its collage paper figures and mixed-media illustrations, this book takes you on a pilgrimage to the holy city of Mecca to perform the hajj. The family performs the rites of the hajj, and the reader experiences the journey with them: "Stand with the pilgrims / As they face the Ka'bah, / Head bare, feet in sandals, / With thousands of others." As they circle the Kaaba (a small stone building that all Muslims face while praying), and join in the diverse crowd filled with young and old people from all over the world, strangers become friends and the readers might feel a little enlightened themselves.

IDEAS FOR FURTHER ENGAGEMENT

- ✋ Find Mecca on the map.
- ✋ Have students make a map of the holy cities of different world religions: Christianity, Judaism, Islam, Hinduism, Buddhism, Sikhism, and others.

It's Ramadan, Curious George. **H. A. Rey and Hena Khan. HMH Books for Young Readers, 2016. 978–0544652262. 14 pp. Fiction. Pre-K and up.**

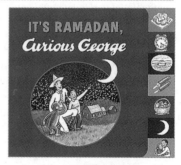

There is little doubt that Curious George is a household favorite for most kids, and in this delightful book Curious George celebrates Ramadan with his friend, Kareem. Author Hena Khan provides a contemporary and relatable story about the Muslim holidays of Ramadan and Eid. It explains the key concepts around Ramadan—fasting, charity, and finally feasting, in child-friendly rhymes. The illustrations offer many opportunities for learning and discussion; for example, they show both pizza and kebabs on the *iftar* table. This book appeals to readers who observe Ramadan, as well as others who would like to learn about Ramadan.

IDEAS FOR FURTHER ENGAGEMENT

- Display this book during Ramadan and use as a read-aloud for Ramadan/Eid-themed storytimes.
- 🖐 Organize a "date" night to celebrate food from all over the Muslim world.
- 🖐 Ask readers to list the traditional dishes and holiday feasts in different religions.

Lailah's Lunchbox. **Reem Faruqi, ill. by Lea Lyon. Tilbury House, 2015. 978–0884484318. 32 pp. Fiction. Gr. 1–7.**

Select Awards: NCSS/CBC Notable Social Studies Trade Book for Young People 2016, ALA Notable Book for Children 2016, Skipping Stones Honor 2016.

Lailah's hesitation about her Muslim faith and traditions are gently explained from a child's point of view. Though she is excited to begin fasting in Ramadan in her new American school, she is unsure of how to explain this practice to her classmates or deal with the temptations of lunchtime. Eventually, and with the help of her librarian and teacher, she gains confidence, acceptance, and admiration among her peers. A great classroom resource, this book was inspired by author Reem Faruqi's personal experiences when she moved to the United States as a young girl.

IDEAS FOR FURTHER ENGAGEMENT

- Discuss the different fasting traditions around Lent, Yom Kippur, and other faiths with the children.
- 🖐 Share awkward moments that new children may experience in school, and what we all can do to make things easier for them.

Reem Faruqi
Feeling Misunderstood

Can you share a little bit about where you grew up, and what inspired you to become a writer?
I grew up in Abu Dhabi, in the United Arab Emirates, and then in Peachtree City, Georgia. My mother is an avid reader and would take us to the library often. I remember loving the scent of books and being mesmerized by so many of them. I also used to write in a diary often, and I often dreamed of becoming an author. It is the most rewarding feeling to see my book in the library!

What inspired you to write about Islam?
I wrote about Ramadan in a school setting for *Lailah's Lunchbox* because I remember the feeling of being misunderstood as a child who was fasting in Ramadan at school in America. I wanted other children to feel comfortable and confident with their faith and with sharing who they are.

In this day and age, the media does not often paint Muslims well, so I wanted to show Muslims as regular people.

What is the one thing that you would like people to know about Muslims?
The word *Islam* means "peace."

If you had a magic wand, what is the one misconception about Muslims that you would banish forever?
The prevalent misconception that Muslim women do not have voices. They do!

What is your favorite story from Islamic traditions?
There is a story about Owais Qarni, who cared for his sick mother and took the utmost care of her. He never met Prophet Muhammad, yet Muhammad spoke highly of him. I was touched by the way Owais lived.

How do we—parents, teachers, and librarians—all of us as a community teach children to respect differences and value diversity?
I believe that if each and every one of us has access to positive stories that represent us, we will easily respect each other's differences and embrace diversity. We are all mirrors of one another.

What is your biggest inspiration from Islam?
The stories of the prophets are always inspiring for me. I especially love the story of Prophet Ayub. I admire how he had steadfast faith even when everything around him was falling apart. I also love

the tale of Zakariya and how he called upon his Lord to grant him a child and was answered.

And finally—biryani or kebabs?

Aloo kebabs! I had them almost every day while in college. Now I make them in batches for my family and I freeze them, so I always have them on hand. Biryani looks too intimidating to make.

Biography

When Reem Faruqi taught second grade, her favorite time was "read aloud" time. Now, her favorite time at home is "read aloud" time to her daughters. Of Pakistani origin, she moved to Peachtree City from Abu Dhabi when she was thirteen years old. Reem based her first children's book, *Lailah's Lunchbox*, on her own experiences as a young Muslim girl who has immigrated to the United States. She has two new books projected for 2019, *Amira's Picture Day* and *Let Me Show You the Way*. Reem Faruqi loves to doodle, write, and take photos. Check out her photoblog at www.reemfaruqi.com. Currently, she lives with her husband and three daughters in Atlanta.

Mabrook! A World of Muslim Weddings. **Na'ima B. Robert, ill. by Shirin Adl. Frances Lincoln Children's Books, 2016. 978–1847805881. 32 pp. Fiction. Pre-K–Gr. 3.**

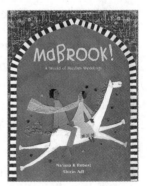

This is a lovely and lively look at wedding celebrations across Muslim cultures from Pakistan, through Morocco, and finally the United Kingdom. While some of the aspects of the wedding ceremony are common across cultures, the colorful celebrations, laughter, and feasting are unique to each country.

Ideas for Further Engagement

- Pair this book with *Sona and the Wedding Game* by Kashmira Sheth and lead a discussion on wedding traditions in different communities.
- Host a henna party with henna styles from around the Muslim world— North African, Indian, Turkish, Sudani, and more.
- Watch the documentary *Algerian Wedding* by Al Jazeera World.

Moon Watchers: Shirin's Ramadan Miracle.
Reza Jalali, ill. by Anne Sibley O'Brien.
Tilbury House, 2017. 978–0884485872.
32 pp. Fiction. K–Gr. 7.

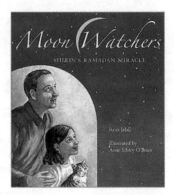

Select Awards: Skipping Stones Honor Award, 2017.

The celebration in Shirin's home in the month of Ramadan begins with a glimpse of the moon. But Shirin's excitement soon turns to disappointment, because her family thinks she is still too young to go without food and water for the whole day. Her father reminds her that Ramadan is about doing good deeds. Keeping her half-day fast, she stumbles on a secret that she decides to keep hidden. With cultural and traditional touches of a Shia-Muslim household, this charming story draws on realistic family tensions as well as the warmth and love that keeps them together.

Ideas for Further Engagement

- Pair this book with *Big Red Lollipop* by Rukhsana Khan to discuss sibling relationships.
- Ask children to find out more about their parents' childhood, and their favorite traditions.

Mommy's Khimar. **Jamilah Thompkins-Bigelow, ill. by Ebony Glenn. Simon and Schuster Books (Salaam Reads), 2018. 978–1534400597. 40 pp. Fiction. Pre–K and up.**

A charming story about an African American Muslim girl's love for her mother that extends to her fascination with her mother's headscarf or *khimar*. She dons her mother's cheerful yellow scarf that lights up her imagination and she pretends to be a shooting star, a superhero, and a queen with a golden train. And when her grandmother drops in from church to pay a visit, she is enveloped in a sunny, loving embrace. With lyrical prose and vibrant images rich with cultural details of a Muslim household, the book also introduces aspects of interfaith families.

IDEAS FOR FURTHER ENGAGEMENT

- A great read for Mothers' Day–themed storytimes/events.
- Draw a picture of what you love most about your mother.
- Find out the other names for headscarfs, such as *hijab*, *chaddor*, and so on.

Muhammad. Demi, ill. by the author. Margaret K. McElderry Books, 2003. 978–0689852640. 48 pp. Fiction. Gr. 2–5.

Select Awards: Winner Middle East Book Award 2004, NCTE/CLA Notable Children's Book in the English Language Arts 2004, CCBC Choices 2004.

This exquisitely illustrated, well-written and researched book makes a perfect introduction to the origins of Islam. The book begins with Muhammad's boyhood and traces his life till he is forty years old, when he receives the revelations of the Quran through the angel Gabriel. These compiled revelations make up the sacred text of the Quran. This book narrates the story of Muhammad's life in a thoughtful and respectful voice. Award-winning author and artist Demi overcomes the challenge of not being able to depict Muhammad pictorially through the creative use of gold leaf.

Ideas for Further Engagement

- Look up the prophets common to Christianity, Judaism, and Islam.
- Create a work of art using gold paint.

***Nabeel's New Pants: An Eid Tale.* Fawzia Gilani-Williams, ill. by Prioti Roy. Two Lions, 2010. 978–0761456292. 24 pp. Fiction. Preschool—Gr. 1.**

It's the night before Eid, and all through Nabeel's house, there is excitement and everyone is busy preparing for the celebrations. After a busy day at his shoe shop, Nabeel goes shopping and buys presents for his wife, mother, daughter, and himself. His pants, however, turn out to be "four fingers too long," and everyone is too busy to help him hem them. He shortens them himself while each of the women then secretly trims his pants, much to Nabeel's surprise the next day. This is a laugh-out-loud book that will give the readers a taste of Eid.

Ideas for Further Engagement

- Discuss traditions that your family has the night before a festival you celebrate.
- 🖐 Break the children into groups and ask them to enact the story of Nabeel as a play.

***Owl & Cat: Muslims Are. . .* Emma Apple. Books by Emma Apple, 2017. 978–0997580464. 58 pp. Fiction. K–Gr. 6.**

With its lovely yet minimalistic illustrations and text, this book showcases Muslims in a simple age-appropriate manner. The bright visuals of an owl and a cat (inspired by the poem "The Owl and the Pussycat") walk us through the diversity of Muslims with humor and show how, just like everyone else, Muslims are defined through their multiple identities.

Ideas for Further Engagement

- Discuss how people from all faiths are similar to one another.
- 🖐 Hand out coloring pages of the owl and the pussycat for children to color or draw.
- 🖐 Look up the poem "The Owl and the Pussycat."

Emma Apple
Understanding the Unseen

Can you share a little bit about where you grew up, and what inspired you to become a writer?
I grew up in small towns in northern New Zealand, playing in forests and on beaches, a place that would stoke any child's imagination. I come from a family of writers and teachers, and have myself always been an artist. Those two things naturally came together, and I was inspired to write and publish stories for children when I had my own children to teach the complexities of life to.

What inspired you to write about Islam?
Any parent knows the challenges of teaching children about God. There are concepts that can be hard to ground in reality for little kids who are just figuring out the world around them. So the solution that I found worked best with my children when they were asking big questions was to come up with stories using the magnitude of nature and scientific knowledge, to help them feel the concepts that are beyond human comprehension and give them real-world foundations for understanding the unseen.

What is the one thing that you would like people to know about Muslims?
I think the most important thing for everyone to remember is that Muslims are regular people, like everyone else. Muslims are neighbors, friends, coworkers, classmates, family. Whatever our faith, our humanity comes first, we're all together on this big blue ball called Earth, and most of us are trying to make it a better place.

If you had a magic wand, what is the one misconception about Muslims that you would banish forever?
The biggest misconception about Muslims is that they are somehow personally responsible for the actions of others in the name of their religion. The fear that this creates for children for whom "Muslim" is a part of their identity, and the comments they hear from others about themselves and their families, can be devastating.

What is your favorite story from Islamic traditions?
The story of Noah is always a fun one to tell with children; all the animals make it animated and interactive. The story of Yunus and the whale is another one that lends itself to imaginative and adventurous retellings.

How do we—parents, teachers, and librarians—all of us as a community teach children to respect differences and value diversity?

Books are, of course, an invaluable way to introduce kids (and adults) to a variety of human experiences. Exposure is the best way to teach kids that even with our perceived differences, we're all in this together, we're not really so different in the end.

What is your biggest inspiration from Islam?

As an artist, I'm inspired by the rich artistic history, and as a writer, by the linguistic history.

And finally—biryani or kebabs?

That's a loaded question! I think I have to say kebabs.

Biography

Emma Apple is an independent children's author-illustrator from New Zealand. She writes unique multicultural books, introducing children to complex concepts and new ideas that help them understand the people and world around them. Her debut book as an independent author-illustrator, *How Big Is Allah?* (2014), quickly reached no. 1 in the Amazon Islamic Children's category, where all of her books have since been featured. As of 2017, Emma has written, illustrated, and published ten children's books under her indie publishing imprint Books by Emma Apple. She is also the founder of the pioneering Muslim women's blog *Muslimas' Oasis,* and the creative professional network Creative Muslim Women (founded 2015).

***Ramadan (Celebrate the World).* Hannah Eliot, ill. by Rashin. Little Simon, 2018. 978–1534406353. 24 pp. Fiction. Pre–K and up.**

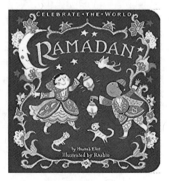

This board book is the first in a series of books that highlights celebrations around the world. With bold colors and whimsical pictures, this book introduces young readers to the basic concepts of Ramadan, which include *suhoor* (the pre-dawn meal), *iftar* (breaking of the fast), and, finally, Eid al-Fitr, the celebration. With diverse images of people from all over the world, the book celebrates the special month of Ramadan as a time of fasting, reflection, good deeds, and being thankful. All children look forward to the end of Ramadan with the anticipation of gifts, sweets, and spending time with their families on Eid.

Ideas for Further Engagement

- Look up sunset timings (that is when the fasting ends) for different countries around the world. Where do people fast for the longest and shortest times?

✋ Have the students use pipe cleaners to create crescent moons and stars and string them all together as decoration.

✋ Ask the children to create a list of ways to help friends and neighbors.

The Apple Tree: The Prophet Says Series. Mariam Al-Kalby, ill. by Yee Von Chan. Prolance, 2013. 978–0988507067. 32 pp. Fiction. K–Gr. 3.

Saima is excited to plant an apple tree with her father, and she dreams of all the fruit she will eat. While at first she is reluctant to share the apples from the tree, she observes the interdependence of different elements of nature. In the course of sharing the apples with birds, animals, and others around her, she learns how to open her heart and give to others. This lesson on giving for the sake of charity is a hands-on way to teach young children about the important values in life.

Ideas for Further Engagement

- Discuss ways in which you can give in your community.
- Pair this book with *The Giving Tree* by Shel Silverstein, or with *Last Stop on Market Street* by Matt de la Pena, to explore different ways of giving.
- Create a giving chart where you can include ideas such as giving in kind and giving of your time.
- ✋ Organize a classroom giving drive for books, coats, or any other item.

The Best Eid Ever. Asma Mobin-Uddin, ill. by Laura Jacobsen. Boyds Mills, 2007. 978–1590784310. 32 pp. Fiction. K and up.

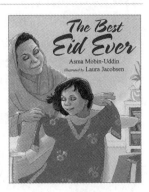

Select Awards: Honorable Mention, Middle East Book Award 2008.

Though Eid-ul-Adha is a day for celebration, Aneesa misses her parents, who have gone on the hajj pilgrimage. Her grandmother tries to cheer her up by cooking her favorite meal and giving her beautiful dresses. At the mosque for prayers, Aneesa befriends two sisters who she learns are refugees and have little to celebrate the holiday with. Aneesa decides to surprise them and with her grandmother's help, they celebrate the true spirit of the holiday.

Ideas for Further Engagement
- Discuss ways in which you can share celebrations of your festival with your friends.
- Talk about special traditions that children may have with their grandparents.
- ✋ Look up the different pilgrimages of different faiths.

***The Grand Mosque of Paris: How Muslims Helped Jews during the Holocaust.* Karen Gray Ruelle, ill. by Deborah Durland DeSaix. Holiday House, 2010. 978–0823423040. 40 pp. Nonfiction. Gr. 3–6.**

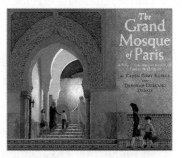

This book about a little-known piece of history recounts how the Muslims of the Grand Mosque of Paris saved the lives of many Jews in Nazi-occupied France. With beautiful and sombre oil paintings, the illustrations hint at both a time of desperation and also one of hope. A timely reminder of the ties of humanity and brotherhood between communities, this book echoes a quote familiar to both Jews and Muslims, "Save one life and it is as if you have saved all of humanity." This advanced picture book is best suited for older readers.

Ideas for Further Engagement
- Discuss something that helps you feel safe.
- ✋ Look up the history of Jews and Muslims in France.
- ✋ Watch *Enemy of the Reich: The Noor Inayat Khan Story* by Robert Gardner, narrated by Helen Mirren.

Quotes for Interpretation
- "The land for the mosque was given by the French government, in exchange for a symbolic payment of one franc, to thank the half-million

Muslim soldiers who had fought for France during the First World War." (8)

- "At the Muslim hospital where Dr. Somia worked, doctors secretly treated injured Allied pilots and parachutists at night, and hid them during the day." (20)
- "Because of Si Benghabrit's actions, the Jewish singer Salim Halili lived a long, successful life and is still revered as the father of modern North African song." (32)

The Little Girl Says Alhamdulillah. **Rabia Gelgi. CreateSpace Independent Publishing Platform, 2016. 978–1535054676. 26 pp. Fiction. Pre-K–Gr. 3.**

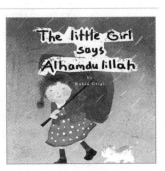

This is a whimsical book that looks at the many ways to thank God (Alhamdulillah in Arabic) for bright blue skies, pouring rain, and a furry friend to share it all with. It is a reminder for us all to celebrate the beauty of nature and the joys of gratitude and friendship.

Ideas for Further Engagement

- Pair this book with *A Bucket of Blessings* by Kabir Sehgal and Suristha Sehgal, or with *Tiny Blessings for Giving Thanks* by Amy Parker.
- List five things people are thankful for.
- Find the words for "Thank you" in different languages.

The Most Magnificent Mosque. **Ann Jungman, ill. by Shelley Fowles. Frances Lincoln Children's Books, 2007. 978–1845070854. 32 pp. Fiction. K–Gr. 3.**

In this book set in Spain during the eighth century, three boys run wild in the gardens of Cordoba's Great Mosque throwing oranges at people. The Caliph catches them and puts them to work on the mosque's grounds for three months, where the boys develop an appreciation of the mosque's beauty. Years later, when the Christian King threatens to tear down the mosque, the three friends—a Muslim, a Jew, and a Christian—band together to convince him otherwise. This is a touching story about people from different religions and traditions working together for the benefit of all.

Ideas for Further Engagement

- Pair this book with *Never Say a Mean Word Again* by Jacqueline Jules.
- ✋ Look up the history of Cordoba, and the different communities that lived there over time.
- ✋ Watch the short film *A House of Many Faiths: Cordoba's Cathedral within a Mosque.*

Snow in Jerusalem. Deborah Da Costa and Ying-Hwa Hu, ill. by Cornelius Van Wright. Albert Whitman, 2008. 978–0807575253. 32 pp. Fiction. Preschool–Gr. 3.

Select Awards: Children's Literature Choice List 2002.

This is a heartwarming story about two boys, one Muslim and one Jew, who discover each other through a white stray cat. Each boy had been feeding the cat and considered it his pet. When the cat is lost and later found by both boys, they argue about whom she belongs to. The cat runs away, and the boys discover a special surprise as they chase her around Jerusalem on a snowy day. The authors deftly weave in different neighborhoods of the historic city where Muslims, Jews, Christians, Armenian Catholics, and others have lived together, and they also provide a brief note on Jerusalem's history. The beautiful watercolor illustrations add to the warmth of this uplifting story.

Ideas for Further Engagement

- Discuss the similarities between the two boys, and how they problem-solve when they both want to find the cat.
- Discuss the importance of pets for children.
- ✋ Lead a discussion with children to reimagine the story from the cat's perspective.

👋 Ask readers to look up the different neighborhoods in Jerusalem.

Yaffa and Fatima: Shalom, Salaam. **Fawzia Gilani-Williams, ill. by Chiara Fedele. Kar Ben, 2017. 978−1467794237. 24 pp. Fiction. K−Gr. 3.**

Yaffa and Fatima are two friends who live side by side in the "land of milk and honey." They work on their date groves, sell their wares next to each other at the market, and share tea, conversation, and a close-knit friendship. The illustrations show them following their different religious traditions—Yaffa is Jewish and Fatima is Muslim, but this difference never mars their closeness. When hit by a drought, both girls resolve to help each other. This retelling of a folktale with both Jewish and Arab origins is a lovely way to talk about the similarities between us and the act of caring for our neighbors.

Ideas for Further Engagement

- Ask readers to do an act of kindness for their neighbors, and share these with the classroom.
- 👋 Research Activity: Look up the origin of words that sound the same, such as *shalom* and *salaam.*

Yo Soy Muslim: A Father's Letter to His Daughter. **Mark Gonzales, ill. by Mehrdokht Amini. Simon and Schuster, 2017. 978−1481489362. 32 pp. Fiction. Preschool−Gr. 2.**

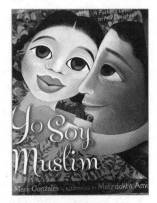

This is a lyrical book that celebrates multiple identities—ethnic, linguistic, racial, indigenous, and religious. Writing in verse as a letter to his daughter, poet Mark Gonzales's deep and profound words weave in the history of the past and the present, draw on the diversity and spirituality of Islam, and question the idea of belonging. The gorgeous illustrations complement the inspiring words to paint a warm and hopeful future for us all.

Ideas for Further Engagement

- Ask children to share something they do together as a family.
- 🖐 Trace your family tree and explore where your ancestors came from.
- 🖐 Write a short poem addressed to your parents.

Chapter Books and Middle Grade Books

The Hijab Boutique. **Michelle Khan. Islamic Foundation, 2011. 978–0860374688. 56 pp. Fiction. K–Gr. 3.**

When Farah, a young Muslim growing up in Los Angeles, has to present an object that defines her mother for International Women's Day, she wonders how her modest mother would compare to her friends' glamorous and accomplished moms. As Farah learns more about her mother, it helps her discover her own cultural and religious identity. This is an eloquent book that illuminates individual choice around wearing the *hijab,* or headscarf. Written from the perspective of a young girl, the story shares her transformation and realization that what is different about us also makes us unique. This book is ideal for the novice reader, given its short length and simple language.

Discussion Starters

- Have you ever received a school assignment that you found challenging?
- Have you made any decision because of your religion, or because you felt compelled to do so?
- What would you have done differently if you were Farah?
- What does eating halal mean? Are there other religions that prescribe eating food in adherence to religious laws?

Ideas for Further Engagement

- 🖐 Research different forms of religious head coverings and their origins. Organize a show-and-tell event around it.

✋ Organize a fair where each child has a tabletop display that shares something about their culture or religion.

Quotes for Interpretation
- "'Um, Ms. Grant,' I blurt out nervously, 'I don't actually have anything to present. My, er, dog ate my homework.'" (14)
- "Non-Muslims interpret the hijab in different ways. Some think that it has to do with politics; others believe that it is a sign of women being oppressed." (27)
- "Women who wear hijabs express themselves through fabric choices, patterns, and different lengths and styles of hijabs." (45)

Many Windows: Six Kids, Five Faiths, One Community. **Rukhsana Khan, Uma Krishnaswami, and Elisa Carbone. Napoleon and Co., 2008. 978–1894917568. 88 pp. Fiction. Gr. 2–7.**

This is a collection of interconnected short stories about six classmates of different faiths whose shared love of basketball brings them together. Sensitively told from the perspective of each child, this book gently touches on how religion impacts our daily lives in relatively minor ways, and it explores how friendship and religious tolerance create community. At the end of the book, the authors provide a useful explanation of different religious faiths and their key principles: Buddhism, Islam, Hinduism, Judaism, and Christianity.

Discussion Starters
- How does religion impact your day-to-day life?
- Name some of the key religious celebrations you celebrate with your family. How do you celebrate them?
- How did this story make you feel?

Ideas for Further Engagement
✋ Celebrate UN Interfaith Week (February 1–7) and ask children to share elements and symbols of their faith.

✋ Chart the dates for all of the festivals mentioned in the book in the upcoming year.

Quotes for Interpretation

- "To pay the Fitr, he only has to give about five dollars, enough to feed a poor person for a day, but instead he gives a lot more. Would a thief do that?" (31)
- "Diwali is a good time to make up if you've had disagreements." (37)
- "Mommy and Daddy say Christmas is about remembering how Jesus said 'Love your neighbor as yourself,' and about helping people who don't have as much as we do." (51)

Growing Up Muslim: Understanding Muslim Beliefs and Practices. **Sumbul Ali-Karamali. Ember, 2013. 978–0385740968. 224 pp. Fiction. Gr. 4 and up.**

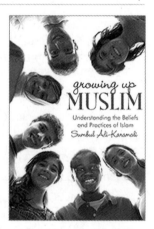

This is a clear and eloquent book that draws on the author's personal experiences growing up in America in order to dispel a number of misconceptions about Islam. The engaging writing, backed by research and peppered with relatable situations, allows readers to learn about various principles of Islam and how they play out in real life. The author also elaborates on the origins of Islam, how it spread, and she surveys modern Muslim demographics. A detailed bibliography provides plenty of additional sources for further reading.

Discussion Starters

- Why do you think the author had to talk about being Muslim at a birthday party or a play date?
- Were there times when you have found it a challenge to express a religious or cultural choice?
- What rules do you follow in your life and why?
- Which example from the book about growing up do you relate to the most? Why?

Ideas for Further Engagement

- ✋ Look up fasting/abstinence traditions in different religions such as Hinduism, Christianity, and Judaism.
- ✋ Organize a potluck party with traditional dishes that are eaten on different religious festivals.

Quotes for Interpretation

- "Ramadan is a month of hunger and thirst and fatigue for Muslims, but it's also a festive time. It means many things to us: discipline, compassion, piety, festivity, connecting with other Muslims, connecting with people of other religions, connecting with God, extra appreciation of food and drink, extra consciousness of good deeds and charity, and a sense of achievement." (61)
- "A person need not belong to any religion to be charitable, but sometimes religion makes people more charitable than they otherwise would be." (82)
- "I'm certainly not saying all Muslims are able to follow all these rules all the time. Every religion has rules like these, which people aspire to follow. But being human sometimes gets in the way." (99)

My Friend Is Muslim (Faith in Friendship). **Khadija Ejaz. Purple Toad, 2015. 978–1624690969. 47 pp. Nonfiction. Gr. 3–7.**

Layla, a mixed-race Muslim girl, is preparing a class presentation on Islam with the help of her friend Nancy. The girls' personable voices explain the different aspects of Islam—from its history to its traditions, beliefs, celebrations, prayers, and the diversity of Muslims around the world. Informative and relatable, this is an easy introduction to Islam and Muslims for those who are unfamiliar with it.

Discussion Starters

- What is religion? How does it impact your daily life?
- What are some of the major world religions?

- What are the similarities between Islam, Christianity, and Judaism?
- What fact struck you as most interesting as you read the book?

Ideas for Further Engagement

✋ Watch the documentary *I Named Her Angel* by Nefin Dinc.

✋ Write a story based on a religious moral.

Quotes for Interpretation

- "Your family is so different. Your mother is a white woman from Russia, your father is a black man from America, but they are both Muslim." (10)
- "Some people think Muslims and Arabs are the same or that all Muslims are Arabs." (11)
- "Muslims don't make images of Allah. We believe that He is beyond human understanding." (25)

The Garden of My Imaan. **Farhana Zia. Peachtree, 2016. 978–1561459216. 192 pp. Fiction. Gr. 3–7.**

Select Awards: Parents' Choice Recommended Award, Parents' Choice Foundation, 2013; Best Children's Books of the Year, Bank Street College of Education, 2014; Social Justice Literature Award, Literacy and Social Justice Special Interest Group, International Reading Association, 2014; South Asia Book Award Honor Book, 2014; Society of School Librarians International Book Awards, Honor Book, Language Arts Grades K–6 Novels; Society of School Librarians International, 2013.

Aliya and Marwa are two Muslim girls in one school; one is from Morocco, and the other's family is from India. One wears the *hijab*, the other does not. One speaks Arabic at home, while the other speaks English and Urdu. Through this story, Zia deftly explores how faith plays a role in children's lives. She also touches on issues of bullying that the two girls face, and how the school authorities respond to them. The book has a helpful glossary at the back with words in Arabic and Urdu.

Discussion Starters

- Have you experienced or observed any bullying at your school? Were you able to do anything to help?
- Why do you think Marwa made Aliya uncomfortable?
- What are one or two ways in which Marwa influenced Aliya?
- Who do you identify with more—Marwa or Aliya?
- Pair this book with *Poppies of Iraq* by Brigitte Findakly and Lewis Trondheim for the perspective of a Christian girl growing up in Iraq.

Ideas for Further Engagement

- ✋ Research the origins of your family and the countries that your grandparents and great-grandparents came from.
- ✋ Create awareness about bullying through anti-bullying activities from www.bullyproofclassroom.com or similar websites.

Quotes for Interpretation

- "'Kids talk about her food though, and they make fun of her hijab. Actually, I don't blame them. It's pretty embarrassing.' 'Embarrassing for whom?' Mom asked. 'Her or you?'" (61)
- "Just because you don't see a lot of people wearing something doesn't make it weird. Anyway, my hijab is not hurting you." (94)
- "Everyone was thankful for a successful month of fasting. We had been good Muslims and upstanding citizens; we had curbed anger and temptation, read from the holy Quran, and given help to the poor by sending money to India. Now we were ready to celebrate!" (165)

My Own Special Way. **Mithaa Alkhayyat, ill. by Maya Fidawi. Orion Children's, 2012. 978–1444003208. 64 pp. Fiction. Pre-K–Gr. 2.**

Select Awards: Shortlisted for 2013 Marsh Award for Children's Literature in Translation.

This is a sweet and humorous story about Hamda, the youngest of five sisters who yearns to be "big enough" to play with her older sisters. She looks at childhood pictures of her sisters and concludes that

she too could be a big girl, if only she wore a veil. She quickly finds out that wearing a veil requires skills. Each of her sisters shares their way of tying the veil, but eventually Hamda finds her own special way. Through cute and appealing illustrations, the book shares the different ways a veil is worn, and it prods girls to look within, and trust themselves to make good choices and persist despite failures.

Discussion Starters

- Do you struggle to keep up with your siblings? How?
- Is there any defining ritual or tradition in your culture that you need to go through to be considered "big"?

Ideas for Further Engagement

- Draw a picture of Hamda in your favorite dress or doing an activity you enjoy.
- Write a short story about "what makes you you."

Quotes for Interpretation

- "I know what makes you big girls. You wear the veil when you go out, and I'm going to wear it too." (22)
- "You're a big girl now, and you found out how to do it all by yourself!" (24)
- "Don't worry. Hind and Fatima and Jamila and Alya all found their special way to wear the veil and you will too." (49)

Ramadan: The Holy Month of Fasting.
Ausma Zehnat Khan. Orca Book, 2018.
978–1459811812. 88 pp. Nonfiction. Gr. 3–7.

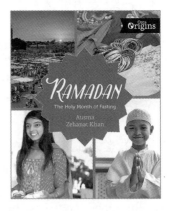

Part of the Origins series by Orca Book Publishers, this book provides a simple and child-friendly introduction to Ramadan and shares relatable stories of different experiences of Muslim children as they fast for Ramadan. The author recounts her first Ramadan fast and what she learned along the way. The book also provides a brief introduction to Islam, the Five Pillars, the stages and spirit of Ramadan, and it shares Ramadan traditions all around the world from Bosnia to Pakistan, and from Palestine to Turkey. Stunning pictures, fun quotes and facts, and easy recipes are woven in throughout the book to make it a unique and comprehensive resource. In the words of the editor, "this book will lead readers towards a place where differences are acknowledged and knowledge facilitates understanding."

Discussion Starters

- Have you ever fasted or given up something you like to eat? How did you feel about the experience?
- What are some of the benefits and drawbacks of fasting?

Ideas for Further Engagement

- 🖐 Watch *Nadia's Ramadan* to learn more about how she fasts and celebrates with her family.
- 🖐 Plan a Ramadan storytime or *iftar* event in your community.
- 🖐 Organize a classroom or community food drive, or volunteer at a soup kitchen.

Quotes for Interpretation

- "Fasting teaches Muslims empathy, and feeling the pangs of hunger and thirst all day, as I did when I was a 9-year-old, teaches us to empathize with others who suffer from hunger and thirst." (16)
- "Eid-al-Fitr and Christmas represent completely different occasions, but they inspire the same feelings of joy and celebration in the communities that observe them." (36)
- "Though Muslims share a common faith, their cultural and religious practices are quite diverse, so there really is no such thing as a single 'Muslim world' or 'Islamic world.'" (59)

Young Adult Books

***Bestest Ramadan Ever.* Medeia Sharif. North Star Editions, 2011. 978–0738723235. 312 pp. Fiction. Gr. 7–12.**

Almira is a typical American teenager who is trying to balance homework, high school friendships, crushes, and fitting in—all while keeping her traditional and observant family at bay. However, things take a turn for the unexpected when she decides to try fasting for Ramadan after failing the year before. As the month of fasting begins, she finds herself at the crossroads of cultural expectations, but with the culmination of each day, she finds opportunities to explore her own faith and take a journey of self-discovery. Told in a funny, down-to-earth voice with a breezy style, this book reflects the realities of many Muslim teens growing up in America.

Discussion Starters

- What religious practices do you observe? Why?
- Have your religious practices ever played a role in your dating choices? How and why?
- Would you have behaved differently with Peter if you were Almira? How?
- Do you think religious practices are different from generation to generation? How?

Ideas for Further Engagement

- ✋ Host an *iftar* event.
- ✋ List some of the values that Ramadan encourages.

Quotes for Interpretation

- "'Your parents allow you to wear nail polish?' As if Muslim girls can't wear something harmless like nail polish." (24)
- "Sometimes I feel weird thinking about boys, because it seems wrong for a Muslim girl to be lusting after them. But isn't that what typical teenage girls do? Am I allowed to be typical?" (30)
- "I look at her short dress and become skeptical on her possible Muslim-

ness. Muslim girls aren't supposed to dress like that (even though many Muslims wouldn't like the way I dress)." (33)

Butterfly Mosque. G. Willow Wilson. 2010. 978–0802118875. 304 pp. Memoir. Adult.

Select Awards: Seattle Times Best Book of the Year 2010.

This is a personal account of author Willow Wilson's relationship with religion, the circumstances that led her to convert to Islam, how she shared the news of her conversion with her friends and family and their reactions, her relationship with her husband, Omar, and her adventures in Egypt and Iran. Wilson recounts many significant decisions and turning points in her life after her conversion to Islam, and the dilemmas she faced: whether she should change her name, how the marriage ceremony should be conducted, whether to wear the *hijab* or not, and her initial hesitations in identifying as a "Muslim" on official paperwork. Her story counters many stereotypes about Islam, shares information about the freedoms granted to women under Islam, and directly addresses the predominant view of Muslims as the "other" in the West. There are multiple opportunities for discussion throughout the book on how religion pervades our daily life and yet offers ample choices as to models of behavior.

Discussion Starters

- Do you think it's "uncool" to be religious?
- Do you see any benefits or harm in being religious?
- Are there people who belong to your religion who you view as "extremists" or people you would not identify with?
- What struck you as most interesting about Willow's life choices?

Ideas for Further Engagement

- Watch the documentary *Inside Islam: What a Billion Muslims Really Think* by Robert Gardner.
- List five ways in which your religion has impacted your culture, or your culture has impacted your religion.

✋ Research the term *fatwa* and its origins.

Quotes for Interpretation
- "When the term 'clash of civilizations' was coined, it was a myth; the interdependence of world cultures lay on the surface, supported by trade and the travel of ideas, the borrowing of words from language to language." (5)
- "There were parts of Shari'a law that were premodern and problematic, but not more so than the Old Testament. Islam had all the hang-ups, along with all the potential for resolution, of any ancient faith." (81)
- "In the West, anything that must be hidden is suspect; availability and honesty are interlinked. This clashes irreconcilably with Islam as it is practiced in the Middle East, where the things that are most precious, most perfect, and most holy are always hidden: the Kaaba, the faces of prophets and angels, a woman's body, Heaven." (137)

Does My Head Look Big in This? **Randa Abdel-Fattah. Scholastic, 2008. 978–0439922333. 368 pp. Fiction. Young adult.**

Select Awards: Winner of the Australian Industry Book Award for Best Australian Book for Young Adult Readers 2006; Long-listed for the Galaxy British Book Awards 2007; Short-listed as a notable young adult book by the Children's Book Council; Short-listed for the Grampian Children's Book Awards UK 2006; Top 100 New York Public Library Books for Teenagers; One of *Kirkus*'s Best Books for Young Adults, USA.

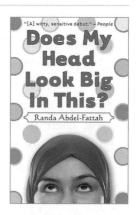

"[A] witty, sensitive debut." — *People*

Does My Head Look Big In This?

Randa Abdel-Fattah

When Amal makes the very personal decision to wear the headscarf or *hijab* at age sixteen, everyone else has an opinion about it. Her parents try to dissuade her, her classmates gives her the silent treatment, and the bullies at school taunt her, but her friends—both Muslim and non-Muslim—stand by her. Amal experiences discrimination and stereotypes because of her outward appearance, but she also has to deal with teenage issues of friendships, crushes, and the conflict of traditions and modernity. The author highlights the diversity within the Muslim community. Through this hilarious story about struggles with cultural and religious identity, Amal and the readers share a journey towards empowerment.

Discussion Starters

- Why do you think Amal decides to wear the *hijab?* Why do her parents try to dissuade her?
- Why does Amal feel scared after she wears her *hijab?*
- Who is she most nervous to appear before with her *hijab?* Do her classmates treat her differently now?
- Are there other religious changes that Amal introduces in her life after wearing the *hijab?*
- How does Amal relate Islam to other religions?
- What are some of the different immigrant experiences the book highlights?
- Has the story changed your view of girls who wear the *hijab* in your school?
- Would you alter your appearance in order to express your faith or culture? In what way?
- Do you think Muslims are better off concealing their identity in today's climate in order to get ahead in society? Why or why not?

Ideas for Further Engagement

- Organize a classroom debate on the value of religion in one's life.

Quotes for Interpretation

- "So when you're a non-pork eating, Eid-celebrating Mossie [a taunting name for Muslim, not mosquito] with an unpronounceable last name and a mother who picks you up from school wearing a hijab and Gucci shades, and drives a car with an 'Islam means peace' bumper sticker, a quiet existence is impossible." (10)
- "The first Muslim she's ever met. It makes me sound like an alien." (146)
- "I wince every time Ms. Walsh says the word 'massacre' with the word 'Islamic,' as though these barbarians somehow belong to my Muslim community. As though they're the black sheep in the flock, the thorn in our community's side. It gives them this legitimacy, this identity that they don't deserve. These people are aliens to our faith." (250)

Enemy Territory. **Sharon E. McKay and Michael Kusugak, ill. by Vladyana Krykora. Annick, 2012. 978–1554514304. 200 pp. Fiction. Young adult.**

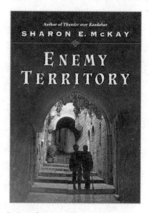

The only thing in common between teenagers Sam and Yusuf, who are roommates at a hospital in Jerusalem, is shared hostility. Sam has an injured leg from being run over by an army truck, and Yusuf lost his left eye in an encounter with the police. With the usual teenage bravado, the two boys decide to slip away into the night to find the famous candy store in the Old City. Their adventure quickly turns into a dangerous situation, and Sam and Yusuf must rely on one another to get themselves to safety. This book is an intense read that lays bare the Israeli-Palestinian conflict and the personal prejudices, myths, and stereotypes that both sides have of each other. The authors present the complexity of the conflict with a balanced perspective and a fast-paced narrative. Eventually the boys develop a friendship and understanding of one another through their banter and shared journey, which helps all of us see how personal friendships can often surpass the politics of hate.

Discussion Starters

- Is there someone you really dislike? Think of something you may have in common with that person.
- How is language intricately connected with culture and religion?

Ideas for Further Engagement

- Watch *Out of Cordoba* by Jacob Bender.
- Look up the history of the Arab-Israel conflict and peace talks.

Quotes for Interpretation

- "Do you ever wonder why so many Jews and Muslims hate each other? I mean, don't we have the same God? Different names of course. And Abraham was our common ancestor. Christians too, right?" (48-49)
- "You think that we are all terrorists. I go to school, same as you. I play soccer, same as you. I have friends, same as you. I want to go to university, same as you." (140)

- "There was more than history here, more than three religions. In this place, past and present were one. And maybe the future was here too." (176)

Muslim Girl: A Coming of Age. Amani Al-Khatahtbeh. Simon and Schuster, 2017. 978–1501159510. 137 pp. Fiction. Young adult.

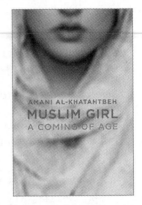

In a poignant, contemporary, straight-from-the-heart monologue, Al-Khatahtbeh shares her experiences of a Muslim childhood, and reflects on what it really means to be a Muslim in America today. This book will resonate strongly at many levels with Muslim teens who grew up in America as they explore their relationship with Islam, their cultural identity, their family life, their friendships, and even their own sense of purpose in life. It provides a visceral insight for anyone interested in understanding the Muslim experience of living in America.

Discussion Starters
- Was your experience growing up in America similar to or different from that of Amani's?
- What are the factors that impact your childhood experiences and access to opportunities?

Ideas for Further Engagement
- ✋ Ask students to interview five people about how 9/11 impacted their lives.
- ✋ Start a class blog where people contribute stories about their experiences growing up in America.

Quotes for Interpretation
- "I hope she doesn't doubt that a Muslim American can be this impacted by 9/11, too. The truth is that 9/11 never ended for us." (9)
- "And then the first time my heritage was held against me as an insult marked the end of the days that I innocently took pride in my culture as a source of joy and the subject of class celebrations during Culture Day, naive to the implications of race and history." (10)

- "One Muslim woman's story is taken to represent Muslim women like a monolith, like an absolute truth that exists for all of us. The intricacies of the different identities that exist among Muslim women far beyond their faith are melted away." (95)

Saints and Misfits. S. K. Ali. Salaam Reads/Simon and Schuster Books for Young Readers, 2017. 978–1481499248. 336 pp. Fiction. Young adult.

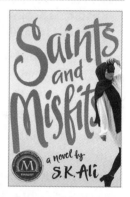

Select Awards: Entertainment Weekly Best Young Adult Book of 2017.

Janna is already battling family dynamics at home and exploring how her Muslim identity affects her at school, when she is assaulted by Farooq, the beloved poster boy at her local mosque. Janna clams up in the presence of Farooq, and her inability to unburden her shame underscores her interactions and her questions around faith. Using inventive ways such as letters to the imam and an Islamic quiz, Ali provides a context for the religious aspects of Islam. The story also shows us the many ways in which Muslims girls get picked on for their choices, as well as how empowered they feel wearing the *hijab* and even the *niqab,* or face veil. The book's colorful and well-rounded characters show the diversity of cultures and the spectrum of religious adherence within the Muslim community.

Discussion Starters

- What are the kinds of questions that Janna and others like her who wear the *hijab* face?
- Does Janna's struggles with identity and peer pressure at high school differ from what all students experience?
- How does the book address stereotypical representations of Muslims and Islam?
- How does Janna stand up to Farooq? What do you think empowered her to do this? Were there other ways she could have handled her situation?
- Is there any artifact or item of clothing that you hold dear because of its religious significance?

Ideas for Further Engagement

✋ Watch the documentary *Wearing Hijab: Uncovering the Myths of Islam in the United States.*

Quotes for Interpretation

- "He's a senior; I'm a sophomore. He's white of Irish background, and I'm brown, a mix of my Egyptian mother and Indian father. He's Christian, I'm Muslim. The non-dating kind." (19)

- "When she first used 'hajeeb' I'd kindly point out it was hijab. She told me some words were too hard for her to pronounce, so 'hajeeb' it is in gym class. . . . I should have asked her why she has no problem pronouncing Genevieve's name." (114)

- "Most girls who cover their faces do it because they want to be the ones to decide who gets to see them. Soon-Lee pauses from writing to consider that. 'Well, when you think of it that way, it sounds kind of powerful. Like no one can sum up your identity without permission. Your real identity, I mean.'" (250)

Sophia's Journal. **Najiyah Daniel Maxfield. Daybreak, 2014. 978–0990625902. 300 pp. Fiction. Young adult.**

This is a historical fiction novel that centers on the coming-of-age story of a young Muslim teenager. Sophia takes a time-travel tumble into the Kansas River while out on a bike ride with her family and wakes up in nineteenth-century Kansas. Adopted by a pioneer family, she is grateful to be alive and helps with daily chores and tries to make the best out of her new life, despite the bigotry and racism she sees all around her. She draws inspiration from her continued practice of her faith, and this leads her to discover Muslim slaves, as well as the fight for freedom and justice by Native Americans. This book is a captivating look at the history of America and the people from many different faiths and beliefs who stood up and did the right thing.

Discussion Starters

- Why do you think Sophia feels she has been brought back in time to 1857? How does she show her gratitude to the pioneer family?
- What commonalities can you draw between Sophia's practice of her faith and the faith of her adopted family? Why do you think she still holds on to her faith?
- Pair this book with *Roots* by Alex Haley to understand where the slaves came from—their histories, homes, and the culture they left behind.

Ideas for Further Engagement

- ✋ Create your own time-travel journal.
- ✋ Look up the history of Islam and Native American history in the United States.
- ✋ Watch the historical documentary *Prince among Slaves* by Andrea Kalin, narrated by Mos Def.

Quotes for Interpretation

- "Sophia was rather shocked that there were so many precise similarities between Christianity and Islam." (65)
- "Everyone feels down or scared sometimes. But that don't mean you's running out o'faith. That jus' means yer faith is being tested." (225)
- "I would rather die fighting for someone's freedom than live knowing I could have helped and didn't." (244)

Notes

1. Tom Burns, "Religion in Children's Literature," in *Children's Literature Review*, ed. Tom Burns, vol. 121 (Detroit, MI: Gale, 2007), available at Literature Resource Center, May 6, 2013, http://lion-witch-wardrobe.weebly.com/religion-in-childrens-literature.html.

2. M. O. Greenby, "The Origin of Children's Literature," https://www.bl.uk/romantics-and-victorians/articles/the-origins-of-childrens-literature.

3. "Publishers fear that discussions of religion may offend the nonreligious, and a sympathetic portrayal of any particular religious group may be seen as attempting to convert readers. Of course, stories can be a tool for conversion, so why isn't religious diversity a danger best avoided in fiction for kids? Because a body of literature that avoids religion is unrealistic: void of many of the belief systems that shape how we perceive and navigate life, how can literature as an art make any claim to reflect human experience?" https://www.thebookseller.com/blogs/religion-children-s-literature-new-taboo-607966.

Chapter 7

Folktales from Islamic Traditions

Drawing Wisdom from Tall Tales

WHETHER IN ARABIC: *KA WAN MA KAN* ("THERE WAS AND there was not"), or in English, "Once upon a time," these magical words have the power to transport us to lands of epics and ancient legends. Each culture has timeless stories that have been passed down from generation to generation: stories of knights and princesses, tales of mystery and magic, and stories of quick wit and resourceful thinking. Children hear these stories even before they learn to read or write. Often passed down through oral storytelling traditions, these folktales are easy to remember and share, and they remain favorites for read-alouds. Most public libraries are well stocked with a global collection of folktales to use in classrooms and homes. However, children in America often grow up immersed in the popular Aesop's fables and similar folktales, but remain unaware of diverse folktales from other cultures.

In this chapter's book list, we've curated folktales from Islamic traditions that open up fantastic worlds and provide insights into the values, beliefs, histories, and traditions of those cultures. We have focused on lesser-known books that spotlight multicultural stories and lend themselves to opening up conversations about various Muslim countries and cultures. While being entertaining and engaging, folktales are also an invaluable way to pass along core beliefs, reiterate cultural values, and share common histories.

Early Arabic literature was comprised of dramatic epics that were recited as long poems. These later took on the form of erudite essays, until a new form appeared: "This was known as *maqamat,* 'assemblies'—amusing anecdotes narrated by a vagabond who made his living by his wits."[1] As caravans of traders, merchants, and explorers traveled up and down the Silk Road, so did their stories. Fables from Persia and India mingled with myths from Iraq and Syria. Legends from Morocco, Mali, and China blended to create multiple versions of the same story. These fluid stories often embraced retellings and were reshaped by the storytellers to reflect local cultural and social norms.

The best-known work to fascinate imaginations around the world through its stories of adventure, magic, and romance is the *Arabian Nights,* better known as *One Thousand and One Nights.* These tales of mystery and intrigue were translated first into French and then into English. Inspirations from this book such as Arab names, settings, and characters have shown up in the works of old masters such as Chaucer, Shakespeare, and Dante and in books by more recent authors such as Tolstoy, Jorge Luis Borges, Salman Rushdie, and Orhan Pamuk. While Western audiences are familiar with "Sinbad the Sailor," "Ali Baba and the Forty Thieves," and "Aladdin," lesser known folktales such as the adventures of Amir Hamza, the sayings of Mullah Nasruddin, and teaching stories derived from the dervish or Sufi traditions are very popular in many Muslim countries. For example, the stories of "Fatima the Spinner and the Tent" and "The Silly Chicken" are known in some form or other across the Middle East all the way to China.

Folktales weave ideals of courage, resourcefulness, and trust into the story in order to teach children (and adults) models of behavior. Children especially love stories where the underdog outwits a powerful enemy, and thus proves that small size, age, or stature is no bar to achieving greatness. Folktales that depict challenging situations in which characters must make a good or bad decision show readers how our actions can have positive or negative consequences. The stories from Islamic traditions are often open-ended and lead to multiple interpretations, without a direct moral or message. They also challenge the more "Western" narratives of bravery, and show different approaches to problem-solving. For instance, in "Neem the Half-Boy," the hero is born as a half-boy, and must find a potion from the dragon's lair to complete himself. Instead of slaying the dragon, the boy sits down to peacefully negotiate with him.

Folktales often serve as repositories of oral histories that remain relevant even today. They can introduce a unique intersection of geography, language arts, and even dramatics into the classroom. Learning about folktales from different countries gives the reader insights into the beliefs, traditions, and customs of those cultures. By encountering the diversity of the world around them through folktales, children can draw parallels with their own lives. Visual cultural cues embedded in the stories—from the tapestry or textiles that reflect the art of a particular region, to the clothes the characters wear and the words they speak, and both traditional and modern elements in the illustrations—all make for lively discussions. Balancing traditional folktales with contemporary stories is an effective way to soak up both a culture's history and its present-day aspects.

Humor is also an important aspect in many of these folktales, and is often used to poke fun at or question authority. The short stories about the Mughal ruler Akbar and his minister Birbal show the clever ways in which Birbal uses humor to advise the monarch, without angering or putting him down. This echoes stories such as "The Emperor's New Clothes," where only children were courageous enough to tell the emperor the truth. Also, classics such as "The Little Black Fish" and "The Conference of the Birds" serve as allegories that encourage people to seek their own paths, with the former even banned in prerevolutionary Iran.

We have also attempted to reclaim orientalist tellings of these tales by featuring writers who take inspiration from their ethnic traditions, situate the story within social and historical contexts, and paint their characters in shades of gray. For example, in the fantasy novel *Throne of the Crescent Moon,* author Saladin Ahmed has the characters heed the call of the Heavenly Chapters to save innocent lives and destroy evil using the hidden power within its verses.

The wisdom and diversity of Muslim experiences in these ancient stories can help retrace those roots back to the present. We hope this book list will provide valuable suggestions that will broaden the horizons of all children, and provide topics for discussions on universal moral values and models of behavior, while also tickling children's imaginations.

Picture Books

Bijan and Manije. Ali Seidabadi, ill. by Marjan Vafaian. Tiny Owl, 2016. 978–1910328149. 28 pp. Fiction. Pre-K–Gr. 3.

Select Awards: Finalist, 2017 Little Hakka International Picture Book Award.

This is an unusual love story from the Persian national epic, the *Shahnameh (Epic of Kings)*, one of the world's longest epic poems, written by the tenth-century poet Ferdowsi. The story centers on Bijan, a brave knight from Iran, and Manije, the daughter of King Afraisaib from Turan. Iran and Turan are archrivals, and so when love blossoms between Bijan and Manije, King Afraisaib renders a harsh punishment on Bijan. Manije is distraught but determined. With a fateful turn of events, Manije manages to save Bijan, and the two live happily ever after. Bright and colorful illustrations bring the story to life.

Ideas for Further Engagement

- Have students compare this story with popular Western romantic folktales such as "Snow White." How is this story similar, and how is it different?
- ✋ Lead a discussion on folk art in Iran; were any of those art forms depicted here?

The Clever Boy and the Terrible, Dangerous Animal. Idries Shah, ill. by Rose Mary Santiago. Hoopoe Books, 2015. 978–1942698234. 38 pp. Fiction. K–Gr. 6.

This is a vividly illustrated and highly entertaining tale told in bright colors and with gentle humor about a young boy who visits a neighboring village only to find the villagers cowering at a "dangerous animal." The boy dispels their fears and manages to lead them to a clever solution, too. This is a lighthearted tale about fearing what (and who) we do not know. This tale is one of the many oral Sufi stories told in books by Idries Shah. The book is also available in bilingual versions in Urdu, Pashto, Dari, and Spanish.

Ideas for Further Engagement

- Discuss "fear of the unknown" and ways to tackle things we fear.
- Pair this book with the story "The Emperor's New Clothes" by Hans Christian Andersen.
- ✋ Use this book for a fun read-aloud session and pair with watermelon as a snack.

Elephant in the Dark. **Mina Javaherbin, ill. by Eugene Yelchin. Scholastic, 2015. 978–0545636704. 40 pp. Fiction. Pre-K–Gr. 3.**

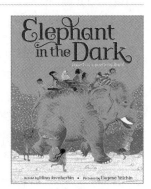

Beautifully illustrated in vivid colors, this folk-tale based on a poem by Rumi takes us to a small Persian village where a merchant has brought back an exotic animal from India. Villagers steal into the barn in the dark of the night, and each of them feels a different part of the animal and comes to his own conclusion about what it is. Squabbling among themselves and knowing only a little of the truth, the villagers miss the big picture, and miss seeing the entire elephant until the merchant rides him the next day.

Ideas for Further Engagement

- Discuss the notion of different perspectives, and how wisdom lies in seeing the whole rather than one single perspective.
- ✋ Conduct a similar activity by hiding a large object under a bedsheet, and ask children to touch different parts of it and guess what the object may be.

Fatima, the Spinner and the Tent. Idries Shah, ill. by Natasha Delmar. Hoopoe Books, 2015. 978–1942698074. 38 pp. Fiction. Gr. 2–6.

Fatima is brought up by her loving father but suffers a series of setbacks in her life. She earns her living with different families, learning their trade and honing her skills as a weaver and seamstress. Her travels take her across oceans from Morocco to Egypt, Turkey, and finally to China, where Fatima realizes the meaning of all the misfortunes in her life. This tale is one of the many oral Sufi stories told by Idries Shah. The book is also available in bilingual versions in Urdu, Pashto, Dari, and Spanish. *This book is best suited for older children.*

Ideas for Further Engagement

- Discuss the value of life's experiences and how they each teach us something.
- Ask children to recount a unique experience they have had, and how it has shaped their outlook.
- ✋ Have the students trace a path through all the countries Fatima lived in.

How Many Donkeys? An Arabic Counting Tale. Margaret Read MacDonald and Nadia Jameel Taibah, ill. by Carol Liddiment. Albert Whitman, 2012. 978–0807534250. 32 pp. Fiction. K–Gr. 3.

Select Awards: 2010 Best English Language Children's Book, Sharjah International Book Fair.

The man of many names: Hoca, Hoja, the Mullah, makes an appearance yet again in this folktale set in Saudi Arabia. Known here as Jouha, he is getting ready to make a trip to the market with his ten donkeys. When his son helps him count, there are ten, but the minute Jouha starts his trip there are only nine. He gets down to count them again and the lost donkey is back. He makes his long trip alternating between feeling lucky and unlucky, but readers will catch on quick. The silly, funny text and counting the numbers in Arabic make this tale a fun read for everyone.

Ideas for Further Engagement

✋ Lead the students in a countdown from one to ten in some of the languages represented in your classroom.

✋ Ask the readers to discuss and draw the symbols for luck in different cultures.

Little Black Fish. **Samad Behrangi, ill. by Farshid Mesghali. Tiny Owl, 2016. 978–1910328194. 48 pp. Fiction. Gr. 2–6.**

Select Awards: Shortlisted for the 2016 Marsh Award for Children's Literature in Translation. The illustrator, Farshid Mesghali, won the 1974 Hans Christian Andersen Award.

This allegorical story about an adventurous little black fish is relayed as a cautionary tale by a grandmother fish to her 12,000 grandchildren. The little black fish wants to explore the world beyond her stream, but her parents and friends tell her that the stream is their world. One fine day, she decides to ignore them and swim beyond the stream. The story follows her adventures in the other world as she meets tadpoles, crabs, and other sea creatures along the way. With stunning illustrations and numerous opportunities to discuss life lessons around freedom, curiosity, bravery, and authority, this book is a must-have in every multicultural library. *The text-heavy story is best for advanced readers.*

Ideas for Further Engagement

• Ask children to recount an experience where they were brave or tried something new.

• Lead a discussion on the idea of freedom.

• Pair this book with the graphic novel version, *The Little Black Fish*, by Rosarium Publishing.

✋ Draw out the scene of the grandmother fish telling this story to the 12,000 fishes.

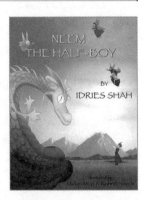

***Neem the Half-Boy.* Idries Shah, ill. by Midori Mori and Robert Revels. Hoopoe Books, 2015. 978–1942698265. 38 pp. Fiction. K–Gr. 6.**

In a faraway kingdom, a queen yearns for a child, yet when a wise man gives her the solution, she only follows it halfway and ends up with a half-boy, Neem. Neem longs to be whole and must venture to a dragon's lair to obtain the potion that can complete him. Faced with an ill-tempered, fire-breathing dragon, Neem uses his cleverness and empathy to figure out a peaceful solution that may surprise readers. This tale is one of the many oral Sufi stories told by Idries Shah and is also available in bilingual versions in Urdu, Pashto, Dari, and Spanish.

Ideas for Further Engagement

- Discuss ways of conflict resolution, and how it's often important to understand the other person's motive in order to reach a resolution.
- Explain the popular negotiation strategy of "Expanding the pie" vs. "Dividing the pie" and how most things are not binary. Break up the class into groups and organize a negotiation activity.

Sally Mallam

Ancient Afghan Tales Offer Timely Perspectives

Sally Mallam was in her early twenties in London when she first heard the author and educator Idries Shah narrate stories of fire-breathing dragons, magical horses, and treasure boxes full of dreams to his children, family, and friends, "These stories were an integral part of [Shah's] exuberant recollections of Afghanistan—where he often recalled the fruit trees that grew the best fruit, where the mountains, flowers, and valleys were the most beautiful and where the men, women, and children were brave, honorable, and wise—or were learning to be so," she remembers.

Idries Shah had collected hundreds of traditional stories from oral and manuscript sources in and around Afghanistan and the Middle East. Mallam even recalls typing these stories from a dictating machine, and the memories of those oral stories remained with her even as she moved on to the United States and pursued a career in publishing and the arts.

"In October 1996 when I visited him in London, I asked him why, though many of these stories had been published in about twenty-five books for adults, his children's stories were not in print anywhere. He gave me the manuscript and—just before he died the following month—agreed that we produce a series of illustrated books from it," she recalls. Mallam mined her network for illustrators and reached out to local Bay Area art schools, working with young and emerging artists to bring Shah's books to life. Mallam, who is a painter and has an art degree, also illustrated *The Man and the Fox*, but only

because "I ran out of money!" she laughs.

While Shah's stories are universal, the gorgeous and detailed illustrations and the outlook of the characters are uniquely Afghan. Unlike Western folktales such as contemporary versions of Aesop's tales, these are not simple moral tales, but something more instructive. "These aren't stories of finding and slaying the dragon, but in stories such as *Neem the Half-Boy*, the young boy learns to understand the dragon's predicament and chooses peaceful negotiation over violent confrontation," Mallam explains.

Like many folktales, these stories were created as a way to pass on a universal understanding of our human nature. Mallam explains, "In the West, the 'Disneyfication' of many stories—to select and retell only those elements that have a strong emotional appeal—has led to the demise of the story as a developmental instrument. [Shah's] stories, however, encourage thinking, problem-solving skills, and perception."

These Sufi stories offer a sophisticated way to learn and observe ourselves and others and to understand a character's motivations and consequent actions. They also allow us to step into a world where we can empathize with the people in the story, and share and acknowledge their point of view even if we don't partake of their traditions and rituals. "A flexible mind open to other perspectives is something we need to develop; too many people, including young children, reflect the prejudices of their group, which are based solely on ignorance, stereotypes, and false assumptions. Providing beautiful stories from cultures that are too often misunderstood can be a first step to breaking down these artificial barriers. Once you hear these ancient tales, they stay with you, and come to mind at different points in your life," Mallam says.

one who pursues his heart's desires while the other takes on a more difficult path, both emphasizing different life choices rather than mere good and bad binaries.

While all the stories reflect universal ideas of courage, perseverance, personal choice, and the importance of critical thinking, they also remain rooted in Afghan culture, which is often misunderstood in the West or seen only through the lens of war, poverty, and oppression. These books are instrumental in helping young readers gain a different perspective of Afghanistan, and they help us appreciate that we are more alike than different and we all have something to learn from each other.

Mallam decided to take Idries Shah's folktales a step further by creating bilin-

---

"Providing beautiful stories from cultures that are too often misunderstood can be a first step to breaking down these artificial barriers."

Citing a few examples, she mentions *The Clever Boy and the Terrible, Dangerous Animal,* which was featured on the Library of Congress's 2002 Christmas list as a great story full of humor; the story emphasizes that though we may be afraid of something which we don't understand, we can learn to overcome fear. "We all can benefit from overcoming irrational fear of 'the other,' especially in the racially charged environment we see today," Mallam states.

In *The Old Woman and the Eagle,* an elderly woman tries to change an unfamiliar eagle into the more familiar pigeon. Children, who are all individual "eagles," readily respond to the story, while adults can relate to the old woman's efforts to alter the unfamiliar to make it acceptable. *The Magic Horse* is a tale of two brothers,

gual versions of the stories. "I remember how difficult it was to learn to read in my own language, so the idea that anyone would have to learn to read in a foreign language seemed crazy," she says. "There are so many children from that region of the world here in the United States. Publishing bilingual editions in Dari and Pashto with English seemed like an obvious next step. Afghan children can share their own stories, images, and writing with children in their new schools."

In 2005, Mallam took things full circle to return these wonderful stories to Afghan children in Dari and Pashto. "I thought that these stories could develop a love of reading and learning and also teach Afghan children about their rich culture and perhaps reinvigorate their ancient storytelling tradition," she says. She also hopes that these books could help alle-viate the influence of Muslim extremism by encouraging flexible minds and critical thinking, which are essentially incompati-ble with extremist beliefs.

The Afghan Ministry of Education wel-comed the "repatriation" of their stories. More than 4.5 million copies of the books have been distributed to children since the program was started. Afghanistan has one of the lowest literacy levels in the world; the problem is not helped by its being a multilingual country, where education is conducted solely in the national languages of Dari and Pashto. "We are now working on nine new bilin-gual minority language editions, so that Afghan children who speak, say, Nuristani at home can begin reading in their mother tongue, and transfer those skills, using the same books, to the national language they will need to further their education."

Mallam firmly believes that anyone who is familiar with these stories understands that they are timeless and hold useful lessons for all of us; as she concludes, "I am still learning from them."

Biography

Sally Mallam spent fifteen years in international business and publish-ing prior to coming to the United States. She joined the Institute for the Study of Human Knowledge (ISHK) in 1983 as its administrative director. In 1996 she initiated the ISHK publishing imprints Malor and Hoopoe Books, and the subsequent development of ISHK's literacy outreach four years later. She is also an artist who has exhibited in the United States and Britain.

Never Say a Mean Word Again: A Tale from Medieval Spain. Jacqueline Jules, ill. by Durga Yael Bern-hard. Wisdom Tales, 2014. 978–1937786205. 32 pp. Fiction. Pre-K–Gr. 3.

Select Awards: 2014 Aesop Prize from the American Folklore Society.

Set in Moorish Spain and based on the legend of a Jewish vizier, this story of a growing friendship between a Muslim and a Jewish boy spins rudeness into kindness. Samuel, the son of the vizier, accidentally runs into Hamza and later annoys him yet again, and in response an angry Hamza says mean words to him. Samuel's powerful father advises him to "Make sure Hamza never says a mean word to you again." Samuel comes up with some absurd ideas, but each plan of his to confront Hamza turns into a play date. This amusing tale turns enemies into friends.

Ideas for Further Engagement

- Explore the idea of friendship and what it really takes to make a friend.
- Discuss the importance of using kind words toward peers.
- ✋ Ask readers to find something in common with each of their classmates: favorite food, family structure, places traveled to, and others.

The Conference of the Birds. Alexis York Lumbard, ill. by Demi. Wisdom Tales, 2012. 978–1937786021. 44 pp. Fiction. K–Gr. 3.

Select Awards: Silver Midwest Book Award for Illustration: Graphic 2012; Silver Midwest Book Award for Interior Layout 2012.

A retelling of a famous Sufi poem by the twelfth-century Persian poet Farid al-Din Attar, this story is a parable of facing your inner fears and putting your hopes in God. A flock of birds are in despair without a leader to guide them. The hoopoe bird proves to be their guide, leading them to King Simorgh the Wise. With the hoopoe's encouragement, all the birds confront and conquer their failings. With rich and beautiful illustrations and lyrical writing, this story touches on the essence of universal spiritual values that we all share.

Ideas for Further Engagement

- Ask students to share whom they look up to for guidance when they have a problem at home and at school.
- ✋ Have the readers pick their favorite bird from the story and draw a picture of it.

The Hungry Coat: A Tale from Turkey. Demi, ill. by author. Margaret K. McElderry Books, 2004. 978–0689846809. 40 pp. Fiction. Gr. 1–6.

Select Awards: Buckaroo Book Award Master List 2004, CCBC Choices 2004, ILA Notable Books for a Global Society 2004, New York Public Library 100 Titles for Reading and Sharing 2004.

While there are many different variations of this folktale in Islamic countries, this story of Nasrettin Hoca is set in Turkey. Using detailed and miniature-inspired paintings, Demi's jewel-toned illustrations paint a vivid picture of ancient Turkey. Hoca rushes to his friends' banquet in his worn-out work clothes and is ignored by everyone. He leaves and returns in a beautiful silk coat and is treated like an honored guest. He proceeds to feed his coat, much to everyone's surprise. This is a funny and thoughtful tale on appearances that questions whether the coat makes the man.

Ideas for Further Engagement

- Discuss how we often judge someone based on how they are dressed. How can we become more aware of this?
- Have students interpret the quote at the end: "He who wears Heaven in his heart is always well dressed."

The Secret Message. **Mina Javaherbin, ill. by Bruce Whatley. Hyperion Books, 2010. 978–1423110446. 32 pp. Fiction. Pre-K–Gr. 2.**

Select Awards: KPBS One Book One San Diego Choice 2010, California Collection Book: 2010–2011, Gold seal recipient from Oppenheim Toy and Book Awards 2010.

This story is based on a poem by the famous poet Rumi and is set in Persia. It is about a merchant and his parrot from India who helped make the merchant's business very successful. The merchant goes on a trip to India to buy items for his business. The parrot sends a secret message to his feathered friends in the forests of India, and this results in an unexpected surprise for the merchant. The story weaves in a number of cultural symbols, such as the silks, jewels, and spices which India was famous for, and the Silk Road which the merchant travels to get to India.

Ideas for Further Engagement

- Pair with a discussion of the Silk Road and how global trade worked historically. Contrast the Silk Road trade with the current shift in global trade.

🖐 Play a game of Telephone with verbal or nonverbal secret messages.

🖐 Organize a bazaar with each child pretending to be a merchant of different wares, while other children roam and barter for goods.

Tunjur! Tunjur! Tunjur! A Palestinian Folktale.
Margaret Read MacDonald, ill. by Alik Arzou-
manian. Two Lions, 2006. 978–0761452256.
32 pp. Fiction. Gr. 1–3.

Select Awards: Notable Social Studies Trade Books for Young People 2007.

This is a whimsical folktale about a young woman who has a lively pot as her child. The pot rattles and rolls around her home, but it soon wants to explore the world outside. Concerned that her child doesn't know right from wrong, the mother is hesitant but finally gives in. The naughty pot gets into some sticky situations and finally gets her comeuppance. This book's bright and colorful art with Arabic touches leaps off the page, and the repetitive phrases lend themselves to repeated readings. Readers will enjoy this moral tale with a light, rolling touch.

Ideas for Further Engagement

- Have the readers discuss situations where they did something wrong and were able to make it right.
- Pair this book with *The Adventures of Pinocchio* by Carlo Collidi.

Chapter Books and Middle Grade Books

Ali Baba and the Forty Thieves: From the One Thousand and One Nights.
Retold by Abdul-Fattah Sabri, ill. by Sura Ghazwan. Real Reads, 2016.
978–1911091011. 64 pp. Fiction. K–Gr. 3.

This is the famous story behind the phrase *"Khulja Sim Sim!"* or "Open Sesame!" Ali Baba's trip to the forest leads him to adventure and riches from the secret treasure cave, but when his brother is killed by thieves, he has to figure out a way to outwit them. His brother's servant girl uses wit and wisdom to dampen the thieves' plans to attack Ali Baba, and she cleverly spoils the thieves' plot to kill him and his family. This is a well-recounted story, with simple language that is perfect for early readers. There are helpful resources and discussion questions at the end of the book.

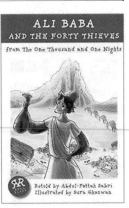

Discussion Starters

- Identify three instances where Ali Baba and Morgiana, Cassim's servant girl, displayed wit and wisdom.
- Do you think the story should be titled Morgiana instead of Ali Baba, since she plays a key role in the story? Why or why not?
- Think of one life lesson from the story that you can pay heed to in your own life.
- Read other titles in this series such as *Aladdin and His Magic Lamp* and *Sindbad the Sailor*.

Ideas for Further Engagement

- 🖐 Design a hiding spot for your treasures and come up with a secret passcode to open it.
- 🖐 Rewrite the story with you as one of the characters.

Quotes for Interpretation

- "Why is it that I am so poor and my brother so rich?" (7)
- "At that moment Cassim realized he would happily exchange several bags of gold coins for one small flask of water." (18)
- "As it was the custom of the time to offer hospitality to strangers, Ali Baba insisted that the 'merchant' spend the night at Cassim's house." (42)

***Akbar and Birbal (Tales of Wit and Wisdom).* Amita Sarin. Penguin Books India, 2005. 978–0143334941. 224 pp. Fiction. K–Gr. 3.**

Akbar, the third Mughal emperor, is regarded as one of India's greatest rulers. His reign was a time of cultural and intellectual advancement and interfaith tolerance. Akbar worked towards the assimilation and integration of his Hindu subjects, appointed many Hindu advisors, encouraged interfaith marriages and celebrations, and abolished the tax on non-Muslims. Birbal

was one such Hindu minister in Akbar's court and a member of his inner council of nine advisors. He was famous for his sharp intellect and keen sense of humor. This well-researched book provides details about Akbar's rule and shares stories of Akbar and Birbal, which are very popular among children and adults alike and form an indispensable part of South Asian folklore.

Discussion Starters

- Recount the history of the Mughal Empire. Analyze key reasons for the success and downfall of the empire.
- Why do you think Akbar trusted Birbal so much?
- Which is one of your favorite stories from the book and why?

Ideas for Further Engagement

- Choose funny or wise snippets from the book and enact them in the classroom.

Quotes for Interpretation

- "In a world that was divided by differences, Akbar and Birbal were searching for similarities that would bring people together and help them to live in harmony." (xiv)
- "Though he was Muslim, and most of his subjects were Hindus, Akbar tried hard to ensure just and fair treatment to all his people, no matter what their race or religion." (xi)
- "Akbar also showed great reverence towards the pictures of the Virgin Mary brought to him by the European Christian priest visiting his court. He donated land to the Christians to build a church and also gave the leaders of the Sikh religion land where they founded Amritsar, their holy land." (58)

Haroun and the Sea of Stories. **Salman Rushdie.**
Granta Books/Penguin, 1991. 978–0140157376.
216 pp. Gr. 5 and up.

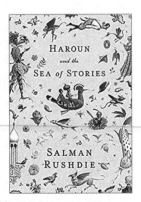

Select Awards: Mythopoeic Fantasy Award for Children's Literature 1991, Writers Guild Award 1991.

This classic children's novel by Rushdie serves as a political allegory, and is especially relevant in today's times. It features Haroun, a twelve-year-old boy, and his father, Rashid, who live in a "sad" city where the politicians can't really be trusted. One day, Rashid loses his ability to tell stories after the betrayal of his wife. Haroun is distraught, but one night he is magically transported to mythical lands of fantasy and adventure, where he meets interesting characters as he tries to restore the poisoned source of the sea of stories and bring back the gift of the gab for his father.

Discussion Starters

- How was it that the citizens listened to Rashid, but did not believe what the politicians said?
- Do you see any similarities in this story with Peter Pan?
- Where do you think stories come from? How can we all think more creatively?
- What do you like to read more—fiction or nonfiction? Why?

Ideas for Further Engagement

- Write a story set in Moody Land, where the mood of the city depends on the mood of its inhabitants.
- Research the meaning of non-English words in the book such as *chup, kitab, kahaani,* and *khattam-shud* in order to understand why Rushdie used them.

Quotes for Interpretation

- "In the sad city people had big families, but the poor children got sick and starved, and the rich children overate and quarreled over their parents' money." (18)
- "What's the use of stories that aren't even true?" (20)
- "He knew what he knew: that the real world was full of magic, so magical worlds could easily be real." (50)

Pea Boy and Other Stories from Iran. **Elizabeth Laird and Shirin Adl. Frances Lincoln Children's Books, 2009. 978–1845079123. 64 pp. Fiction. Gr. 2–6.**

This is a delightful book that features seven unique folktales from Iran, including stories of a vain young female cockroach who learns to grow up and take care of herself, a young boy who makes a quick promise he later regrets, a clever boy who happens to be in the right place at the right time, a beautiful tale of a sparrow trying to understand the interplay of nature and discovering her own strength in the process, and the pea boy who uses his wits to follow his father's wishes and provide for his family. The stories lend themselves to many avenues for discussion about morals and values such as being grateful for what we have, being responsible and careful with our words and actions, being thoughtful about whose advice we seek, and our place in this world.

Discussion Starters

- What are some of the core values and life skills you learned from these stories?
- Pair the *Pea Boy* story with *Gobble You Up!* by Gita Wolf.
- Read *A Fistful of Pearls and Other Tales from Iraq* by Elizabeth Laird.

Ideas for Further Engagement

✋ Pick your favorite story and write it with a different ending.

Quotes for Interpretation

- "Iran is a country full of stories: of jinns and fairies and demons, faithful mice and frivolous cockroaches, foolish young weavers and curious sparrows." (9)
- "How does it feel then, cruel sparrow, to be the greatest thing on earth?" (37)

Tales from the Arabian Nights: Stories of Adventure, Magic, Love, and Betrayal. **Donna Jo Napoli, ill. by Christina Balit. National Geographic Children's Books, 2016. 978–1426325403. 208 pp. Fiction. Gr. 3–7.**

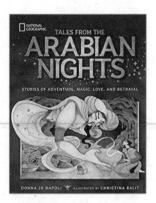

This is an engrossing retelling of fantasy and folklore from the *Thousand and One Nights* collection common throughout the Middle East and South Asia. It begins with Scheherazade's story and her ability to keep King Shahriyar enthralled with her tales in order to save herself from being killed, and it moves on to the more familiar tales of Aladdin and Sinbad the Sailor, as well as lesser-known ones such as "Maaruf the Cobbler" and "The Three Apples." It is a comprehensive resource with an introduction, information boxes to provide context, and a detailed map and postscript. This book is ideal for older elementary and middle grade children, though its beautiful illustrations may capture the attention of younger readers too.

Discussion Starters

- Can you draw any similarities in the morals or plot between any of these stories and the Western stories like "Little Red Riding Hood" and "The Three Little Pigs" that you are familiar with?
- "The carpenter's door is falling apart." What does this phrase mean?

Ideas for Further Engagement

- ✍ Write a story with a cliffhanger; that is, don't disclose what happens in the end but only allude to it.
- ✍ Write down a few examples of wit that you learned from the stories.
- ✍ List a few cultural practices or objects that you encountered while reading these stories that were new to you.

Quotes for Interpretation

- "This storytelling tradition puts an emphasis on careful listening and mental jockeying. The listener is rewarded frequently by gifts to the ear—songs and poems—as well as gifts to the spirit: characters who make us laugh, love stories that hold us entranced, fantastical creatures and devices that amaze us." (7)

- "Scheherazade wins not through trickery, but through understanding human nature, and through faith in her own abilities and in the transformative power of storytelling. She dares to fathom the meaning of life with every bit of intelligence she has. As a result, she embodies the spirit of the times and places of the tales she spins." (7)
- "In many places the mentally ill were cast out of society, even as recently as a century ago. But the Muslim world was tolerant; therapy was needed, not banishment." (64)

The Kidnapping of Amir Hamza. **Mamta Dalal Mangaldas and Saker Mistri. Magpin, 2010. 978–0944142868. 56 pp. Fiction. Gr. 3–6.**

Select Awards: First Prize for Children's Books by the Federation of Indian Publishers 2008.

Hamzanama, or the "story of Hamza," was such a favorite of the Mughal emperor Akbar that he commissioned grand illustrations of the epic. These adventure stories of daring princesses, dragons, flying demons, and other characters have been popular all over the Islamic world. *The Kidnapping of Amir Hamza* is one such story retold with intricate Mughal miniature illustrations inspired by the originals. This is a fantastic fantasy story that has an interactive section on Mughal art too.

Discussion Starters
- Who are the stories from the *Hamzanama* based on?
- What can you find out about the *dastangoi* tradition of storytelling?
- Can you think of any other stories of valiant kings that are parallels to the martial adventures of Hamza?

Ideas for Further Engagement
- ✋ Look up the Indonesian puppet theater version of Amir Hamza, titled *Wayang Menak.*
- ✋ Organize a story-building activity based on a theme from the book. Form a circle with the first child beginning the story, then each child adding one sentence until the last child who concludes the story.

Quotes for Interpretation

- "Listening to stories seems to have been so important to Akbar that he took his storyteller on many of his expeditions." (5)
- "In Mughal times, storytellers like Darbar Khan were expected not only to recite stories perfectly from memory, but also to elaborate on favorite parts and even invent new episodes." (6)
- "Often the storytelling continued for many hours and was accompanied by music and dancing." (13)

***The Ogress and the Snake and Other Stories from Somalia.* Elizabeth Laird. Frances Lincoln Children's Books, 2009. 978-1845078706. 96 pp. Fiction. Gr. 3–6.**

This set of eight folk stories set in Somalia is presented with rich detail—lively tea-house chatter, evil stepmothers, cunning hyenas, clever cats, and fantastical creatures—and ranges from a talking head to a flying sorceress. Masterfully translating from local storytellers, Elizabeth Laird brings these trickster tales to life and manages to transport you to Jigjiga in Somalia, where she collected these stories.

Discussion Starters

- Pair the "Ogress and the Snake" story with "Hansel and Gretel."
- Which is your favorite story? Why?
- Do you have a different story about why dogs became man's best friend and a cat became a woman's best friend?

Ideas for Further Engagement

- ✍ Read the traditional rhyme at the beginning of the book: ("Can you see what I see? Can you hear what I hear? No! What do you see? What do you hear? Tell us!") List some traditional ways that stories from other cultures begin.
- ✍ Listen to popular Somali music.

Quotes for Interpretation

- "Friends are the greatest riches of all." (49)
- "And it's only common decency to help when a poor soul asks, even if he doesn't have a body." (83)
- "She was a girl of such beauty that birds fell out of the sky when they flew overhead, flowers turned on their stalks to watch her go past, and camels fell to their knees as she went by." (85)

***The Seven Voyages of Sinbad the Sailor.* Retold by John Yeoman, ill. by Quentin Blake. Pavilion Books, 2009. 978–1843651291. 119 pp. Fiction. Gr. 2–4.**

This engaging retelling of the stories of Sinbad the Sailor, or rather Sinbad the merchant, is perfect to enthrall young readers. In each voyage that Sinbad makes, he is faced with new perils and meets fantastical creatures, but somehow he manages to come out unscathed. Each story has creative twists and turns and showcases numerous elements and traditions of the cultures of the time. Beautiful watercolor illustrations animate and complement the stories.

Discussion Starters

- Which voyage of Sinbad was your favorite and why?
- What values and skills do you think Sinbad relied upon to survive all the adventures he faced in his voyages?
- Do you like to travel? Why or why not?
- How has travel evolved since the Sinbad stories were first told?

Ideas for Further Engagement

- Research trading routes in the past, and current trading routes.
- Divide students into groups and have them enact one of Sinbad's voyages.

Quotes for Interpretation

- "These stories have been famous for a long time. They were first translated into French, and then almost immediately into English, over two hundred years ago; but the stories themselves were first told hundreds of years before that." (6)

- "The Sinbad stories (unlike the others in *The Arabian Nights*) must be based on the yarns that the real travelers of that time told on their return." (6)

- "It is our custom and our duty . . . whenever we find a shipwrecked man, to take him up and to feed and clothe him. Far from accepting money from him, we set him ashore at a convenient port of safety with a gift of money from ourselves." (75)

The Wise Fool: Fables from the Islamic World.
Shahrukh Husain, ill. by Micha Archer.
Barefoot Books, 2015. 978–1782852551.
64 pp. Fiction. Gr. 2–4.

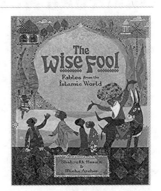

This book serves as an introduction to Mulla Nasruddin, a legendary character whose adventures and misadventures have been cherished for centuries in countries all the way from China to Turkey. Eccentric, engaging, and irreverent, Nasruddin always has a twinkle in his eye, a sliver of wisdom in his ramblings, and a few good surprises up his sleeve.

Discussion Starters

- Pair this book with *Stories to Solve, Folktales from Around the World*, told by George Shannon, illustrated by Peter Sis.
- What is the one lesson that stuck with you and you will try to implement in your life?

Ideas for Further Engagement

- Hold a riddle contest with riddles from around the world.
- Find out all the different names that the Mulla is known by in different countries such as Iran, Iraq, Turkey, Morocco, and China.
- Look up when and where the International Nasreddin Hodja Festival is celebrated.

Quotes for Interpretation
- "Was he a real person or is he entirely fictional?" (5)
- "Now listen very carefully, because the sound of these coins is payment for the steam from your food. That's a fair exchange, I believe, for a miser like you!" (7)
- "The Mulla loved stories. He loved the way they brought events to life." (10)

Shahrukh Husain
The Timelessness of Folktales

Can you tell us a little about where you grew up and what inspired you to be a writer?

I was born in Karachi, Pakistan, spent a couple of early years in London while my father finished his studies, and then I returned to Pakistan. I started writing when I was far too young, so it's hard to know what inspired me. It was just something I did. I would make up stories and as soon as I could, I began writing them down.

It's very likely the influence of the storytelling culture in which I grew up. My mother's family in particular had a story for every occasion; they even used anecdotes to tell us off or to demonstrate right and wrong. And I always felt a powerful urge to tell—and hear—those stories again and again. Later, when my own toddlers reacted with the prompt demand "Again!" after I'd finished telling them a story, it struck me that I must have been a bit of a pest!

When did you first hear stories of Mulla Nasruddin?

I think they were always there floating in the ether—but he really settled in my consciousness in 1967 when I was seventeen and started puzzling over the meaning of some of the more obscure tales.

At the time a regional cultural development had been formed between Turkey, Pakistan, and Iran, and when I mentioned the "Hoja" to a senior Iranian diplomat in Karachi, he said: "We don't like talking about him in Iran." I was startled, but I delved into the tales and realized that it was because many of the stories subtly oppose the government of the day and can be downright critical.

But a "fool" or jester, as in Shakespeare, gets away with criticizing society and government while an ordinary person can be severely punished as a rebel. But the Mulla triumphed, and his stories continued to thrive everywhere despite this gentleman's objection.

Since these were mostly oral tales, how and why did you decide to commit them to the written word with illustrations?
I'd often toyed with the idea of retelling the tales, and then Penguin India approached me to retell them. It was exciting because I had noticed the Mulla's

Mulla Nasruddin's experiences are compact and punchy little packets of humor and wisdom, and they cross boundaries of time and space as well as age. Parents can enjoy them as much as children of all ages.

What makes these stories different as compared to Western fairy tales such as Aesop's or Grimm?
The Brothers Grimm are a different proposition altogether; they are folktales with a narrative, often quite long, that is intended to show how life can be, and which often suggests that things come right in the end and the underdog will

---

"Mulla Nasruddin's experiences are compact and punchy little packets of humor and wisdom, and they cross boundaries of time and space as well as age. Parents can enjoy them as much as children of all ages."

---

presence among storytellers and academics in England, certainly, but also in Spain and Canada. Then I was utterly thrilled when Tessa Strickland asked me to do an illustrated book for Barefoot Books.

Images enhance and complement words and help fix verbal impressions in the mind. It was great because I had dozens more stories in my head and some distinct ideas of the Mulla's characters; for example, his fondness for food, especially baklava, his love of traveling, his way of dealing with neighbors, and his occasional laziness.

I do believe very strongly that folktales and myths have a universality about them that reveal our common humanity, underscore the excesses of the ruling classes, and equalize the fate of rich and poor.

win. Fables with their short and compact format are comparable but have a clearly stated moral.

Mulla Nasruddin's tales, though also short, are anecdotal and often have a twist in the tale. There's an element of light-heartedness, irony; he has no hesitation in poking good-natured fun at everything and everyone, including himself. But behind the jokes and irony lies concern about the serious aspects of life: poverty, injustice, the effects of extreme power, snobbery, greed, foolishness, and the individual ego.

Nasruddin lived in the age of a cruel king and took the opportunity to challenge him by playing the fool—humor allows the clown to get away with a surprising amount of cheek.

Has oral storytelling gotten lost in this visual and wired world we live in?
No! And thank God for it. There's an international revival of oral storytelling. New technology reinforces it, just like the images of color and form in picture books are always a great way of fixing different worlds and narrative events in our minds—they are a fabulous boost to the imagination and a joy to the eye.

Why do you feel it is important to read folk stories?
Stories should be read and shared for enjoyment. I also love the fact that traditional tales are informative in so many ways. They look at cultures, human character, and experience in a way that enters our subconscious and subtly delivers life lessons in order to help us manage our expectations. They show us that difficulties on our individual journeys can be overcome.

The written word is the best way of getting to places you've never reached before, and children's literature helps us to cross boundaries. When my children were growing up, I learned a lot while reading to them. Not only was I reminded of stories I'd forgotten, but I understood the hidden meaning in some that I'd never worked out before. I also came across new stories, and I connected with the wisdom of children and the complexities of life in a simple way.

What is the one thing that you would like people to know about Muslims?
Muslims come in so many shapes, sizes, colors, customs, beliefs, traditions, and factions—you get the picture—so I want people to know about Islam, rather than Muslims. The Islamic scholar Sheikh Mohammad Akram Nadwi said: "I know of no other religion in which women were

> **"Traditional tales . . . look at cultures, human character, and experience in a way that enters our subconscious and subtly delivers life lessons in order to help us manage our expectations. They show us that difficulties on our individual journeys can be overcome."**

so central in its formative history." Here are some examples I can think of.

Nusayba bint Ka'ab was a female warrior at Uhud and other battles. The Prophet Muhammad is said to have commented about her: "Wherever I looked . . . I saw her fighting in front of me." Aysha bint abu Bakr, the Prophet's wife, was consulted on Islamic matters by scholars and jurists from around the world and was referred to as a *muftiyya* (a female mufti or religious leader). Fatima al-Fihri founded the world's first university, Al Qarawiyyin, an institution of Islamic learning.

There are many others like them. They utilized the rights that Islam gave them before social and cultural strictures took hold. They can be found in the book *Al-Muhaddithat: The Women Scholars in Islam.*

If you had a magic wand, what is the one misconception about Muslims that you would banish forever?
That Muslims are a hermetically sealed, monolithic bloc of a community and they all think the same way—mostly

negatively. And Muslims, like members of other faiths, should not be defined by the worst examples of their faith or be expected to answer for the misdemeanors of those they themselves disagree with. I have no idea why a man kills or shouts a religious phrase before doing something terrible, so how—and why—should I have to answer for him?

What is your favorite story from Islamic traditions?

Oh, so many great little stories—one of them is about an occasion when the Prophet Muhammad's close associate Omar visited the mosque and was annoyed to find a group of men jeering at him. He saw that the Prophet remained focused on his prayers even though he could hear them, so Omar ignored them too. The Prophet acknowledged his forbearance with a smile. When Omar had completed his prayers, he passed the men again, who were still taunting the Prophet. Omar was known for his quick temper, and this time he reprimanded them.

The Prophet looked sad and disappointed. "I don't understand," Omar said, going over to him. "You smiled when I failed to defend you from those men, but now, when I've challenged them, you look upset." "Omar," the Prophet said, "when you ignore offensive behavior, the angels defend you; when you join in that behavior, they withdraw."

How do we—parents, teachers, and librarians—all of us as a community teach children to respect differences and value diversity?

Stories are the most powerful method of teaching—children identify with the main characters and experience the cause and effect of their actions. The narrative must be followed by debate and discussion so that they can begin to see the subtleties of the tale. Children should be encouraged to express their doubts and voice their questions, always in a respectful manner, and these should be addressed openly and sensibly. Rather than avoid misunderstandings and hurt feelings that such questions can bring up, our discussions should address these and manage them in such a way that no one is judged or made to feel "wrong" for asking or feeling a certain way. The point is to let children work through their prejudices and reservations and hopefully to dissipate stereotypes. It's not about converting people to one belief or another, it's about opening their minds to alternative ways of thinking and developing their ability to accept those differences without being forced to agree with them. In other words, agree to differ with a *"vive le difference"* attitude. As the Quran says: "You have your faith and I have mine." We need to be taught to respect each other as soon as we can understand.

Finally, biryani or kebabs?

Can I be greedy? Kebabs (with a salad) to start and then *biryani*. I'd happily forego pudding.

Biography

Shahrukh Husain, a prolific writer of fiction, nonfiction, and screenplays, writes for both adults and children. Her work focuses on the retelling of myths for a modern audiences. Her book *The Wise Fool: Fables from the Islamic World*, which retells stories about Mulla Nasruddin, introduces this thirteenth-century jester to new audiences.

Young Adult Books

Alif the Unseen. G. Willow Wilson. Grove, 2013. 978–0802121226. 448 pp. Young adult.

Select Awards: 2013 World Fantasy Award.

Alif, an enterprising computer programmer, backs himself into a corner when he creates a potent software to spy on his ex-lover. His neighbor, friend, and former messenger between Alif and his ex-lover Dina unexpectedly becomes Alif's accomplice. The State police starts to chase them, and they're not sure why until they unfold the mysteries of the *Alf-Youm* (*One Thousand and One Nights*), a gift from Alif's ex-lover. They meet interesting characters along the way, including Vikram the jinn. A cat-and-mouse chase follows until Alif must sacrifice to the State and confront the Hand, his ex-lover's future husband. Alif is sure he's doomed, until a friend from the past rescues him and they try to fix what they can in the dystopian city they live in. Wilson weaves in references to the rich cultural history of Islam, a number of stories from *One Thousand and One Nights*, and creatively spins a gripping story asking us all to question the divides between the seen and the unseen, the digital and the analog, and the real and the unreal.

Discussion Starters

- Did the story's setting remind you of any modern-day country? Which one and why?
- What would you have done if you were in Dina's place?

Ideas for Further Engagement

- 🖐 Organize a classroom debate about the importance of using fantasy stories as political resistance.
- 🖐 Research examples of cultural appropriation, and especially the appropriation of elements of Eastern culture by the West.

Quotes for Interpretation

- "A daughter would have been preferable. If she was pretty and well-mannered, a daughter could marry up; a son could not. A son needed his own prospects." (55)

- "The censors don't bother with fantasy books, especially old ones. They can't understand them. They think it's all kids' stuff. They'd die if they knew what *The Chronicles of Narnia* were really about." (105)

- "It happens, you know—one culture invents something and claims it's from somewhere else, and then the people of somewhere else adopt it as their own. History is full of palimpsests like that." (131)

Ayat Jamilah: Beautiful Signs (A Treasury of Islamic Wisdom for Children and Parents). **Collected and adapted by Sarah Conover and Freda Crane, ill. by Valerie Wahl. Eastern Washington University Press, 2011. 978–0910055947. 189 pp. Fiction. Young adult.**

This is a collection of stories commonly known in oral form and now preserved in this lively and profound book. It features stories from all over the Muslim world, from Indonesia, Azerbaijan, Nigeria, and Syria to China and more. The moral lessons from Sufi mystical teachings, stories from the Quran, and hadiths or sayings of the Prophet Muhammad are nicely balanced by the wit and humor of the folk hero Mulla Nasruddin. The notes provide more context and information for further research and discussion.

Discussion Starters
- What do you infer from the quote "Trust in God, but tie your camel"?
- Can you think of a phrase to replace "This too shall pass" that would please the king?

Ideas for Further Engagement
- Find out the meaning of *Kan wan ma kan . . .* and other similar beginnings of the stories.
- Look up some morals that are common across religions and find sayings from each religion to support the morals.

Quotes for Interpretation
- "The cure of ignorance is to ask and learn." (40)

- "Contentment and peace will come when you widen your perspective." (42)
- "He who is unthankful for little, is unthankful for much." (162)

Malika: Warrior Queen Part One. Roye Okupe and Chima Kalu. YouNeek Studios, 2017. 978–0996607056. 144 pp.

Built in a fantasy world set in fifteenth-century West Africa, this graphic novel follows the victories and trials of Malika, the queen and commander of the kingdom of Azzaz. Despite her martial skill, Malika continues to be haunted by her past even as she manages the various factions in her royal court and the impending threat of the Ming Dynasty. With a strong woman at the helm of the story, and machinations of enemies both within the walls of her royal court and the empire itself, *Malika* is a powerful tale of history and power. Okupe uses fantasy, mines inspiration from African empires and mythology, and nods to the *Arabian Nights* while creating a completely new context.

Discussion Starters
- What are some of the inspirations for ancient African empires mentioned in the book?
- Read the sequel, *Malika: Warrior Queen Part Two.*

Ideas for Further Engagement
- Look up the real-life inspirations for the provinces of Fon, Kano, and Mandara.
- Research some West African myths on kings and spirits.
- Listen to some Afrobeat music and discuss the ways in which it fuses local and global sounds.

Quotes for Interpretation
- "The doom of darkness must yield to the light of the perfect warrior." (50)
- "An iron fist may have united your kingdom, but it will take a gentle hand to prevent division . . . Or rebellion." (59)

- "Today we may lose. Tonight we may perish. But I would rather die a thousand deaths, in a thousand lifetimes, than become a slave on my own lands!" (94)

The City of Brass (The Daevabad Trilogy).
S. A. Chakraborty. Harper Voyager, 2017.
978–0062678102. 544 pp. Adult.

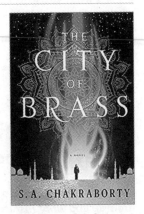

The title of this debut novel comes from a story in *One Thousand and One Nights.* Inspired by the world of myth, fantasy, and the supernatural, *City of Brass* creates a complex alternate world of magic, intrigue, and danger. One of the last remaining Nahid healers, Nahri is unaware of her past until it is revealed through a zar, or exorcism gone wrong. She summons Dara, a djinn warrior from the past, and then embarks on a perilous journey and battles creatures of air, land, and water to get to the magical city of Daevabad. Though a safe haven for her at the moment, the city itself is full of political intrigue and simmering social tensions. Nahri finds a friend in young prince Ali, who has secret sympathies of his own. Reimagining Middle Eastern folklore and showcasing its diversity in an inventive fantasy, Chakraborty conjures up a rich and layered world that examines timeless issues.

Discussion Starters
- What parallels can you draw between the shafits and the majority-minority divides in our present society?
- What are some of the inspirations from the original story of the "City of Brass" from the *Thousand and One Nights?*

Ideas for Further Engagement
- 🖐 Read the second sequel in the trilogy, *Kingdom of Copper.*
- 🖐 Write a short fictional story with one of the characters from the book.

Quotes for Interpretation
- "There was only one creature that line referred to, only one being that struck terror in hardened warriors and savvy merchants from the

Maghrib to the Hind. An ancient being said to live for deceiving mankind. A djinn." (37)

- "To keep walking a path between loyalty to your family and loyalty to what you know is right. One of these days, you're going to have to make a choice." (382)
- "Often the mightiest things have the humblest beginnings." (398)

S. A. Chakraborty
Fantasy Spun from History

Can you tell us a little about where you grew up and what inspired you to be a writer?

I grew up in New Jersey, near the coast and just outside of New York City. I was a big bookworm as a kid and a huge history buff; in fact, I didn't want to be a writer—I wanted to be a historian. I would read all the history books I could get my hands on at the library, particularly those giant picture books about ancient civilizations. It definitely got my imagination spinning.

The title of your book refers to a story within the "Thousand and One Nights." Are there any themes or other similarities that you drew from that story for your novel?

There are quite a few. The "City of Brass" is one of my favorite stories from the *Thousand and One Nights*: the tale of a pseudo-archaeological expedition gone very wrong. It takes a long view of history, warning the reader to look upon the ruins of once-great empires and contemplate their destruction. This was a theme I wanted to carry into my own book, in which the world's history plays a heavy

role in the characters' lives and decisions. It's also a bit of a twist: being brought to an ancient, mysterious city in a folktale is supposed to be a magical experience . . . and this doesn't quite pan out for the characters in the original tale or my book.

How did the story for your book come together? What were some the writings and research that inspired you?

The book began as a world-building experiment to pass the time. I studied history in college and was hoping to go back to graduate school to study the medieval Islamic world when my daughter was a bit older. But I loved the period, and since I was still reading up on it, I figured I might as well do something with my research. So, I began re-creating a fantasy world that incorporated parts of beloved sailors' tales from the Indian Ocean, the great library of Baghdad, and the coral castles and salons of the Swahili coast. It's difficult to list particular sources since there were so many, but for students interested in learning more, I keep a reading list at my website, www.sachakraborty.com.

book. Was this depiction an integral part of the storytelling?
Absolutely. I have an affection for trade and travel journals from the medieval world, and it's incredible to see how vast and diverse the Islamic community was at that time. It's remarkable that someone could travel from Spain to Malaysia, and from Siberia to the Swahili Coast, trading on their knowledge of the Quran and finding a community to pray with despite all the geographic, linguistic, and cultural

> *"It's remarkable that someone could travel from Spain to Malaysia, and from Siberia to the Swahili Coast, trading on their knowledge of the Quran and finding a community to pray with despite all the geographic, linguistic, and cultural borders they would pass."*

In the book, the main protagonist, Nahri, grapples with a new world and the ongoing political and social complications of the city of Daevabad. What kinds of parallels can we draw to current political events?
I'm not sure I'd draw parallels to current political events because, sadly, the issues that come up in the book—foreign occupation, political repression, racism, sectarianism, and the ways they feed into each other—are fairly universal to the human experience. I think you could apply the same framework Nahri sees in Daevabad to any number of societies in both history and today.

The world-building in the novel is incredibly complex and layered, and it also paints a picture of a very diverse Muslim community. As a reader, it was really delightful to see nuggets of Middle Eastern folklore throughout the

borders they would pass. There's a diversity and flexibility that allowed this, and it's a broad history that I think we should cherish. There is strength in this diversity: religions don't last millennia and grow to nearly two billion followers while not allowing room for different types of expression, and I wanted to show this.

We often like to share our own stories—how is the story behind the book connected to your personal story? Were there any personal life experiences that you wished to reflect or showcase through the book?
I think the creation of the book is more personal than the story itself. I delved into these histories and wrote this story while going through a lot of personal changes: my conversion to Islam, becoming a mother, an abrupt career change that left me unmoored—writing this book and briefly escaping into another world

was something I did for my own mental health. I write because I enjoy sharing stories, but also because I simply love doing it for myself.

What is your biggest inspiration from Islam?

I'm a convert, so this is a rather lengthy and personal question, though I will say I was drawn by the idea of a more personal connection with God, as well as the focus on social justice. In Islam, I felt like I had room to grow; to fall and pick myself back up again as long as I kept trying to improve.

If you had a magic wand, what is the one misconception about Muslims that you would banish forever?

I get this question often, and honestly, I don't know that I would banish anything because I'm not sure our first priority should be what outsiders think of us. I believe we're called to account for our deeds and intentions first, and make our community the best it can be.

How do we—parents, teachers, and librarians—all of us as a community teach children to respect differences and value diversity?

I think it's a constant process of questioning and reevaluation. Are we making sure everyone from our community has the chance to make their voice heard—and are we then listening to them, even when it gets uncomfortable? What are our own biases? How do we counter them and teach our children better?

Biography

S. A. Chakraborty is a speculative fiction writer and history buff from New York City. Her debut novel, *The City of Brass*, is out now with Harper Voyager and is the first book in *The Daevabad Trilogy,* an epic fantasy set in the eighteenth-century Middle East. When not reading, she enjoys hiking, knitting, and re-creating unnecessarily complicated medieval meals for her family. You can find her online most frequently at Twitter (@SChakrabs), where she likes to talk about history, politics, and Islamic art.

***The Honey Thief.* Najaf Mazari and Robert Hillman. Viking, 2013. 978–0670026487. 304 pp. Adult.**

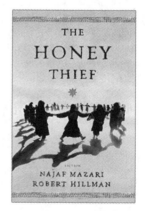

This book is a collaboration between two authors, one an acclaimed Australian writer, Robert Hillman, and the second, Najaf Mazari, who grew up in Afghanistan and fled to Australia as a refugee when members of his ethnic group, the Hazaras, were under threat in Afghanistan. This insightful book shares the history and experiences of the Hazara people through stories about upheavals and uprisings, and folklore about music, food, and snow leopards. Each of these heartwarming stories provides a window into the lives of the Hazaras and the nuanced culture and history of Afghanistan, and showcases the brotherhood, determination, and resilience of its people. The delectable recipes and food tips at the end are a pleasant surprise.

Discussion Starters
- Which was the most memorable story to you and why?
- What did you learn about the Hazara people from the book?

Ideas for Further Engagement
- ✋ Watch the documentary *I Am Hazara*.
- ✋ Research the history of Afghanistan and in particular its history of conflict and the displacement of its indigenous people.

Quotes for Interpretation
- "The great massacres became part of who we are—we, the Hazara. I say 'part of who we are' rather than 'part of our history' because history is a thing apart; something you can study, if you wish, and write books about. The massacres are not 'history' in that sense; they have a place in our minds and our hearts from which they can't be torn." (55)
- "Joy comes into our lives always within range of sorrow. The two are sisters." (106)
- "We are a people who should never have survived our history of five thousand years; we are a people who should no longer exist. And yet we do, and there is beauty in that fact alone." (253)

The Wrath and the Dawn. **Renee Ahdieh. G. P. Putnam's Sons Books for Young Readers, 2015. 978–0399171611. 416 pp. Gr. 7 and up.**

Select Awards: New York Public Library Best Book for Teens 2015, YALSA 2016 Best Fiction for Young Adults Pick.

In Ahdieh's debut novel, she weaves an intricate story of a young girl, Shahrzad, who volunteers to be the next bride of evil Prince Khalid, despite knowing that

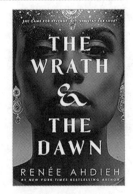

he marries a new girl every day only to kill her the next morning. With equal doses of fear and bravado, she takes on the challenge to kill Khalid to avenge the death of her best friend, Shiva. Shahrzad is depicted as a strong-willed, confident, and witty girl who stands up for herself and initially keeps Khalid at bay with her magical stories from the *Thousand and One Nights*. Khalid warms up to her honesty and enigma, but is not sure if she's worth the hefty price he has to pay for her love. Shahrzad's childhood friend and ex-lover, Tariq, complicates matters further. This is a highly readable, vivid love story with a good measure of politics, humor, and thrills.

Discussion Starters

- Would you have volunteered to be Prince Khalid's next bride like Shahrzad? Why or why not?
- Do you think Khalid was justified in killing his brides? Why or why not?
- What did you think of Shahrzad's relationship with her handmaiden, Despina?
- Do you think Shahrzad betrayed Tariq by falling in love with Khalid?
- Read *The Rose and the Dagger*, the sequel to this book.

Ideas for Further Engagement

- ✋ Design a movie poster for the book.
- ✋ List five things that you think would have been different if this story had been set in a Western setting.

Quotes for Interpretation

- "You see things the way you live your life. Without fear." (70)
- *"Honey catches more flies than vinegar." (124)*
- "We are not meant to be alone, Shahrzad. The more a person pushes others away, the clearer it becomes he is in need of love the most." (137)

Throne of the Crescent Moon. **Saladin Ahmed. DAW, 2012. 978–0756407780. 384 pp. Adult.**

Select Awards: Hugo Award Nominee for Best Novel 2013, Nebula Award Nominee for Best Novel 2012, Locus Award for Best First Novel 2013.

The last of the ghul hunters of the Crescent Moon kingdom, a world-weary Doctor Abdoullah Makshlood is contemplating retirement, but a personal connection to a horrifying murder forces him to take on one last adventure. He is accompanied by Raseed, the warrior dervish whose sword skills complement Makhshlood's magical sorcery, and together they battle unworldly creatures. Aided by a young shape-shifting tribeswoman, who seeks to avenge the death of her tribe, and with the help of the Doctor's learned friends and healers, they seek to root out and destroy the disturbing unseen source of evil black magic. They also find themselves embroiled in the power struggles of the iron-fisted Khalif and a plot to overthrow him by a Falcon Prince who steals from the rich to give to the poor. Ahmed conjures this grand epic in the style of the *Thousand and One Nights* with stunning prose, magic, demons, sword fights, the power of faith, and the inner struggles of his characters to build a rich, layered, and truly unique fantasy.

Discussion Starters
- Are there any real-world places that resemble the Little Square and the Crescent Moon Palace?
- Which popular character from folklore does the Falcon Prince remind you of? Do you think his means justifies his ends?

Ideas for Further Engagement
- Find out the origins of supernatural creatures such as ghuls, ifrits, and djinns.
- Organize a film festival featuring fantasy films from different cultures.

Quotes for Interpretation
- "We are obligated to fight the servants of the Traitorous Angel." (31)

- "Remember what the Chapters say: 'God speaks through these Chapters, not through the mouths of priests.'" (75)
- *"To save one child from the ghuls is to save the whole world."* (157)

***When Dreams Travel.* Gita Hariharan. Penguin, 2011. 978–0143104285. 288 pp. Adult.**

This novel begins where the *Thousand and One Nights* ends. It follows the characters of Shahrzad, her sister Duniyazad, and the sultan Shahryar when the curtains fall and they step off stage. Through Duniyazad's and her companion Dilshad's travels and ruminations, the novel seeks to reclaim the voices of women who were silenced by the sultan's sword. Weaving together ideas on power, gender, dreams, and memory, Hariharan's feminist reinterpretation of the classic book is a must read. Her web of stories plays with the characters in bygone and contemporary times to tell an inventive and thought-provoking tale.

Discussion Starters
- What was Duniyazad's role in the original story? What role does she play here?
- Why does Shahryar think that his wife is changing from Wise Shahrzad to Wily Shahrzad?
- Which other monument does Shahrzad's tomb remind you of?
- What do you think are the causes of Shahrzad and Shah Zaman's disappearance?

Ideas for Further Engagement
- ✋ Look up the meanings of all the characters' names: Shahryar, Shah Zaman, Shahrzad, Duniyazad, and Dilshad.

Quotes for Interpretation
- "I don't have a sword, so it seems I cannot rule. I cannot rule, I cannot travel, I don't care to weep. But I can dream." (20)

- "The sultan, powerful, noble, deluded, has seen the light. He has been brought to his senses by a woman; and with, of all things, her stories; her ready tongue, her cleverness." (21)
- "In this abnormal climate where imagination—through the medium of the word—asserts its power over the blood-shedding sword, everyone forgives everyone." (21)

Note

1. Muslim Heritage, "Literature and Music in the Muslim Civilization," www.muslim heritage.com/article/literature-and-music-muslim-civilisation.

CONCLUSION

THE LAST FEW TUMULTUOUS AND CHALLENGING YEARS HAVE GALVANIZED the need for hope and change. The 2016 presidential election and events that followed have reignited a passion in many of us to be engaged citizens. People from all walks of life came together to protest the Muslim ban, participate in women's marches, stand for electoral offices, hold their representatives accountable, express their concern over the various discriminatory policies proposed by the Trump administration, and stand in solidarity with the people affected by them.

The power of a democracy is in the hands of its citizens. Through our engagement, vigilance, and actions, we can ensure that all people who live in America have access to liberty, equality, and justice. With increased globalization, it is anticipated that by 2045, a majority of the American population will be people of color. Our children are growing up in a multicultural society and it is up to us—parents, educators, and librarians—to equip them for this changing new world. A world where we celebrate differences and value diversity.

Our book is a suggested toolkit that is designed to sensitize the next generation to the issues faced by Muslims in America, and encourage understanding and empathy. One book, even just one story can open windows to different worlds. It can, proverbially, put you in someone else's shoes, hear their voice, get under their skin, and peek into their soul. Stories help us make sense of ourselves and the world around us. Each of the books reviewed in this volume is an invitation to fight fear with knowledge.

We urge you to use these books in your communities and classrooms in order to have conversations about diversity, address fears, and create a sense of belonging and respect as we all raise the next generation of leaders. We hope that these stories will entertain, engage, and illuminate the path so that we can transform the shadows of today into a new light for tomorrow.

APPENDIX A

Frequently Asked Questions on Islam

OVER THE LAST YEAR, WE HAVE PRESENTED OUR COUNTER ISLAMOPHOBIA through Stories campaign to varied audiences of parents, teachers, and librarians. As these educators returned to their communities and introduced these books, they have also had to field a barrage of questions from children on the whys and whats of Islam. And sometimes they had questions of their own.

We are frequently asked some of these questions about Islam and its practices. We understand that it can be a challenge to answer questions about cultures and practices that may be unfamiliar. In this day and age of information overload, it is also hard to ascertain which sources are reliable. As a result, we have compiled this appendix, in which Sumbul Ali-Karamali answers some questions that have been frequently posed to us.

Sumbul Ali-Karamali is an American Muslim mother and former lawyer who grew up in a suburb of Los Angeles. In addition to her degree in English from Stanford University and her law degree from the University of California at Davis, she has a degree in Islamic law from the University of London's School of Oriental and African Studies. She has written extensively on Islam in a style that is readable, relatable, and often humorous.

Her first book, *The Muslim Next Door: The Qur'an, the Media, and That Veil Thing* (2008), won the 2009 Independent Publishers Awards Bronze Medal. It was featured on the American Academy of Religion's Islam section list as a recommended text for teaching Islam in classrooms, as well as the *Huffington Post's* list of Eleven Must-Read Books by Muslim Authors. It was selected for Silicon Valley Reads 2012, a 14-city-wide reading program.

During Sumbul's book tour, several secondary-school teachers complained to her about the absence of age-appropriate books on Islam for middle school and high school students. As a result, she wrote *Growing Up Muslim: Understanding the Beliefs and Practices of Islam,* a nonfiction chapter book which is a great resource for teachers, students, and anyone else who wants academically reliable information on Islam and Muslims.

In the interview below, Sumbul answers a few frequently asked questions on Islam and Muslims. Please note that these are nutshell answers to complex questions, and they are meant only to provide brief introductory definitions. For complete answers, please read *The Muslim Next Door: The Qur'an, the Media, and That Veil Thing* and/or *Growing Up Muslim: Understanding the Beliefs and Practices of Islam.*

How did you first come to write on Islam?
I've answered questions about Muslims all my life, because I was usually the only Muslim my friends, teachers, classmates, and lawyer colleagues knew. When I was working as a corporate lawyer, I also began to receive requests for book recommendations on Islam—but I didn't have any! So I earned a degree in Islamic law and started writing books to answer the kinds of questions I've been asked all my life.

What has changed since you first started answering questions?
Growing up Muslim is different for my kids than it was for me. There was more ignorance and unawareness of Islam when I was a child, but there was also less widespread hostility, and there was no Islamophobia industry (as there is now) fomenting fear about Islam. In addition, there is a 1,400-year-old historical west-

ern European tradition, which we in America have inherited, of viewing Islam through the lens of the enemy. This tradition was revived in 1979, when the Iranian revolution brought Islam back into public awareness. It's a historical prejudice that's invisible to us because it's part of our culture and we're accustomed to it. This historical attitude, combined with the media's inclination to feature Muslims only in the context of violence, has given us a wildly distorted image of Islam and Muslims, about which there is still enormous ignorance. The good news: many more non-Muslim Americans are sincerely and generously attempting to learn about Islam, build cross-cultural bridges, and ally with Muslims against anti-Muslim prejudice.

The word "jihad" is often used to denote acts of violence by Muslims. What does "jihad" really mean?
The word *jihad* means "effort" or "struggle." Any kind of struggle. My childhood featured a jihad to get good grades! In a religious sense, the "greater jihad" is the internal struggle to make oneself a better person; the "lesser jihad" is the external struggle to make society a better place.

Can you elaborate on the ways of internal and external jihad?
The internal jihad is about improving oneself and ridding oneself of wicked impulses, such as lying and backbiting. The external jihad is about improving society, and there are several ways to do this. First, we should use "jihad by the word," which means using verbal persuasion to correct injustice. Or we may use "jihad by the hand," which means doing good works to correct societal injustice. As a last resort, Muslims may undertake "jihad by the sword," which means taking up arms to correct injustice, but this is strictly limited: jihad by the sword can be undertaken only (a) in self-defense or to overthrow an oppressor, (b) by a leader of all Muslims (no such person exists anymore), or (c) if the self-defense is immediate.

Moreover, some Islamic scholars say that in a jihad to overthrow an oppressor, the oppression must *actively* prevent Muslims from practicing their religion.

Even if a world leader of all Muslims were to declare a jihad in self-defense or to overthrow an oppressor, extremely strict rules of engagement would apply to any jihad by the sword. Here are just a few: Muslims *may not* kill noncombatants (civilians), kill children or the elderly, kill anyone taking refuge in holy buildings, arbitrarily destroy property, uproot trees, commit rape, commit terrorism (the clandestine use of force), cheat or use treachery, poison the water supply, torture anyone (including animals), or commit suicide. They can't kill other Muslims, either.

Note that these rules of engagement—established since very early Islam—are, if anything, more restrictive than our modern international rules of warfare.

Why then do Al-Qaeda and ISIS claim that their fight is a jihad?
To legitimize themselves, of course. But what these groups are doing is not jihad. Terrorism has *never* been allowed in Islam, not in over a thousand years of history, and even in early Islam it was severely punished. Al-Qaeda and ISIS members are not jihadists, but criminal mass murderers under Islam. These groups have been repeatedly denounced as such by Islamic scholars and institutions. Note that roughly 90 percent of the victims of these groups are other Muslims.

Can you explain what Sharia is?
Not in such a small space. *Growing Up Muslim* has an explanation of it. But here are a few points to remember:
1. "Sharia" has no fixed meaning. It means "the righteous path" or "the way of God." But loosely, it really just means "Islam."
2. There are certain main principles of Sharia, called the *maqasid al-sharia*, that are derived from the Quran. All Islamic rules must abide by the maqasid, which I articulate here as six principles:

> The right to the protection of life.
> The right to the protection of family.
> The right to the protection of education.
> The right to the protection of religion.
> The right to the protection of property (or access to resources).
> The right to the protection of human dignity.

What then is Sharia law?

The term "Sharia law" is a misnomer (and not an Islamic term), because Sharia is not law, at least not in the way we think of law, which is an earthly, enforceable, and rigid system. Rather, Sharia is the abstract way of God.

Usually when people talk about Sharia, they actually mean *fiqh*, which is an enormous body of Islamic religious rules and principles derived from the Quran and Sunnah. It's similar to the Jewish *halakha*. Most of the detailed rules of Islam come from *fiqh*. Fiqh is not homogenous, or static—it is comprised of a variety of legal opinions and discussions (with frequent disagreements between scholars). Although some of it is old and outdated (what religion doesn't have old and outdated bits?), *fiqh* continues to change and develop with time and context. All religions adapt and modernize, and Islam is no exception.

What really bothers me when I speak to secondary schools is that students seem to be under the impression that if Muslims don't follow a rigid set of laws, then they are thrown in prison or otherwise punished. That's the problem with calling Sharia "law." Muslims practice religion in a variety of ways or not at all; that's no different from any other religious group.

Are Muslim-majority countries governed by Sharia? As an Islamic state, are they bound to follow it?

Sharia (or more accurately, *fiqh*) is not the law of the land anywhere in the world. Nearly all Muslim-majority countries, even Iran, are constitutional states with civil codes. Nothing in the Quran requires an "Islamic state," whatever that may be. Those under his leadership practiced a variety of religions. In fact, even very early Islamic religious rules (*fiqh*) determined that Muslims must follow the government of the lands they live in, whether the government is "Islamic" or not. Moreover, every great historical Islamic empire was a multireligious empire, where minority religious communities were allowed to follow their own religious laws.

Is the hijab a mandatory requirement for all women in Islam?

I'd rather call it a headscarf, since we're speaking English. *Hijab* just sounds scary and alien. Whether covering one's hair is a religious duty for Muslim women is open to interpretation, and therefore it's a personal choice. The Quran simply requires modesty for both men and women, and it does so in language nearly identical for men as for women. What constitutes modesty depends on the time and place, culture, and personal interpretation.

The headscarf is *not* about oppression. The Prophet Muhammad never oppressed women, and in fact implemented numerous feminist reforms in the seventh century. Here is a little-known but crucial fact: Islam and Muhammad gave women more rights in the seventh century than English women would have for another thousand years. (No kidding.)

What is a fatwa? Does one have to follow it once a fatwa is issued?
A fatwa is neither divine nor an order. It is not a law. A fatwa is the nonbinding legal opinion of a recognized Islamic religious scholar (or, as developed in later years, of an institution such as an Islamic religious school) on a point of religious law that results from applying recognized legal reasoning to a particular issue.

What is the one thing you would like people to know about Islam?
There is so much I would like people to know (that's why I wrote my books), because there is an ocean of tall tales and outright falsehoods about Islam. Sometimes I feel as if I'm chipping away at a wall of misconceptions with nothing but a spoon. But if I had to pick one thing, I'd point to the tradition of pluralism and multireligious respect in Islam.

The Quran, which Muslims believe is the literal word of God, contains some of the oldest statements of religious freedom in the world. The Quran specifically prohibits forced conversion. It says: "There shall be no coercion in matters of faith" (2:256); "If your God had willed, everyone on earth would have believed; are you then going to compel the people to become believers?" (10:99); and "To you your religion, to me my religion!" (109:6).

Moreover, it is stated in the Quran, and it's absolutely established in Islam, that you do not have to be Muslim to go to heaven. The Quran says, "The Muslims, the Jews, the Christians, the Sabians, and any who believe in God and the Last Day and do good have their reward with their Lord" (2:62). The Quran is especially respectful of "People of an Earlier Revelation" (also called "People of the Book"), which originally included Jews and Christians and all kinds of Muslims, but which over the centuries has also grown to include Hindus, Zoroastrians, Buddhists, and others.

The Quran values diversity, too. It says God could have made everyone into one people, but elected not to (11:118). And God in the Quran says, "We made you into different races and tribes for you to learn from one another" (49:13).

Any last words?

Well, yes. I think it's important to realize that there isn't anything special about Muslims. We're just like any other community of people: good, bad, and in between; pious and impious; peaceful and confrontational; educated and uneducated. Most Muslims live in what are now developing countries, and they have the same problems as everyone else who lives in developing countries. Not every act of a Muslim is motivated by religion, just like not every act of a Christian is motivated by Christianity. Mostly, Muslims are just motivated by trying to get through life. Like everyone else.

APPENDIX B

Suggested Guidelines to Evaluate
Muslim Children's Literature

WE ARE MINDFUL THAT MANY NEW CHILDREN'S BOOKS FEATURING MUSLIM protagonists and topics will continue to be released. Here are some pointers to keep in mind as you evaluate these books for inclusion in your classrooms and libraries.

Literary Quality
- In general, the book should meet the rigorous standards of well-written literature. Review the plot, characters, setting, tone, and illustrations to see that they meet high-quality standards.
- Determine if the book lends itself to being read and reread, and is nuanced enough to merit revisiting multiple times.
- Research if the book has been nominated for or awarded any multicultural or diverse book awards, such as the Middle East Book Award.

Theme
- Evaluate the book to determine if it fits under one of the four themes identified in our book: Muslim Kids as Heroes, Inspiring Muslim Leaders and Thinkers, Celebrating Islam, and Folktales from Islamic Traditions.
- Review the book to determine if it shares the Muslim experience or the Muslim American experience. In each case, also look into where the

Muslim protagonists or traditions in the book are from, and how the book complements your existing collection.

- Evaluate the book to determine if it provides opportunities to understand Muslims and their cultural traditions and experiences.
- Examine the value of the story and the book's appeal for all children. Identify universal themes that would help a non-Muslim child find connections with the Muslim protagonist or story.
- Assess if Muslim children would feel proud of their heritage after reading the book.

Accuracy and Currency

- Carefully examine the book to make sure that facts are presented accurately and in a balanced fashion. Also, determine if different points of view are shared in the book.
- Determine if the nonnative or privileged characters end up "saving" the other characters.
- Examine if the characters have or develop agency through the story, and if they can problem-solve their way through the challenges that present themselves in the story.
- Review if the events are historically accurate and plausible for that context and time period.
- Determine if the book has phrases and words from a particular Muslim or other culture, and includes a glossary and pronunciation guide.

Author and Publisher

- Consider the background and personal experience of the author to determine if the author has the requisite experience to provide an "insider" perspective.
- Has the author/illustrator researched, visited, or lived among the culture she is writing about?
- Evaluate other books from the publisher and the general focus of the publisher. Ask if any sensitivity readers were employed by the author or publisher prior to the publication of the book.

Illustrations

- Carefully examine the book's illustrations, and compare them with other Muslim children's books you have in your collection.
- Review if Muslim women and girls are only shown in *hijabs*. Examine if the book represents the diversity of the Muslim community and is free of stereotypical illustrations.
- Determine if ethnic features or costumes are exaggerated or out of proportion.

APPENDIX C

Time Line of Muslims in America

WE'VE INCLUDED A SHORT CHRONOLOGY OF EVENTS TO TRACE THE HISTORY of Muslims in America along with key immigration patterns and American global policies.

800 BCE-1000 AD: Ancient Middle Eastern mariners travel to the unknown territories of the Americas.

1492: Louis De Torre, an Arab guide, accompanies Columbus on his famous voyage to America.

1539: A Moroccan guide, "Estevan the Arab," explores the American Southwest.

16th-19th centuries: Muslims from West Africa arrive as slaves in the Americas.

1776: Private Nathan Badeen, from Syria, dies fighting in the American Revolution.

1777: The kingdom of Morocco is the first country to recognize the new United States as a sovereign nation.

1812: Bilali Mahomet of Sapelo Island, Georgia, leads fellow slaves in preparing to fight the British during the War of 1812.

19th century-World War I: Muslim immigrants from the Ottoman Empire and South Asia arrive in the United States.

1850–1920: Many people from Greater Syria come to the United States and find work in factories or as peddlers.

1856: The U.S. military imports camels for military operations in the Southwest. Arab camel drivers are hired and brought to America to work with the animals.

1861-1865: More than 5,300 Arab/Muslim Americans serve in the Civil War.

Ca. 1875: First major wave of Muslim immigration to the United States begins.

1892: Kawkab America, the first Arabic-language newspaper in America, begins publication.

1893: The World's Columbian Exposition in Chicago draws many merchants from the Arab world. Some Arab American families in the Great Lakes area trace their ancestry to these merchants.

1893: Former U.S. consul Alexander Russell Webb, a white convert, represents Islam at the World Parliament of Religion in Chicago.

1918: A second major wave of Muslim immigration begins, and an estimated 14,000 Arab Americans serve in World War I.

1923: One of the most famous books of the period, *The Prophet* by Khalil Gibran, is published.

1924: The National Origins Act restricts immigration from non-European countries.

1925: Noble Drew Ali establishes the Moorish Science Temple in Chicago.

1930: Wallace D. Fard creates the Nation of Islam in Detroit.

1934: The first new mosque constructed in the United States is built in Cedar Rapids, Iowa.

1941-1945: An estimated 30,000 Arab Americans serve in World War II.

1947–1960: Muslim immigrants arrive from the Indian subcontinent and Eastern Europe.

1957: The Islamic Center of Washington is opened, and is dedicated by President Dwight D. Eisenhower.

1963: Muslim students form the Muslim Student Association at the University of Illinois.

1965: President Lyndon Johnson signs the Hart-Celler Act, which leads to greatly increased immigration from Asia, the Middle East, and Africa.

1981: The Islamic Society of North America is founded.

1990: Some Arab Americans and Muslim Americans are targets of hate crimes because of the first Gulf War. President George H. W. Bush calls for an end to hate crimes against Muslims and Arabs and signs the Hate Crime Statistics Act.

1991: Siraj Wahhaj is the first Muslim to offer the invocation in the U.S. House of Representatives.

1992: W. D. Mohammed is the first Muslim to give the invocation in the U.S. Senate.

1994: The Council of American-Islamic Relations is formed in Washington, DC.

1996: Hillary Rodham Clinton hosts the first Eid al-Fitr, the festival marking the end of Ramadan, at the White House. The U.S. Navy commissions a Muslim chaplain.

2001: Members of al-Qaeda murder approximately 3,000 people in coordinated attacks in New York City and Washington, DC.

2001: The USA PATRIOT Act is signed into law.

2001: The Transportation Security Administration is created.

2002: The Homeland Security Act is enacted, and a national terror threat-level advisory system is implemented.

2003: The United States invades Iraq in what President George W. Bush calls "a war on terrorism."

2005: The Fiqh Council, a group of Muslim American scholars of Islamic law, issues a fatwa against religious extremism and terrorism; over 100 other Muslim American groups endorse the statement.

2007: Keith Ellison becomes the first Muslim American to be seated in the U.S. Congress, representing Minnesota.

2008: Andre Carson is the second Muslim elected to the U.S. Congress.

2016: Ilhan Omar is the first Muslim woman to be elected to the Minnesota House of Representatives.

January, 2018–July, 2018: Numerous executive orders were signed into effect by President Donald Trump suspending entry into the United

States for people from several majority Muslim countries. These orders have been contested in various courts in the United States. For a detailed time lime and status, please visit the ACLU website at https://www.aclunc.org/sites/muslim-ban/.

APPENDIX D

Glossary: A Few Unfamiliar Words

abayah (**Arabic**): A long, loose, flowing, full-length dress worn by women.

Alf-Youm (**Arabic**): *One Thousand and One Nights.*

alhamdullilah (**Arabic**): "Thank God."

Al-Kitab al-mukhtasar fi hisab al-jabr wa-1-muqabala (**Arabic**): *The Compendious Book on Calculation by Completion and Balancing,* by Al-Khwarizmi.

Al Qanun Fi Al-Tibb (**Arabic**): *The Canon of Medicine,* written by Ibn Sina (Avicenna).

bachaposh (**Farsi**): A girl dressed up and disguised as a boy.

Basant (**Hindi/Urdu**): The festival of spring in South Asia.

biryani (**Urdu**): A spicy rice dish popular all over South Asia made with seasoned rice, various kinds of meat, or vegetables.

bismillah (**Arabic**): A Muslim invocation that means "In the name of Allah."

chai (**Farsi/Hindi/Russian/Turkish/Urdu**): A beverage concocted from a blend of black tea, spices, and milk.

chup (**Hindi/Urdu**): "Be quiet!"

djinn (**Arabic**): A spirit created out of smokeless fire who has supernatural powers.

Eid (**Arabic**): A Muslim festival, in particular Eid al-Fitr (celebrated after the month of fasting) and Eid al-Adha (celebrated after the pilgrimage to Mecca).

el-qirkat **(Arabic):** Also known as *alquerque,* a strategy board game.

falafel (Arabic): A Middle Eastern dish which is a mixture of vegetables formed into patties and fried.

ghul **(Arabic):** An evil creature that robs graves and feeds on dead bodies.

Grameen Bank (Bangla): Village Bank.

Hadith (Arabic): A narrative record of the sayings of the Prophet Muhammad and his companions.

haft seen **(Farsi):** The tabletop arrangement of seven symbolic items traditionally displayed on Nowruz or the Iranian New Year.

hajj (Arabic): The pilgrimage to Mecca, one of the religious duties of Muslims.

henna (Arabic): A reddish-brown dye created from the leaves of the henna plant and used to color hair and in decorative patterns on the hands and legs.

hijab **(Arabic):** Headscarf.

hummus (Arabic): A Middle Eastern dip made from pureed chickpeas.

ifrit **(Arabic):** A supernatural creature who is the most powerful and dangerous djinn.

iftar **(Arabic):** Meal eaten at sunset to break the fast in Ramadan.

imaan **(Arabic/Urdu):** Faith.

imam (Arabic): The priest who leads the prayers at the mosque.

insan **(Arabic):** Human.

Janjaweed (Arabic): Armed militia in the Darfur region of western Sudan.

Jigjiga (Arabic/Somali): A city in Somalia.

Kaaba (Arabic): A small stone building that contains a sacred black stone. Muslims face the Kaaba while praying.

kahani **(Hindi/Urdu):** Story.

kasr **(Arabic):** An ancient Islamic castle or fortress.

Ka wan ma kan **(Arabic):** Proverb meaning "There is and there is not."

kebab (Arabic/Urdu): A marinated skewer of cubed and cooked meat.

khattam-shud **(Farsi):** Exhausted, spent, or "completely finished."

khimar **(Arabic):** A head-covering or veil worn by some Muslim women that is similar to the hijab.

Khulja sim sim (Urdu): "Open Sesame!"

kitab (Arabic/Urdu): Book.

kufi (Arabic): A short round cap worn by some Muslim men.

mabrook (Arabic): "Congratulations!"

mahajon (Bangla/Hindi): A moneylender.

malafa (Arabic): A long, colorful cloth worn by the women of Mauritania.

maqam (Arabic): A system of melodic modes used in traditional Arabic music.

maqamat (Arabic): Plural of maqam. Also refers to gatherings or assemblies.

Masnavi (Farsi): A collection of spiritual couplets written by Rumi.

mullah (Arabic/Farsi/Turkish/Urdu): A Muslim scholar of Islamic theology and law.

musaharati (Arabic): The drum-beater who walks around neighborhoods waking people up for the pre-dawn meal during Ramadan.

niqab (Arabic): A face veil.

Nowruz (Farsi): The Persian New Year celebrated on the first day of spring in Iran.

paheli (Hindi): Puzzle.

pakora (Hindi/Urdu): A fried savory snack that is popular across South Asia.

Ramadan (Arabic): Muslim month of fasting.

salaam (Arabic): A greeting in most Muslim countries.

samosa (Hindi/Urdu): A stuffed triangular pastry.

sandesh (Bangla/Hindi): A sweet dessert made of milk and sugar.

Shahnameh (Farsi): *The Book of Kings*, a long epic poem written by the Persian poet Ferdowsi.

shalom (Hebrew): A Jewish greeting.

shalwar-kameez (Hindi/Urdu): A traditional garment that consists of a loose tunic and trousers.

Shia (Arabic): A sect of followers of Islam who believe in Ali and the imams as the rightful successors to the Prophet Muhammad.

souk (Arabic): a marketplace in Africa and the Middle East.

tagine (Arabic): A traditionally cooked stew from northwestern Africa made in covered earthenware.

vizier (Arabic/Turkish): A high-ranking executive officer in the Ottoman Empire.

yarmulke (Hebrew): A brimless cap worn by Jewish men.

zalabia (Arabic): A popular dessert in the Middle East, Africa, and Asia that is made from deep-fried batter soaked in a sugar syrup.

APPENDIX E

Suggested Educational Resources

WE'VE COMPILED A USEFUL LIST OF EDUCATIONAL ORGANIZATIONS, reports, and websites for educators.

Educational Organizations
- Anti-Defamation League (www.adl.org)
- Art in History, Inc. (www.artinhistory.com)
- Cultural Jambalaya (www.culturaljam.org)
- Dar al Islam (www.daralislam.org)
- Global Oneness Project (www.globalonenessproject.org)
- Institute of Arabic and Islamic Studies (www.islamic-study.org)
- Islamic Network Group (https://www.ing.org)
- Middle East Outreach (www.meoc.us)
- Pulitzer Center (www.pulitzercenter.org)
- Qatar Foundation International (www.QFI.org)
- Sultan Qaboos Cultural Center (www.sqcc.org)
- Teaching Tolerance (www.teachingtolerance.org)
- Unity Productions Foundation (www.upf.tv/)
- U.S. Institute of Peace (www.usip.org)

Reports

- SAALT 2017 Report: "Power, Pain and Potential: South Asian Americans at the Forefront of Growth and Hate in the 2016 Election Cycle": http://saalt.org/wp-content/uploads/2017/01/SAALT_Power_rpt_final3_lorez.pdf
- 2016 Noor Kids "Muslim Children's Identity Study" (www.noorkids.org)
- CAIR 2017 Report: "The Empowerment of Hate": http://islamophobia.org/images/2017CivilRightsReport/2017-Empowerment-of-Fear-Final.pdf
- Pew Research, "Muslims and Islam: Key Findings in the U.S. and around the World": www.pewresearch.org/fact-tank/2017/08/09/muslims-and-islam-key-findings-in-the-u-s-and-around-the-world/
- Runnymede 20th anniversary report: Islamophobia Still a challenge for us all: https://www.runnymedetrust.org/uploads/Islamophobia%20Report%202018%20FINAL.pdf

Lesson Plans

- "Islamophobia Lesson Outline," by Fakhra Shah: https://docs.google.com/document/d/11g9AwWwdWkiCvbYeprwwJ2G9URzkG7CBe0AUJxyukWY/edit
- "Black Muslims in the United States: An Introductory Activity": www.teachingforchange.org/black-muslims
- "Islamophobia Lesson Plan": https://bctf.ca/uploadedFiles/Public/SocialJustice/Issues/Antiracism/Islamophobia%20Lesson%20Plan%20-%20Part%201.pdf
- "15 Years since 9/11 Lesson Plan," by Fakhra Shah: https://docs.google.com/document/d/1xhTD8GJUGv10u7rmyBDCUKJQgAWWWzZcp36yaUbJihs/edit
- Zinn Education Project, "History of Muslims in the United States": https://zinnedproject.org/2014/04/a-peoples-history-of-muslims-in-the-united-states/
- SAALT, "In the Face of Xenophobia: Lessons to Address Bullying of South Asian American Youth": http://saalt.org/wp-content/uploads/2012/09/In-the-Face-of-Xenophobia.pdf

- Teaching Tolerance, "In a Time of Islamophobia, Teach with Complexity": www.tolerance.org/blog/time-islamophobia-teach-complexity
- Teaching Tolerance, "What's Missing in the Teaching of Islam in the U.S.": www.tolerance.org/blog/time-islamophobia-teach-complexity
- *Washington Post*, "On the Importance of Teaching Islamic Art": https://www.washingtonpost.com/posteverything/wp/2017/01/06/its-harder-than-ever-to-teach-islamic-art-but-never-more-important/?postshare=8221483724359012&tid=ss_tw&utm_term=.1bd24ad9316d

Articles

- "UNESCO Guide for Educators on Countering Islamophobia": http://unesdoc.unesco.org/images/0021/002152/215299e.pdf
- VICE, "How to Support Muslims in Trump's America": www.vice.com/read/how-to-support-muslims-in-trumps-america?utm_source=vicetwitterus
- Huffington Post, "How Should We Combat Islamophobia?": www.huffingtonpost.com/daniel-tutt/how-should-we-combat-islamophobia_b_3149768.html
- CAIR, "A Muslim Parent's Guide to Talking to Muslim Children after an Act of Violent Extremism": www.islamophobia.org/157-talking-to-muslim-children-after-an-act-of-violent-extremism/173-a-muslim-parent-s-guide-to-talking-to-children-after-an-act-of-violent-extremism.html
- Noor Kids, "How to Talk to Muslim Kids about Trump": http://noorkids.com/blogs/news/guide-how-to-talk-to-muslim-kids-about-trump

INDEX